BOLLINGEN SERIES XCIX

A COMPLETE LIST OF THE COLLECTED WORKS OF C. G. JUNG
APPEARS AT THE BACK OF THIS VOLUME

THE PSYCHOLOGY OF KUNDALINI YOGA

NOTES OF THE SEMINAR

GIVEN IN 1932 BY

C. G. JUNG

EDITED BY SONU SHAMDASANI

BOLLINGEN SERIES XCIX

PRINCETON UNIVERSITY PRESS

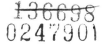

PUBLISHED BY PRINCETON UNIVERSITY PRESS, 41 WILLIAM STREET,
PRINCETON, NEW JERSEY 08540

THIS EDITION OF THE NOTES OF JUNG'S SEMINARS IS BEING PUBLISHED IN THE UNITED STATES OF AMERICA BY PRINCETON UNIVERSITY PRESS AND IN ENGLAND BY ROUTLEDGE LTD. IN THE AMERICAN EDITION, THE VOLUMES OF SEMINAR NOTES CONSTITUTE NUMBER XCIX IN BOLLINGEN SERIES, SPONSORED BY BOLLINGEN FOUNDATION

THE TEXT HERE PUBLISHED IS THAT WHICH MARY FOOTE, ITS ORIGINAL EDITOR, ISSUED PRIVATELY IN 1933

LIBRARY OF CONGRESS CATALOGING-IN-PUBLICATION DATA

JUNG, C. G. (CARL GUSTAV), 1875–1961.
THE PSYCHOLOGY OF KUNDALINI YOGA : NOTES OF THE SEMINAR GIVEN IN 1932
BY C. G. JUNG / EDITED BY SONU SHAMDASANI.
P. CM. — (BOLLINGEN SERIES ; 99)
ISBN 0-691-02127-9 (CL : ALK. PAPER)
1. KUNDALINI—PSYCHOLOGY. I. SHAMDASANI, SONU, 1962– .
II. TITLE. III. SERIES.
BL1238.56.K86J86 1996
294.5'43—DC20 95-44198

THIS BOOK HAS BEEN COMPOSED IN BASKERVILLE

PRINCETON UNIVERSITY PRESS BOOKS ARE PRINTED ON ACID-FREE PAPER AND MEET THE GUIDELINES FOR PERMANENCE AND DURABILITY OF THE COMMITTEE ON PRODUCTION GUIDELINES FOR BOOK LONGEVITY OF THE COUNCIL ON LIBRARY RESOURCES

PRINTED IN THE UNITED STATES OF AMERICA BY PRINCETON ACADEMIC PRESS

1 3 5 7 9 10 8 6 4 2

IN MEMORIAM

Michael Scott Montague Fordham
(1905–1995)

TABLE OF CONTENTS

LIST OF ILLUSTRATIONS

PREFACE

From 3 to 8 October 1932 the Indologist Wilhelm Hauer presented six lectures concurrently in English and German at the Psychological Club in Zürich, entitled "Der Yoga, im besondern die Bedeutung des Cakras" (Yoga, especially the meaning of the cakras). Following these, Jung devoted four lectures to a psychological interpretation of Kundalini yoga.

Hauer's English lectures, Jung's English lectures of 12, 19, and 26 October and Jung's German lecture of 2 November (which was translated by Cary F. Baynes) were compiled by Mary Foote[1] from stenographic notes taken by her secretary, Emily Köppel, and privately published in mimeographed form under the title *The Kundalini Yoga: Notes on the Lecture Given by Prof. Dr. J. W. Hauer with Psychological Commentary by Dr. C. G. Jung* (Zurich, 1933). In her editorial preface Foote noted that the text had been corrected by both Hauer and Jung.

A German edition edited by Linda Fierz and Toni Wolff entitled *Bericht über das Lecture von Prof. Dr. J. W. Hauer.* 3–8 October (Zurich, 1933), and bearing the title *Tantra Yoga* on the spine, differed in content from the English edition. In addition to a German translation of Jung's English lectures, it contained the text of Hauer's German lectures, an account of Toni Wolff's lecture " Tantrische Symbolik bei Goethe" (Tantric symbolism in Goethe) given to the club on 19 March 1932,[2] and an account of Jung's lecture " Westliche Parallelen zu den Tantrischen Symbolen" (Western parallels to tantric symbols) of 7 October 1932.

Jung's lectures were published in abridged form without annotations in *Spring: Journal of Archetypal Psychology and Jungian Thought* (1975 and 1976).

This present unabridged edition is based on the text of Mary Foote's first edition. Hauer's lectures have not been reproduced, with the exception of his final English lecture, which Jung attended and which forms the bridge to his lectures. This particular lecture demonstrates the relation between Hauer's and Jung's approaches. Where Hauer's exposition is referred to in Jung's lectures, the specific context has been supplied in a footnote.

[1] For information on Mary Foote, see Edward Foote, "Who was Mary Foote," *Spring: An Annual of Archetypal Psychology and Jungian Thought* (1974): 256–68.

[2] Her lecture, which contained interpretations of Goethe's work through the symbolism of Kundalini yoga, was published in full in her *Studien zu C. G. Jungs Psychologie* (Zurich: Daimon, 1981), 285–318.

In addition, Jung's comments in Hauer's German lectures in the Fierz and Wolff edition and the résumé of his 1930 lecture "Indian Parallels" contained in Olga von Koenig-Fachsenfeld's edition, *Bericht über das Deutsche Seminar von C. G. Jung, 6–11. Oktober 1930 in Küsnacht-Zürich* (Stuttgart, 1931) have been newly translated by Katherina Rowold and Michael Münchow respectively and included, together with Sir John Woodroffe's translation of the *Ṣaṭ-cakra-nirūpaṇa,* the tantric text that was the subject of Hauer's and Jung's commentaries. This has been reproduced from the fifteenth edition of Woodroffe's *The Serpent Power* (Madras, 1992), from which the illustrations of the cakras have also been reproduced (citations, unless otherwise indicated, are to this edition). For reasons of space, his copious explanatory notes have not been reproduced.

In editing the transcript, silent changes have been restricted to minor alterations in punctuation, spelling, and grammar. The *Spring* edition has been of assistance in this regard. With few exceptions, the orthography of the Sanskrit terms in the Foote edition has been followed. The spelling of these terms in the *Ṣaṭ-cakra-nirūpaṇa* and other texts cited has been maintained in the original form.

Sonu Shamdasani

ACKNOWLEDGMENTS

I would like to thank Ulrich Hoerni and Peter Jung for their assistance in a myriad of ways with the preparation of this seminar, and particularly the former for many helpful suggestions and for his comments on the manuscript; Franz Jung for kindly enabling me to consult his father's library and locating items for me; C. A. Meier and Tadeus Reichstein for sharing their recollections of the proceedings; Paul Bishop for locating Tadeus Reichstein; Beat Glaus for assisting the consultation of Jung's correspondence; Eric Donner, Michael Münchow, and Katherina Rowold for translations; Natalie Baron for assistance with transcription; Anthony Stadlen for supplying a copy of a letter of John Layard; Ernst Falzeder and André Haynal for inviting me to lecture at the Department of Psychiatry at the University of Geneva, which enabled me to undertake research in Switzerland; David Holt for the gift of copies of Jung's German-language seminars and lectures at the Eidgenössische Technische Hochschule; William McGuire for his comments on the manuscript; and the late Mary Foote, for her invaluable work transcribing and editing Jung's English-language seminars. Finally, I would like to thank the Erbengemeinschaft C. G. Jung for permission to consult and quote from Jung's unpublished manuscripts and correspondence with Wilhelm Hauer and Surendranath Dasgupta.

S.S.

MEMBERS OF THE SEMINAR

The following list accounts for persons whose names appear in the original multigraphed transcript, and others known to have attended. In the transcript only surnames are given. Here, the full names together with the country of residence where possible have been given. The actual attendance was far higher (see p. xxxviii). Biographical details on many of these individuals have recently been culled together by Paul Bishop.[1]

Alleman, Mr. Fritz (Switzerland)
Bailward, Mrs.
Baumann, Mr. Hans (Switzerland)
Barker, Dr. Culver (U.K.)
Baynes, Mrs. Cary F. (U.S.)
Bertine, Dr. Eleanor (U.S.)
Crowley, Mrs. Alice Lewisohn (U.S.)
Dell, Mr. Stanley W. (U.S.)
Diebold, Mrs.
Fierz, Mrs. Linda (Switzerland)
Foote, Mary (U.S.)
Hannah, Miss Barbara (U.K.)
Kranefeld, Dr. Wolfgang (Germany)
Mehlich, Mrs. Rose
Meier, Dr. C. A. (Switzerland)
Reichstein, Dr. Tadeus (Switzerland)
Sawyer, Mrs. Carol Fisher (U.S./Switzerland)
Shaw, Dr. Helen (U.K./Australia)
Sigg, Mrs. Martha Böddinghaus (Switzerland)
Spiegelberg, Dr. Friederich (Germany)
Spiegelberg, Mrs. (Germany)
Thiele, Miss
Trüb, Dr. Hans (Switzerland)
Wolff, Miss Antonia (Switzerland)

[1] See Paul Bishop, "The Members of Jung's Seminar on *Zarathustra*," *Spring: A Journal of Archetype and Culture* 56 (1994): 92–112.

LIST OF ABBREVIATIONS

Analytical Psychology = *Analytical Psychology: Notes of the Seminar Given in 1925 by C. G. Jung.* Edited by William McGuire. Princeton (Bollingen Series XCIX) and London, 1989.

CW = *The Collected Works of C. G. Jung.* 21 vols. Edited by Sir Herbert Read, Michael Fordham, and Gerhard Adler; William McGuire, executive editor; translated by R.F.C. Hull. New York and Princeton (Bollingen Series XX) and London, 1953–83.

ETH = Jung papers, Wissenschaftshistorische Sammlungen, Eidgenössische Technische Hochschule, Zurich.

HS = Wilhelm Hauer, "Yoga, Especially the Meaning of the Cakras." In Mary Foote, ed., *The Kundalini Yoga: Notes on the Lecture Given by Prof. Dr. J. W. Hauer with Psychological Commentary by Dr. C. G. Jung.* Zurich, 1932.

Interpretation of Visions = C. G. Jung, *Interpretation of Visions: Notes of the Seminar in Analytical Psychology, Autumn 1930–Winter 1934*, ed. Mary Foote. 11 vols. Zurich.

Jung: Letters = *C. G. Jung Letters.* 2 vols. Selected and edited by Gerhard Adler in collaboration with Aniela Jaffé; translated by R.F.C. Hull. Princeton (Bollingen Series XCV) and London, 1973 and 1975.

MDR = C. G. Jung, *Memories, Dreams, Reflections.* London, 1983.

Modern Psychology 3 and *4* = *Modern Psychology. The Process of Individuation.* Vols. 3, *Eastern Texts. Notes on the Lectures Given at the Eidgenössische Technische Hochschule, Zurich, by Prof. Dr. C. G. Jung, October 1938–March 1940*, and 4, *Exercita Spiritualia of St. Ignatius of Loyola.* 2d ed. Zurich, 1959.

Tantra Yoga = *Bericht über das Lecture von Prof. Dr. J. W. Hauer. 3–8 October.* Edited by Linda Fierz and Toni Wolff. Zurich, 1933.

INTRODUCTION

JUNG'S JOURNEY TO THE EAST

26 January 1930. Throughout India gatherings took a pledge that began:

> We believe that it is the inalienable right of the Indian people, as of any other people, to have freedom and to enjoy the fruits of their toil and have the necessities of life, so that they may have full opportunities of growth. We believe also that if any government deprives a people of these rights and oppresses them, the people have the further right to alter it or to abolish it. The British Government in India has not only deprived the Indian people of their freedom but has based itself on the exploitation of the masses, and has ruined India economically, politically, culturally, and spiritually. We believe that India must sever the British connection and attain Purna Swaraj or complete independence.[1]

Civil disobedience was proclaimed, Gandhi commenced his salt march, and Nehru was imprisoned.

*

Munich, 30 May. At a memorial for his deceased colleague, the sinologist Richard Wilhelm, Jung echoed these dramatic events:

> If we look to the East: an overwhelming destiny is fulfilling itself. . . . We have conquered the East politically. Do you know what happened, when Rome subjugated the near East politically? The spirit of the East entered Rome. Mithras became the Roman military god. . . . Would it be unthinkable that the same thing happened today and we would be just as blind as the cultured Romans, who marvelled at the superstitions of the Christians? . . . I know that our unconscious is crammed with Eastern symbolism. The spirit of the East is really *ante portas*. . . . I consider the fact that Wilhelm and the Indologist Hauer were invited to lecture on yoga at this year's congress of German psychotherapists, as an extremely significant sign of the times.[2] Consider what it means, when the

[1] In Jawaharlal Nehru, *An Autobiography* (London, 1989), 612.

[2] Hauer spoke on "Der Yoga im Lichte der Psychotherapie" (Yoga in the light of psychotherapy), in *Bericht über den V. Allgemeinen Ärztlichen Kongress für Psychotherapie in Baden-Baden, 26–29th April, 1930,* edited by E. Kretschmer and W. Cimbal (Leipzig, 1930).

> practising doctor, having to deal directly with suffering and therefore susceptible people, establishes contact with an Eastern system of healing![3]

This grand analogy encompassed what Jung saw as the epochal political and cultural significance of the impact of Eastern thought upon Western psychology, and set the stage for his encounter with Kundalini yoga.

In the sixties, Jung was adopted as a guru by the new age movement. Not least among the reasons for this was his role in promoting the study, aiding the dissemination, and providing modern psychological elucidations of Eastern thought. For journeyers to the East, he was adopted as a forefather. At the same time, these interests of Jung together with their appropriation by the counterculture were seen by many as confirmation of the mystical obscurantism of his psychology.

YOGA AND THE NEW PSYCHOLOGY

The emergence of depth psychology was historically paralleled by the translation and widespread dissemination of the texts of yoga.[4] Both were topical, exotic novelties. Newly arrived gurus and yogins vied with psychotherapists over a similar clientele who sought other counsel than was provided by Western philosophy, religion, and medicine. Hence the comparison between the two was not to be unexpected (not least by the potential customers). While a great deal had already been written comparing Eastern and Western thought,[5] the advent of the new depth psy-

[3] "Richard Wilhelm: In Memoriam," in *CW*, vol. 15, §90; translation modified. Elsewhere Jung contended that the violence of colonial imperialism presented the West with an imperative to understand Eastern thought: "The European invasion of the East was an act of violence on a grand scale. It has left us with the duty—noblesse oblige—of understanding the spirit of the East." "Commentary on 'The Secret of the Golden Flower,' " in *CW*, vol. 13, §84; translation modified. Where indicated, for the sake of literalness and accuracy, I have modified the translations from the *CW*. For a prolegomena to the consideration of Hull's translations, see my "Reading Jung Backwards? The Correspondence between Michael Fordham and Richard Hull Concerning 'The Type Problem in Poetry' in Jung's *Psychological Types*," *Spring: A Journal of Archetype and Culture* 55 (1994): 110–27.

[4] For an overview of the introduction of yoga in the West, see Georg Feuerstein, "East Comes West: An Historical Perspective," in Feuerstein, *Sacred Paths* (Burdett, N.Y., 1991). On the introduction of Eastern thought in general, see *Eastern Spirituality in America: Selected Writings*, edited by Robert Elwood (New York, 1987). For a model case study, see Peter Bishop, *Dreams of Power: Tibetan Buddhism, the Western Imagination and Depth Psychology* (London, 1992).

[5] See especially Raymond Schwab's monumental study *The Oriental Renaissance: Europe's Rediscovery of India and the East, 1680–1880*, translated by G. Patterson-Black and V. Renning (New York, 1984).

chologies heralded a new and more promising yardstick for comparison. For the depth psychologies sought to liberate themselves from the stultifying limitations of Western thought to develop maps of inner experience grounded in the transformative potential of therapeutic practices. A similar alignment of "theory" and "practice" seemed to be embodied in the yogic texts that moreover had developed independently of the bindings of Western thought. Further, the initiatory structure adopted by institutions of psychotherapy brought its social organization into proximity with that of yoga. Hence an opportunity for a new form of comparative psychology opened up.

As early as 1912, in *Transformation and Symbols of the Libido*, Jung provided psychological interpretations of passages in the *Upanishads* and the *Rig Veda*.[6] While this opened the possibility of a comparison between the practice of analysis and that of yoga, possibly the first explicit comparison was made by F. I. Winter in "The Yoga System and Psychoanalysis."[7] He contrasted psychoanalysis, as depicted in the work of Freud and Jung, with Patanjali's *Yoga Sutras*. Before Jung himself took up the subject, his work was already being compared to yoga—and the "new paths in psychology" that he sought to open up since leaving the auspices of the International Psychoanalytical Association promised to be the most fertile crossroads between Eastern and Western approaches.

An account of Jung's encounter with Eastern thought would be incomplete without mention of Count Hermann Keyserling and his School of Wisdom at Darmstadt, which provided a collegiate environment for Jung's explorations. Keyserling dealt with yoga in his *The Travel Diary of a Philosopher*, which was a much-acclaimed work. He contended that the new psychology actually represented a rediscovery of what was already known by the ancient Indians: "Indian wisdom is the profoundest which exists. . . . The further we get, the more closely do we approach the views of the Indians. Psychological research confirms, step by step, the assertions contained . . . within the old Indian science of the soul."[8]

[6] Gopi Krishna later criticized Jung's interpretation of a Vedic hymn concerning the producion of fire through the rubbing of sticks in which Jung saw 'unequivocal coitus symbolism' (See *Psychology of the Unconscious*, translated by Beatrice Hinkle, *CW*, supplement B, §§243–45), stating that "the terms used clearly point to the fire produced by Kundalini." *Kundalini for the New Age: Selected Writings of Gopi Krishna*, edited by Gene Kieffer (New York, 1988), 67.

[7] F. I. Winter, "The Yoga System and Psychoanalysis," *Quest* 10 (1918–19): 182–96, 315–35. Jung had a set of this journal from 1910 to 1924 and from 1929 to 1930 in his library.

[8] Count Hermann Keyserling, *The Travel Diary of a Philosopher*, translated by J. H. Reece (New York, 1925), 255–56. On Keyserling's encounter with India, see Anne Marie Bouisson-Maas, *Hermann Keyserling et L'Inde* (Paris, 1978).

What was distinctive about Keyserling's approach was that he viewed yoga as a psychological system superior to any in the West: "The Indians have done more than anyone else to perfect the method of training which leads to an enlargement and deepening of consciousness. . . . Yoga . . . appears entitled to one of the most highest places among the paths to self-perfection."[9] Several of his characterizations of the difference between the East and the West paralleled those of Jung, such as the following: "The Indian regards psychic phenomena as fundamental; these phenomena are more real to him than physical ones."[10]

It was at Darmstadt in the early 1920s that Jung met the sinologist Richard Wilhelm, and their 1928 collaboration over the Chinese alchemical text *The Secret of the Golden Flower*, which Wilhelm translated into German and for which Jung wrote a psychological commentary,[11] provided Jung with a means to assay the comparative psychology of East and West. Jung (who did not know Sanskrit) subsequently had similar collaborations with figures such as Heinrich Zimmer, Walter Evans-Wentz, Daisetz Suzuki, and in this instance Wilhelm Hauer, who represented the leading commentators on Eastern thought in Jung's day.[12]

The comparison between yoga and psychoanalysis was further explored by Keyserling's associate Oskar Schmitz in *Psychoanalyse und Yoga*,[13] which Schmitz dedicated to Keyserling. Schmitz claimed that of the schools of psychoanalysis it was Jung's rather than Freud's or Adler's that lay closest to yoga: "With the Jungian system for the first time the possibility enters that psychoanalysis can contribute to human higher de-

[9] Keyserling, *The Travel Diary of a Philosopher*, 124–25.

[10] Ibid., 95. Cf. Jung: "The East bases itself upon psychic reality, that is, upon the psyche as the main and unique condition of existence." "Psychological Commentary on 'The Tibetan Book of the Great Liberation,'" in *CW*, vol. 11, §770. (Jung's commentary was written in 1939 and first published in 1954). Such characterizations follow a long line of orientalist speculations in which Indian thought was characterized as dreamlike (Hegel) or as being dominated by imagination (Schlegel). See Ronald Inden, *Imagining India* (London, 1990), 93–97.

[11] Jung, *CW*, vol. 13.

[12] This period of scholarship is increasingly coming in for reappraisal. See *Heinrich Zimmer: Coming into His Own*, edited by Margaret Case (Princeton, 1994), and *A Zen Life: D. T. Suzuki Remembered*, edited by Masao Abe (New York, 1986). Expressions of reciprocal admiration between Jung and his colleagues were frequent. For example, on receiving his commentary to the *The Tibetan Book of the Great Liberation*, Evans-Wentz wrote to Jung that it was an honor to be able to include a contribution from "the foremost authority in the West on the Science of the Mind" (Evans-Wentz to Jung, 13 July 1939, *ETH*).

[13] Oskar Schmitz, *Psychoanalyse und Yoga* (Darmstadt, 1923).

velopment. . . . It is not a method of yoga, and does not even want to be one, but possibly Jung's system is such."[14] Jung's response to Schmitz's work was equivocal:

> Inasmuch as I regard the psychoanalytical and psychosynthetic methods likewise as means of self-improvement, your comparison with the yoga method seems thoroughly plausible to me. It appears to me, however, as one must emphasize, that it is merely an analogy which is involved, since nowadays far too many Europeans are inclined to carry Eastern ideas and methods over unexamined into our occidental mentality. This happens, in my opinion, neither to our advantage nor to the advantage of those ideas. For what has emerged from the Eastern spirit is based upon the peculiar history of that mentality, which is most fundamentally different from ours.[15]

TANTRISM AND KUNDALINI YOGA

The omnipresence of yoga classes alongside aerobics, weight training, massage, and other sects of the contemporary body cults at sports and fitness centers makes it easy to forget that yoga is an ancient spiritual discipline.

Yoga partakes of two notions generally held in common in Indian philosophy and religion—reincarnation, and the quest for emancipation from the cycle of birth, death, and rebirth. Mircea Eliade stated that for yoga and Sāṃkhya philosophy to which it is related, in contrast to other Indian schools of thought, "the world is *real* (not illusory—as it is, for example, for Vedānta). Nevertheless, if the world *exists* and *endures*, it is because of the 'ignorance' of spirit."[16] What distinguishes yoga is its essentially practical cast. Surendranath Dasgupta noted: "The yoga philosophy has essentially a practical tone and its object consists mainly in demonstrating the means of attaining salvation, oneness, the liberation of purusha."[17] Many different definitions and accounts of yoga have

[14] Ibid., 65, translated by Eric Donner.

[15] Jung to Schmitz, 26 May 1923, "C. G. Jung: Letters to Oskar Schmitz, 1921–31," *Psychological Perspectives* 6 (1975): 81; translation modified.

[16] Mircea Eliade, *Yoga: Immortality and Freedom*, translated by Willard R. Trask (Bollingen Series LVI; reprint, London, 1989), 9.

[17] Surendranath Dasgupta, *Yoga as Philosophy and Religion* (London, 1924), 124. On the translation of *puruṣa*, which is often rendered as "self," see lecture 2, nn. 11 and 12. Jung met Dasgupta when he was in Calcutta in 1938 (Jung to Dasgupta, 2 February 1939,

been given. Eliade stated: "Etymologically, *yoga* derives from the root *yuj*, 'to bind together,' 'hold fast,' 'yoke.' . . . The word *yoga* serves, in general, to designate any *ascetic technique* and any *method of meditation.*"[18] For Feuerstein, "Yoga is a specifically Indian tradition consisting of sets of varyingly codified and/or systematized ideas, attitudes, methods and techniques primarily intended to induce a transformation in the practitioner (*yogin*) and transmitted from one teacher to one or more disciples in a more or less formal setting."[19] The earliest traces of yoga have been traced to the third millennium B.C.[20] There are several main schools of yoga: Raja yoga, Hatha yoga, Jnana yoga, Bhakti yoga, Karma yoga, Mantra yoga, Laya yoga, and Kundalini yoga. To characterize the latter, it is useful to consider several general features of the tantric movement.

Tantrism was a religious and philosophical movement that became popular from the fourth century onward and influenced Indian philosophy, mysticism, ethics, art, and literature. Agehananda Bharati stated, "What distinguishes tantric from other Hindu and Buddhist teaching is its systematic emphasis on the identity of the absolute [*paramārtha*] and the phenomenal [*vyavahāra*] world when filtered through the experience of worship [*sādhanā*]."[21] Tantrism was anti-ascetic and anti-speculative, and represented a transgressive countercurrent to mainstream Hinduism. It rejected the prevalent caste system and represented a transvaluation of values. In tantrism there was a celebration of the body, which was seen as the microcosm of the universe. In contrast to the masculinist cast of traditional Hinduism, Eliade noted that in tantrism, "for the first time in the spiritual history of Aryan India, the Great Goddess acquires a predominant position. . . . We also recognize a sort of reli-

ETH). The following year Jung invited Dasgupta to lecture in Zurich: "We should be much obliged if you would give us a talk about the relation of mind and body according to yoga in your Saturday lecture at the Psychol. Club. As a theme for the lecture at the Polytechnicum I would propose Psychology or Philosophy of Yoga (specially Patanjali Yoga Sutra)." (Jung to Dasgupta, 17 April 1939, *ETH*). Dasgupta lectured to the Psychological Club in May.

[18] Eliade, *Yoga: Immortality and Freedom,* 4.

[19] Feuerstein, *The Yoga-Sutra of Patanjali: An Exercise in the Methodology of Textual Analysis* (London, 1979), 1.

[20] Vivian Worthington, *A History of Yoga* (London, 1989), 11.

[21] Agehananda Bharati, *The Tantric Tradition* (London, 1992), 18. Narendra Nath Bhattacharyya noted that "although Tantra in its earlier stage opposed the Vedantic philosophy of illusion and admitted the reality of the world . . . [later] superimposed elements brought it into line with Vedanta." *History of the Tantric Religion: A Historical, Ritualistic and Philosophical Study* (New Delhi, 1982), 14.

gious rediscovery of the mystery of woman."[22] The different outlook of tantrism was reflected in its practice, which often utilized elements absent from traditional religious rituals. Zimmer stated that tantrism "insists on the holiness and purity of all things; hence, the 'five forbidden things' . . . constitute the substance of the sacramental fare in certain tantric rites: wine, meat, fish, parched grain, and sexual intercourse."[23] In what are known as the "right-handed" schools these are used in rituals symbolically, whereas in the "left-handed" schools they are used literally.

Apropos the contemporary perception of tantrism Jacob Needleman aptly noted that "the moment one hears the word 'tantrism,' various wild and lurid associations spring forth in the Western mind which add up to a *pastiche* of psychospiritual science fiction and sexual acrobatics that would put to shame even the most imaginative of our contemporary pornographers and quite eclipse the achievements of our hardiest erotic warriors."[24] The intersection of the new age movement and the sexual revolution in the sixties led to increasing interest in tantrism in the West accompanied by numerous "how to do it" manuals that focused on its ritualized sexual practices—often glossed in the process was that in tantrism, such practices were directed not toward the liberation of sexuality per se but toward liberation from the cycle of rebirth.

Jung specified his psychological understanding of tantric yoga as follows:

> Indian philosophy is namely the interpretation given to the precise condition of the non-ego, which affects our personal psychology, however independent from us it remains. It sees the aim of human development as bringing about an approach to and connection between the specific nature of the non-ego and the conscious ego. Tantra yoga then gives a representation of the condition and the developmental phases of this impersonality, as it itself in its own way produces the light of a higher suprapersonal consciousness.[25]

At a time when psychology was characterized by the reign of behavior-

[22] Eliade, *Yoga: Immortality and Freedom*, 202. For a reevaluation of the role of women in tantrism, see Miranda Shaw, *Passionate Enlightenment: Women in Tantric Buddhism* (Princeton, 1994).

[23] Heinrich Zimmer, *Philosophies of India*, edited by Joseph Campbell (London, Bollingen Series XXVI, 1953), 572.

[24] Jacob Needleman, "Tibet in America," in Needleman, *The New Religions* (London, 1972), 177.

[25] Résumé of Jung's lecture "Indische Parallelen" (Indian parallels), 7 October 1931, in *Bericht über das Deutsche Seminar von Dr. C. G. Jung, 5–10. Oktober in Küsnacht-Zürich*, edited

ism, the positivist experimental epistemology, and the growing dominance of psychoanalysis, and when developmental phases could hardly be associated with anything other than what was becoming the alpha and omega of the study of personality—the child—Kundalini yoga presented Jung with a model of something that was almost completely lacking in Western psychology—an account of the developmental phases of higher consciousness.

In Kundalini yoga the body is represented as consisting in a series of cakras: *mulādhāra, svādhiṣṭhāna, maṇipūra, anāhata, viśuddha, ājñā,* and *sahasrāra.* These are located in different parts of the body and linked by channels (*nāḍīs*), the most important of which are the *iḍā, piṅgalā,* and *suṣumṇā.* Most commentators concur that the cakras and the *nāḍīs* are not intended as physiological depictions of the body in the contemporary Western sense but represent a subtle or mystical body. Feuerstein described them as "idealized version of the structure of the subtle body, which are meant to guide the yogin's visualisation and contemplation."[26]

Jung's lectures are principally taken up with providing a modern psychological interpretation of the cakras. Narendra Nath Bhattacharyya stated that the cakras are best understood through seeing their different components as constituted by a process of historical layering:

> From a historical point of view it may be suggested that the *padmas* or *cakras* were originally conceived of in terms of human anatomy for the purpose of physiological study. . . . At a subsequent stage, in conformity with the tantric idea that the human body is the microcosm of the universe, worldly objects such as the sun, moon, mountains, rivers, etc., were connected with these *cakras.* Each *cakra* was again thought to represent the gross and the subtle elements . . . quite in accordance with the tantric idea that the deities reside within the human body and that the aspirant has to feel the deity within the body itself. These *cakras* came to be conceived of as the seat of the male and female principles, symbolized by the male and female organs. . . . The presiding deities of the *cakras* were originally tantric goddesses. . . . The theory of letters, of the alphabet symbolising different *tattvas* was also grafted, and in this way we

by Olga von Koenig-Fachsenfeld (Stuttgart, 1932), 66–67; my translation. On the relation of this lecture to the lecture of the same title in the appendix to this volume, see xxxiv.

[26] Feuerstein, *Yoga: The Technology of Ecstasy* (Wellingborough, 1990), 258.

> come across the functioning of a very elaborate and complicated process which the *cakras* are supposed to represent in their qualitatively transformed capacity.[27]

The Kundalini is represented in the form of a serpent coiled around the spine that lies sleeping in *mulādhāra,* the lowest cakra. Feuerstein defined the Kundalini as "a microcosmic manifestation of the primordial Energy, or Shakti. It is the Universal Power as it is connected with the finite body-mind."[28] The object is to awaken Kundalini through ritual practices and to enable her ascent up the *suṣumṇā nāḍī* through the cakra system. When it reaches the topmost cakra the blissful union of Śiva and Śakti occurs. This leads to a far-reaching transformation of the personality.[29]

JUNG'S ENCOUNTER WITH YOGA

In *Memories, Dreams, Reflections,* Jung recounted how during his "confrontation with the unconscious" around the time of the First World War, "I was frequently so wrought up that I had to eliminate the emotions through yoga practices. But since it was my purpose to learn what was going on within myself, I would do them only until I had calmed myself and could take up again the work with the unconscious."[30]

In Hauer's last English lecture (see appendix 3), Jung gave an account of how his interest in Kundalini was awakened through an encounter with a European woman brought up in the East who presented dreams and fantasies that he could not understand until he came across Sir John

[27] Bhattacharyya, *History of the Tantric Religion,* 324–25.

[28] Feuerstein, *Yoga: The Technology of Ecstasy,* 264.

[29] For a fascinating firsthand account of the awakening of the Kundalini accompanied by a lucid psychological commentary, see Gopi Krishna, *Kundalini: The Evolutionary Energy in Man,* with a psychological commentary by James Hillman (London, 1970). For a comprehensive guide to the practice of Kundalini yoga, see Swami Satyananda Saraswati, *Kundalini Tantra* (Bihar, 1993).

[30] Jung, *MDR,* 201; translation modified. It is not known what specific practices Jung utilized. However, Fowler McCormick, recalling an analytical interview with Jung in 1937, spoke of Jung's recommendation of a procedure not without similarities to the śavāsana asana of Hatha yoga: "Dr. Jung said that under periods of great stress the one thing which was useful was to lie down flat on a couch or a bed and just lie quietly there and breathe quietly with the sense that . . . the wind of disturbance blew over one." Fowler McCormick interview, Jung Oral History Archive, Countway Library of Medicine, Harvard Medical School, 17.

Woodroffe's *The Serpent Power*,[31] which consisted of translations of the *Ṣaṭ-cakra-nirūpaṇa* and the *Pādukā-pañcaka*, together with extensive commentaries.[32]

Woodroffe was primarily responsible for making the tantric texts known in the West through his translations and commentaries.[33] He stated: "All the world (I speak of course of those interested in such subjects) is beginning to speak of Kundalinî Shakti."[34] This was in no small part due to his sympathetic treatment of a subject that had been treated with derision. He described his intention as follows: "We, who are foreigners, must place ourselves in the skin of the Hindu, and must look at their doctrine and ritual through their eyes and not our own."[35]

Jung claimed that the symbolism of Kundalini yoga suggested that the bizarre symptomatology that patients at times presented actually resulted from the awakening of the Kundalini. He argued that knowledge of such symbolism enabled much that would otherwise be seen as the meaningless by-products of a disease process to be understood as meaningful symbolic processes, and explicated the often peculiar physical localizations of symptoms.[36] With the hegemony of the biochemical ap-

[31] Arthur Avalon (pseud. Sir John Woodroffe), *The Serpent Power* (London, 1919). The copy in Jung's library is the first edition and contains many marginal annotations. Woodroffe was born in 1865. He studied at Oxford and became a barrister. He was an advocate at the Calcutta high court and a fellow and Tagore law professor at the University of Calcutta. From 1904–22, he was on the standing council for the Government of India and Puisne judge of the high court of Calcutta. He was knighted in 1915, and returned to become a reader in Indian law at Oxford from 1923 to 1930. He died in 1936. (From *Who Was Who, 1929–1940* [London, 1941], 1485.) No evidence has emerged that he had any direct contact with Jung.

[32] The *Ṣaṭ-cakra-nirūpaṇa* (Description of the six centers) was the sixth chapter of Purṇananda-Svāmī's *Śri-tattva-cintāmaṇī*, composed in 1577.

[33] Heinrich Zimmer recalled: "The values of the Hindu tradition were disclosed to me through the enormous life-work of Sir John Woodroffe, alias Arthur Avalon, a pioneer and a classic author in Indic studies, second to none, who, for the first time, by many publications and books made available the extensive and complex treasure of late Hindu tradition: the Tantras, a period as grand and rich as the Vedas, the Epic, Puranâs, etc.; the latest crystallisation of Indian wisdom, the indispensable closing link of a chain, affording keys to countless problems in the history of Buddhism and Hinduism, in mythology and symbolism." "Some Biographical Remarks about Henry R. Zimmer," *Artistic Form and Yoga in the Sacred Images of India*, translated by G. Chapple and J. Lawson (Princeton, 1984), 254.

[34] Ibid., 639.

[35] John Woodroffe, *Shakti and Shâkta: Essays and Addresses on the Shâkta Tantrashâstra*, 3d ed. (London, 1929), x. Jung had a copy of this book in his library.

[36] On the bearing of Kundalini yoga to the question of the localization of consciousness, see C. A. Meier, *The Psychology of Jung*, vol. 3.: *Consciousness*, translated by D. Roscoe (Boston, 1989), chap. 4, "The Localization of Consciousness," 47–64.

proach to so-called mental disorders and the rise of an endless succession of "wonder" drugs such as Prozac, Jung's insistence on the psychogenic and symbolic significance of such states is even more timely now than then. As R. D. Laing stated in this regard, "It was Jung who broke the ground here, but few have followed him."[37]

Jung's published writings specifically on Indian religion consisted of two essays, "Yoga and the West" (1936) and "The Psychology of Eastern Meditation" (1948), together with a foreword to Zimmer's 1944 *Der Weg zum Selbst* (The way to the self), which Jung edited.[38] His most extensive work on these topics was presented in his seminars—commencing with the "Western Parallels" seminars in 1930 (see appendix 1), 1931, and 1932 and the Kundalini seminars in 1932, and culminating in his commentaries on Patanjali's *Yoga Sutras*, the *Amitāyur-Dhyāna-Sūtra* and the *Shrichakrasambhara* in 1938–39 at the Eidgenössische Technische Hochschule in Zurich.[39] Given the format, Jung's statements in this seminar must be taken provisionally, as constituting work in progress.

In 1937 he was invited by the British Government to take part in the twenty-fifth anniversary celebrations at the University of Calcutta the following year. Jung took the opportunity to travel in India for three months, during which time he received honorary doctorates from the Universities of Allahabad, Benares, and Calcutta.[40] On his return he

[37] R. D. Laing, *The Politics of Experience and the Birds of Paradise* (London, 1985), 137. Jung's view that so-called pathological experiences may in actuality be misrecognized experiences of the arousal of Kundalini is confirmed and developed by Lee Sannella, *The Kundalini Experience: Psychosis or Transcendence?* (Lower Lake, Calif., 1992).

[38] Jung, *CW*, vol. 11. In addition, an interview of Jung by Shin'ichi Hisamatsu in 1958 was published under the title "Gespräch mit einem Zen-Meister" (Conversation with a Zen master), edited by Robert Hinshaw and Lela Fischli, in *C. G. Jung im Gespräch: Interviews, Reden, Begegnungen* (Zurich, 1986).

[39] *Modern Psychology 3*. In 1933 Jung gave a series of seminars in Berlin on the subject of dream analysis, in which the contrast between Eastern and Western thought played a certain role, and in which Zimmer presented a talk on the psychology of yoga (*Bericht über das Berliner Seminar von Dr. C. G. Jung vom 26. Juni bis 1. Juli 1933* [Berlin, 1933]). In addition, from 1933 to 1937, the Eranos conferences, where Jung presented major studies on the archetypes, the process of individuation, and alchemy, were focused on the contrast between Eastern and Western thought: "Yoga and Meditation in the East and the West" (1933), "Symbolism and Spiritual Guidance in the East and the West" (1934 and 1935), "The Shaping of the Idea of Redemption in the East and the West" (1936 and 1937), and such contrasts continued to play an important role in the following years. Recently recovered notes of the original German wording of Jung's Eidgenössische Technische Hochschule seminars are under examination, and a definitive text is being prepared for publication.

[40] The deputy registrar of Benares Hindu University wrote to Henri Ellenberger on 28 March 1967 that "Professor C. G. Jung was awarded D. Litt (Doctor of Letters) Honoris Causa on 20th December 1937 by this University." The registrar of the University of Cal-

wrote his impressions in two articles: "The Dreamlike World of India" and "What India Can Teach Us."[41] Fowler McCormick, who accompanied Jung on this trip, recalled an experience of Jung's that had tantric overtones:

> As we would go through temples of Kali, which were numerous at almost every Hindu city, we saw the evidences of animal sacrifice: the places were filthy dirty—dried blood on the floor and lots of remains of red betelnut all around, so that the colour red was associated with destructiveness. Concurrently in Calcutta Jung began to have a series of dreams in which the colour red was stressed. It wasn't long before dysentery overcame Dr. Jung and I had to take him to the English hospital at Calcutta. . . . A more lasting effect of this impression of the destructiveness of Kali was the emotional foundation it gave him for the conviction that evil was not a negative thing but a positive thing. . . . The influence of that experience in India, to my mind, was very great on Jung in his later years.[42]

In "Yoga and the West" Jung delimited his brief as follows:

> I will be silent on the meaning of yoga for India, because I cannot presume to pass judgment on something I do not know from personal experience. I can, however, say something about what it means for the West. Our lack of direction borders on psychic anarchy. Therefore any religious or philosophical practice amounts to a *psychological discipline*, therefore *a method of psychic hygiene*.[43]

cutta wrote to Ellenberger on 10 May 1967 that "the degree of Doctor of Law (Honoris Causa) was conferred upon Dr. Charles Gustave Jung in absentia by this University at a special Convocation held on 7th January, 1938. . . . Dr. Jung could not be present at the convocation owing to indisposition." Ellenberger archives, Hôpital Sainte-Anne, Paris.

[41] Jung, *CW*, vol. 12 (1939). A further account of Jung's time in India is found in *MDR*, 304–14. Jung frequently related anecdotes of his experiences there in his seminars and letters. He subsequently maintained correspondences with many of the individuals he met there.

[42] Fowler McCormick interview, Jung Oral History Archive, Countway Library of Medicine, Harvard Medical School, Boston, 25–26.

[43] Jung, "Yoga and the West," in *CW*, vol. 11, §866; translation modified. After his trip to India, however, Jung became less circumspect in this regard: "Tantric yoga is in rather bad repute in India; it is criticised because it is connected with the body, particularly with sex," *Modern Psychology 3*, 42; and "Yoga is mainly found in India now as a business proposition and woe to us when it reaches Europe," ibid., 69.

Thus Jung's interest, in contrast with Dasgupta's, were with yoga not as "philosophy and religion" but as psychology. Hence his definition of yoga was a psychological one: "Yoga was originally a natural process of introversion. . . . Such introversions lead to characteristic inner processes of personality changes. In the course of several thousand years these introversions became gradually organized as methods, and along widely differing ways."[44] Jung's concern was not primarily with the canonical and organized methods and teachings of yoga but with the putative natural processes of introversion that originally underlay them. This perspective legitimized the liberties that he took with the former in the seminar that follows. Jung saw the inner processes to which yoga gave rise as universal, and the particular methods employed to achieve them as culturally specific.[45] For Jung, yoga represented a rich storehouse of symbolic depictions of inner experience and of the individuation process in particular. He claimed that "important parallels with yoga [and analytical psychology] have come to light, especially with Kundalini yoga and the symbolism of tantric yoga, Lamaism, and Taoistic yoga in China. These forms of yoga with their rich symbolism afford me invaluable comparative material for the interpretation of the collective unconscious."[46] Jung's aim was to develop a cross-cultural comparative psychology of inner experience. Hence he was concerned to differentiate his approach from indigenous Eastern understandings, as represented in the missionary efforts of the Ramakrishna movement and such advocates as Romain Rolland,[47] the Western appropriation of Eastern teachings, such as by the theosophists, Hauer's historico-existential approach, and the spiritual valorization of Eastern thought by Keyserling's School of Wisdom, and contrastingly to demonstrate the specificity of a psychological viewpoint.

Throughout his writings on Eastern thought, while Jung promoted

[44] Jung, "Yoga and the West," §873; translation modified.

[45] On reading Gopi Krishna's account of his experiences, the Jungian analyst John Layard noted that his descriptions of the awakening of the Kundalini "correspond so closely to what I have referred to as my 'feinting experiences,' with similar noises & sensations, which were truly terrifying, & mixed up also with highly mystical ones, also of course Psychosexual, that I'm wondering whether something of the same kind may have been happening to me—The devilish outcome of an almost divine experience. We in the West are so lacking in the true religiosity that we have lost the threads, & get good things so muddled up with bad, that we have lost the purity of divine dirt!" (John Layard to Anthony Stadlen, 17 October 1968; personal possession of Anthony Stadlen.)

[46] Jung, "Yoga and the West," §875; translation modified.

[47] Romain Rolland, *Prophets of the New India,* translated by Malcolm Smith (London, 1930).

and endorsed their study he cautioned against their practice by Westerners: "There are many different kinds of yoga and Europeans often become hypnotized by it, but it is essentially Eastern, no European has the necessary patience and it is not right for him. . . . The more we study yoga, the more we realize how far it is from us; a European can only imitate it and what he acquires by this is of no real interest."[48] For Jung the danger was one of mimetic madness: "The European who practices yoga does not know what he is doing. It has a bad effect upon him, sooner or later he gets afraid and sometimes it even leads him over the edge of madness."[49] This led him to conclude that "in the course of the centuries the West will produce its own yoga, and it will be on the basis laid down by Christianity."[50]

With the mushrooming of yoga and meditational practices in the West, such statements have come in for a great deal of criticism. However, such cautions are frequently found in the works of writers on yoga contemporary to Jung both in the East and in the West. Thus Dasgupta wrote:

> If anyone wishes methodically to pursue a course which may lead him ultimately to the goal aimed at by yoga, he must devote his entire life to it under the strict practical guidance of an advanced teacher. The present work can in no sense be considered as a practical guide for such purposes. . . . The philosophical, psychological, cosmological, ethical, and religious doctrines . . . are extremely interesting in themselves, and have a definitely assured place in the history of the progress of human thought.[51]

Likewise, Eliade wrote:

> We have no intention of inviting Western scholars to practice yoga (which, by the way, is not so easy as some amateurs are wont to suggest) or of proposing that the various Western disciplines practice yogic methods or adopt the yogic ideology. Another point of view seems to us far more fertile—to study, as attentively as possible, the results obtained by such means of exploring the psyche.[52]

[48] Jung, *Modern Psychology 3*, 17.
[49] Ibid., 71.
[50] Jung, "Yoga and the West," in *CW*, vol. 11, §876.
[51] Dasgupta, *Yoga as Philosophy and Religion*, vii.
[52] Eliade, *Yoga: Immortality and Freedom*, xvii.

Keyserling was also critical of the adoption of yoga practices in the West:

> It is very significant that the Indian breathing exercises, which have been popularized by Swami Vivekananda through his lectures in America, have not helped a single American to a higher condition, but, on the other hand, are reported to have brought all the more into hospitals and lunatic asylums. . . . It has not been proved, even of the most harmless exercises, . . . that they are appropriate to the organism of the European.[53]

Jung's conclusion that something analogous to yoga would arise on the basis of Christianity was also close to Keyserling's view on the Christian basis of Western psychology:

> The Indian concepts are alien to us Westerners; most people are incapable—it is just the theosophists who prove this—of acquiring an inner relation to them. Moreover, physiologically we are all Christians, whether our consciousness recognizes this or not. Thus every doctrine which continues in the Christian spirit has a better chance of taking hold of our innermost being than the profoundest doctrine of foreign origin.[54]

WILHELM HAUER[55]

Wilhelm Hauer was born in Württemberg in 1881, six years after Jung. He had a Protestant theological education and was sent in 1906 by the Basel Mission to India. Like Richard Wilhelm, Hauer was more impressed by the spirituality he met than by that which he brought with him. He later recalled:

[53] Keyserling, *The Travel Diary of a Philosopher,* 276. Swami Vivekânanda's address at the World's Congress of Religions in Chicago in 1893 made a great impact, and together with his subsequent lectures, did much to promote interest in Indian thought. His lectures were published as *Yoga Philosophy: Lectures Delivered in New York, Winter of 1895–96 by the Swâmi Vivekânanda on Râja Yoga, or Conquering the Internal Nature,* 5th ed. (New York, 1899). See also Eugene Taylor, "Swami Vivekânanda and William James," *Prabuddha Bharata* 91 (1896): 374–85. Jung had copies of several of Vivekânanda's works in his library.

[54] Ibid., 165.

[55] Information concerning Hauer has been drawn from his own works and from the comprehensive biography by Margerete Dierks (which includes a full bibliography of Hauer's writings), *Jakob Wilhelm Hauer, 1881–1962* (Heidelberg, 1986).

> My five years' experience in India has widened and deepened my religious views in a way I had never expected. I went to India as a missionary in the ordinary sense, but I came back from India a missionary in a different sense. I learned that we have only the right to state, to testify to what is in us, and not expect others to be converted to our point of view, much less to try to convert them.[56]

Together with his pastorate, Hauer undertook studies in comparative religion. This included a spell at the University of Oxford. In 1921 he abandoned the former and took up a post as a university lecturer at Tübingen. In 1927 he became a professor of Indian studies and comparative religion and published widely on these topics. It was Hauer's talk "Der Yoga im Lichte der Psychotherapie" (Yoga in the light of psychotherapy) that drew the attention of Jung. Hauer commenced by stating:

> I know possibly enough about it to recognize that yoga, seen as a whole, is a striking parallel to Western psychotherapy (although fundamental differences lie there) but to compare the individual parts of yoga with the different orientations of Western psychotherapy with its special methods—this I noticed soon—the detailed knowledge and above all the conclusive experiment are lacking for me.[57]

In the remainder of his talk he gave a factual account of yoga and left the comparison between the two to his audience. Hauer presented himself as an Indologist seeking psychotherapists with whom he could have a dialogue concerning the similarities and differences between yoga and psychotherapy. It was Jung who took up the invitation.

Opinions concerning Hauer vary considerably among scholars. Zimmer recalled:

> My personal contact with Jung started in 1932. At that time, another Indic scholar, most unreliable as a scholar and as a character as well, but endowed with a demoniac, erratic vitality made up of primitive resistances and ambitions, drew the attention of doctor-psychiatrist-psychologists to the subject of yoga. Now, after his long collaboration with Richard Wilhelm on Chinese wisdom, Jung was ready to

[56] *The World's Religions against War. The Proceedings of the Preliminary Conference Held at Geneva, September 1928, to Make Arrangements for a Universal Religious Peace Conference* (New York, 1928), 60.

[57] Hauer, "Der Yoga im Lichte der Psychotherapie," 1; my translation.

> take over similar stuff from Indic scholars. Hauer had a seminary [*sic*] on Kundaliniyoga at Zuerich, and I introduced myself at this forum with a lecture on the types of yoga in Indian tradition, in the spring of 1932.[58]

By contrast, Feuerstein stated that "J. W. Hauer . . . to whom we owe a great deal in the study of yoga and Samkhya . . . not only possessed a rich knowledge of Indian thought, but was also well acquainted with Western culture. . . The central theme of all his works is man as a religious being, and Hauer himself was a sincere god-seeker and mystic."[59] C. A. Meier described Hauer as a "typically dry German scientist," "an excellent Sanskritist," and a "very nice chap."[60]

THE GENESIS OF THE KUNDALINI SEMINARS

According to Barbara Hannah,

> It was in the autumn of 1932 that the Indologue, J. W. Hauer, at that time a professor of his subject in Tübingen, came to Zurich to give us a seminar on Kundalini yoga. This was a thrillingly interesting parallel to the process of individuation, but, as always happens when a perfected Indian philosophy is placed before a European audience, we all got terribly out of ourselves and confused. We were used to the unconscious taking us into this process very gradually, every dream revealing a little more of the process, but the East has been working at such meditation techniques for many centuries and has therefore collected far more symbols than we were able to digest. Moreover, the East is too far above everyday reality for us, aiming at Nirvana instead of at our present, three-dimensional life. Jung was confronted with a very disorientated group who had greatly appreciated but been unable to digest Hauer's brilliant exposition of Kundalini yoga. When this was over, therefore, Jung devoted the first three lectures of his English seminar to a psychological com-

[58] Zimmer, "Some Biographical Remarks about Henry R. Zimmer," in *Artistic Form and Yoga in the Sacred Images of India*, 259–60. Zimmer's lecture, "Einige Aspekte des Yoga" (Some aspects of yoga) took place on 18 June 1932 and preceded the Kundalini seminars.

[59] Feuerstein, "The Essence of Yoga," in *A Reappraisal of Yoga: Essays in Indian Philosophy*, edited by G. Feuerstein and J. Miller (London, 1971), b.

[60] Interview with the editor, 30 June 1994.

mentary on Hauer's lectures which got us all back—the richer for the experiences—into ourselves.[61]

Hannah gives the impression that Jung's seminar was a spontaneous improvisation to therapeutically counsel his disoriented auditors. This account has been uncritically followed by subsequent commentators.[62] By contrast, Meier, who was also present, stated that while Hannah might have found Hauer's seminars confusing he found them perfectly clear, and added that there was no general confusion.[63] He also stated that Jung's psychological commentary was from the outset part of a planned collaboration. Hauer, as the specialist, was to present a scholarly philological and historical account to provide the root support for Jung's psychological interpretation.[64]

Further evidence that Jung's seminar was by no means simply a spontaneous improvisation is given by the fact that in both 1930 and 1931 he presented lectures on Kundalini yoga and the symbolism of the cakras.[65] The first of these appears to be Jung's first public presentation of the subject (see appendix 1). As the second largely reduplicates this, it has not been included in this volume. There also exists a series of undated manuscripts of Jung's which demonstrate the careful preparation that he put into his seminars.[66] Jung was lecturing on the topic of Kundalini yoga and giving symbolic interpretations of the cakras before his collabo-

[61] Barbara Hannah, *Jung: His Life and Work: A Biographical Memoir* (New York and London, 1976), 206. For general background to Jung's seminars, see William McGuire's introduction to *Dream Analysis: Notes of the Seminar Given in 1928–1930 by C. G. Jung* (Princeton, Bollingen Series XCIX, 1984).

[62] Harold Coward, *Jung and Eastern Thought* (with contributions by J. Borelli, J. Jordens, and J. Henderson) (Delhi, 1991) (citations are to the Indian edition), 110–11; John Clarke, *Jung and Eastern Thought: A Dialogue with the Orient* (London, 1994), 110.

[63] Meier, interview with the editor. On Hannah's confusion see appendix 3, 92.

[64] Meier, interview with the editor.

[65] On 11 October 1930, Jung's lecture was on Indian parallels (see appendix 1). On 7 October 1931 Jung presented a lecture covering the same ground (also in German), under the same title: see *Bericht über das Deutsche Seminar von Dr. C. G. Jung, 5–10. Oktober in Küsnacht-Zürich*, 66–73. Of this event, Emma Jung wrote to Oskar Schmitz on 12 October: "The seminar was very well attended again—we were quite surprised that despite the critical times so many participants came from Germany, too. Pictures and phantasies were again treated, of various female patients, but which all contained the 'Kundalini' symbolism." "C. G. Jung: Letters to Oskar Schmitz, 1921–31," 94–95.

[66] The following are the manuscripts upon which it appears that Jung drew directly for these seminars: 1) a three-page handwritten manuscript headed "Tantrism"; 2) a four-page handwritten manuscript headed "Avalon Serpent," consisting of references and quotations from 1–76 and 210–72 of *The Serpent Power* (1st ed.); 3) a three-page handwritten manuscript headed "Chakras"; and 4) a two-page typewritten manuscript headed "Die Beschreibung der beiden Centren Shat-chakra Nirupana" (The description of each center

ration with Hauer, which gave him the opportunity to expand rather than to commence his work on this topic.

On 13 June 1931 Hauer presented a lecture, "Ueberblick über den Yoga" (Overview of yoga), to the Psychological Club in Zurich. Jung's correspondence with Hauer sheds new light on the active organizational role he took in the seminars. The earliest reference I have located concerning Hauer's lectures is Emma Jung's letter to Schmitz on 12 October 1931, in which she wrote: "I am just now corresponding with Prof. Hauer in regard to a seminar which he would hold for us in Zurich also for a week. He suggests the second half of March and as the theme, yoga practices, I think. Would you be there too?"[67] In the first letter located between Hauer and Jung, Hauer thanked Jung for sending him his new book: "I am sure that I will also derive sundry benefits from it for the upcoming seminar. Again and again I have the strong impression that for psychotherapy on the whole the way lies in the direction at which you are pointing."[68] Hauer mentioned his forthcoming book on yoga,[69] and wrote:

> I wanted to ask you, if (in the conviction that your analytical psychology and those elements of yoga which could be made effective for the West belong together in a very profound way), I could dedicate my book to you.[70] If you so desire, I will send you the printed

Shat-chakra Nirupana)—this manuscript appears incomplete, as it breaks off midway through the description of the *anāhata* cakra. Manuscripts 1) and 3) closely correspond to the text of "Indische Parallelen" (see appendix 1), which suggests that Jung used them directly to lecture from. In addition, there exists a two-page manuscript headed "Tantr. Texts. VII Shrichakrasambhara," which he evidently used in preparation for his Eidgenössische Technische Hochschule lectures on this text (*Modern Psychology 3*), and a two-page manuscript headed "Prapanchasara Tantra," which consists mainly in references and quotations from 25–87 of Zimmer's *Artistic Form and Yoga.* The *Prapanchasāratantram* was vol. 18 of Woodroffe's *Tantrik Texts* (Calcutta, 1935), in *ETH.*

[67] Emma Jung to Schmitz, 12 October 1931, "C. G. Jung: Letters to Oskar Schmitz," p. 95. Schmitz died later that year and hence was unable to attend. Jung wrote a foreword to Schmitz's fairy tale of the otter, in his *Märchen aus dem Unbewussten* (Fairy tales from the unconscious) (Munich, 1932), which took the form of a memorial to Schmitz. See *CW*, vol. 18, §§1716–22.

[68] Hauer to Jung, 20 November 1931, *ETH*, translated by Katherina Rowold. The work in question was in all likelihood Jung's collection of papers *Seelenprobleme der Gegenwart* (Soul problems of the present) (Zurich, 1931).

[69] J. W. Hauer, *Der Yoga als Heilweg* (Yoga as a way of salvation) (Stuttgart, 1932).

[70] Hauer's book *Der Yoga als Heilweg* carried a dedication to "C. G. Jung, the researcher of a new way for mankind." Copies of this work, together with Hauer's *Die Bhagavadgita in neuer Sicht mit Uebersetzungen* (The Bhagavadgita in a new light, with translation) (Stuttgart, 1934), are in Jung's library, bearing personal inscriptions to Jung. Neither contains marginal annotations.

> sheets for inspection as soon as I receive them. I hope that the book will be printed at the latest by the time I give my seminar in Zurich. . . . With regard to my seminar I would like to express once more the wish that it could, if possible, take place between April 15 and April 30, since I can hand over from the office of dean of the faculty of Philosophy until then.[71]

Jung replied that the news that Hauer wanted to dedicate his book to him was a happy surprise, and that "I am aware of the profound congeniality between my view and yoga."[72] Concerning the timing of the seminar, he added: "I would be willing to schedule your seminar for the spring, if the necessary audience were present around that time. But if this is not the case, we will have to arrange it for the autumn."[73] It seems that it was not possible for the necessary audience to be present, for Jung subsequently wrote to Hauer: "By the way, how do you feel about the proposal to hold the planned seminar in the autumn? It would be very nice if it could be arranged. Interest in it is very lively here. I would be very grateful, if you could soon inform me as to which date would be convenient for you. For us the beginning of October would be most suitable."[74] Hauer replied: "I will gladly hold the seminars in the autumn. Beginning in October would be good for me."[75] A few months later, Jung wrote to Hauer:

> Following our recent discussion in the Club on your seminar in the autumn, I am approaching you with the polite request to give your opinion on our proposition: in light of the current economic situation the organisation of a seminar is not entirely easy. The Psychological Club is prepared in this case to take charge of the organisation and above all to put the hall at your disposition free of charge. Our lecture hall accommodates 60 seats. In the meeting it was generally felt that it would be desirable that the fees would not exceed Fr. 20 per person. It was equally emphasized that a course exceeding a duration of one week (6 lectures) would not be desirable. In this case, one week of sold-out seminar would bring you a remuner-

[71] Hauer to Jung, 20 November 1931, in *ETH*; translated by Katherina Rowold.

[72] Jung to Hauer, 30 November 1931, in ibid.

[73] Ibid.

[74] Jung to Hauer, 1 March 1932, in ibid.

[75] Hauer to Jung, 22 March 1932, in ibid.; my translation.

> ation of Fr 12000.[76] With regards to method, I would propose at least one hour of lecturing and 1 to 1½ hours of answering questions and discussion.
>
> According to instructions, I would like to ask you to give us your opinion with regards to this proposition, so that the Club has a definitive basis for the organisation of the seminar.
>
> With regard to any English lectures, to be held in parallel with the German ones, I could not yet tell you anything definite. The American economic crisis, you must know, has made itself felt here in that the number of visitors has been very considerably reduced. For all that, it would not be impossible for me to gather an English audience for you. However, I would advise you, not in the least to save time and effort, to provide the English only with an hour of lecturing at a time. In the German seminar I will assist you with the psychological side.[77]

From this it appears that Hauer was to be paid the proceeds of the registration fees. It also indicates that the attendance at Jung's English-language seminars had fallen off because of the American economic crisis and that the dual-language format was used to maximize the fee. During the summer Jung wrote to Hauer:

> The rumour about your seminar is already creating a stir. Zimmer, in Heidelberg, has asked me if he could come. Since I know him personally, I have agreed. However, Spiegelberg of Hellerau, has also asked me and has used your name as a reference. Other information that I have about Dr. Spiegelberg does not sound enthusiastic, hence I would like to ask you if you are keen on this Spiegelberg, who seems to be an intellectual Jew. I have to admit that I am a bit in two minds and that I am fearing for the quality of the atmosphere. However, I want to leave the decision entirely to you since you seem to know Spiegelberg.[78]

[76] This figure should probably be "Fr 1200." The membership list of the Psychological Club for 1933 lists sixty members and twenty-eight guests, of whom about a dozen seemed to reside outside Switzerland. Professor Tadeus Reichstein, who attended the seminars, recalled that there was a fee for both Hauer's and Jung's seminars (interview with the editor, 23 November 1994).

[77] Jung to Hauer, 10 May 1932, in *ETH*; translated by Katherina Rowold.

[78] Jung to Hauer, 23 June 1932, in ibid. Friedrich (later Frederick) Spiegelberg, who wrote a review of Hauer's *Yoga als Heilweg* in the *Deutsche Allgemeine Zeitung* 71 (1932), did attend the seminar, with his wife.

Hauer's lectures were titled "Der Yoga, im besondern die Bedeutung des cakras" (Yoga, the meaning of the cakras in particular) and took place between 3 and 8 October. In 1930 Jung had presented a German seminar on 6–11 October and similarly in 1931 he presented a German seminar on 5–10 October. Hence Hauer's lectures followed these in format and timing.

Following Emma Jung's invitation, Hauer stayed at Jung's house during the lectures.[79] Meier stated that Hauer's German seminar took place from 10:00 A.M. to noon with a tea break. Reichstein stated that between thirty and forty people attended Hauer's lectures and that between forty and eighty attended Jung's seminar, and that it was often difficult to get a seat for the latter. He recalled that it was difficult to attend Jung's seminars for many of those present wanted to preserve an exclusive atmosphere and prevent others from attending. Consequently, Reichstein (who won the Nobel prize for chemistry) went directly to Jung, who gave him permission to attend.[80] After each lecture, Jung, Hauer, and Toni Wolff had lunch together.[81] Mrs. Hauer had painted enlarged copies of the illustrations of the cakras from *The Serpent Power*, which were used for the lectures.[82]

Hauer's German and English lectures covered the same ground. The latter were shortened versions of the former. In his English lectures he omitted his own German translation of the *Ṣaṭ-cakra-nirūpaṇa*, which he presented in his German lectures.

While the lectures were in progress Jung's ongoing seminar on visions was suspended. Jung also presented a synoptic illustrated lecture entitled "Western Parallels to Tantric Symbols" on the evening of 7 October.[83]

HAUER'S LECTURES

Hauer commenced with a historical overview of yoga and an explanation of his overall approach. He defined yoga as follows: "Yoga means to grasp the real essence, the inner structure of a matter, in its living reality as a

[79] Letters of Emma Jung to Hauer, cited in Dierks, *Jakob Wilhelm Hauer, 1881–1962*, 283.

[80] Reichstein, interview with the editor.

[81] Meier, interview with the editor.

[82] Meier donated these to the Jung Institute when it was founded, and they remain there (interview with the editor). Jung described them as "very wonderful" (Jung to Mrs. Hauer, 11 January 1933, *ETH*).

[83] "Westliche Parallelen zu den tantrischen Symbolen," in *Tantra Yoga*, 153–58.

dynamic substance, and the laws of that matter."[84] He claimed that the profundity of Kundalini yoga was that it viewed reality as "a balanced polarity of woman and man power."[85] He stated that its practice developed in the following way: "First the inner reality is grasped, then the symbol is used to crystallize this in the imagination, and then comes the real practice of meditating on the six cakras."[86] He compared it favorably with the classical yoga of Patanjali, in which he saw a tendency to lose the god in the self of man, and with Hatha yoga, in which he saw "a psychotechnical tendency leading away from the central powers to the more psychical, even physiological powers."[87] He explained this tendency as follows:

> One meditates upon the symbol, and appropriates its contents partly intellectually, partly psychically, and arrives in this way at a certain kind of psychic change; perhaps sometimes one may arrive at a stratum, in which happen the radical developments of the soul. But not often. The danger to people who deal with the cakras from without is that they remain in the region of these psychic processes . . . and the real change in the inmost structure of their being would not take place.[88]

For Hauer this presented the main difficulty lying in the way of gaining an understanding of Kundalini yoga. He argued that the way to overcome this was through grasping it on the basis of one's own inner experience: "I understand an inner reality only in so far as I have it within myself and am able to look at this reality that has come up into my conscious from the depth of my subconscious; or if it has come from without, it must have become absolutely living in my own conscious."[89] Hence he stated: "I freed myself to a great extent in the beginning from the Indian way of looking at things. I find that I do not reach the inner meaning if I do not look at them in my own way, from my own point of view."[90] The rest of Hauer's lectures were taken up with an explication of the metaphysics that underlay Kundalini yoga and the symbolism of the cakras.

Meier recalled that the tone of Hauer's German lectures was dry and there was little time for dialogue except in the tea breaks. By contrast, Jung's seminars came alive.[91] Reichstein stated that Hauer was a fanatic and that there was no real discussion, for he was "so persuaded of his

[84] Hauer, *HS*, 1. [85] Ibid., 8. [86] Ibid., 14.

[87] Ibid., 13. Hauer's distinction between these two types of yoga was challenged by Zimmer, who claimed that Hauer was overstating the difference. See 15–16.

[88] Ibid., 14. [89] Ibid., 1–2. [90] Ibid., 19.

[91] Meier, interview with the editor.

views" and "only accepted what he himself said." Reichstein described Jung's seminars as "very impressive" and noted that there was a "possibility for open discussion."[92] Speigelberg recalled that Jung asked "many questions from the Indologists about Indian yoga practices . . . and about the interrelation of that Indian system and Western psychology as a whole. I think this seminar is still the last word that has ever been said about the deeper psychological meanings of yoga practice."[93] News of the lectures spread far. Shortly afterward, Hans Trüb wrote to Martin Buber that "I would like to speak to you of Hauer's seminar. Overall it was for me inspiring as anticipated. The 'purusa'-atman was for me a complete new revelation—above all, the very foreign way (Kundalini yoga) to it for us."[94]

Hauer's method seemed to have influenced Jung's. In his seminars Jung attempted to lead the participants to an understanding of Kundalini yoga on the basis of their own inner experience, namely, the process of individuation. Consequently the account of Kundalini yoga with which they were presented was triply filtered—first through Woodroffe's translations and commentaries, then through Hauer's, and finally through Jung's. Not surprisingly, the three were often at variance, both in their terminology and in their understanding of the processes involved. Hence a good deal of the questions from the floor queried these differences.

It is important to note that for those who attended Jung's seminars, they were not simply a course in hermeneutics but engendered particular experiences. Thus Reichstein recalled having dreams that depicted the movement of the Kundalini serpent during and after the seminars, and that "at least a few" others had similar experiences.[95]

PSYCHOLOGY AND YOGA: PROBLEMS OF COMPARISON AND COLLABORATION

Shortly after his lectures, Hauer wrote to Jung: "The week in Zurich has provided me with much stimulation and perhaps I may entertain the hope that the threads of our co-operation have been tightened a little as

[92] Reichstein, interview with the editor.

[93] Frederic Spiegelberg interview, Jung Oral History Archive, Countway Library of Medicine, Harvard Medical School, Boston, 1–2.

[94] Hans Trüb to Martin Buber, 27 November 1932, Buber Archive, Hebrew University of Jerusalem; my translation.

[95] Reichstein, interview with the editor.

well."[96] The feeling seems to have been reciprocal, for Jung replied, "I would like to extend our collaboration in a special way," and invited him to participate in an interdisciplinary journal that Daniel Brody of Rhein Verlag had proposed to him.[97]

The following year Hauer founded the German Faith Movement. In his work *Germanic Vision of God*, Hauer proclaimed the advent of a specifically German (or Indo-Germanic) religion that would provide a liberation from the "alien" Semitic spirit of Christianity. Hauer stated: "The new phase of the German Faith Movement which began with the meeting in Eisenach in July 1933, must be understood in close relation with the national movement which led to the foundation of the Third Reich. Like the latter, the German Faith Movement is an eruption from the biological and spiritual depths of the German nation."[98] He unsuccessfully attempted to have it recognized as the official religion of National Socialism.

In 1935 Hauer contributed an essay entitled "Die indo-arische Lehre vom Selbste im Vergleich mit Kants Lehre vom intelligiblen Subject" (The Indo-Aryan teaching on the self in comparison with Kant's teaching on the intelligible subject) to the Festschrift volume for Jung's sixtieth birthday.[99]

In his 1936 essay "Wotan" Jung took Hauer and the German Faith Movement as exemplars of his thesis that the political events in Germany could be psychologically explained as stemming from the renewed activity of the old Germanic god Wotan.[100]

In 1938 Hauer again presented a series of lectures at the Psychological Club in Zurich between 7 and 12 March, on "Der Quellgrund des Glaubens und die religiöse Gestaltwerdung" (The basic source of faith and the development of religious forms). Meier recalled that Hauer lectured on "the symbolic meaning of the flag (svastika), which met with extremely severe criticism and opposition."[101] Their divergent views of

[96] Hauer to Jung, 11 November 1932, in *ETH*; translated by Katherina Rowold.

[97] Jung to Hauer, 14 November 1932, *Jung: Letters*, vol. 1, 103. The project never materialized. Brody was the publisher of the proceedings of the Eranos conferences, the *Eranos Jahrbücher*.

[98] Hauer, "Origin of the German Faith Movement," in J. W. Hauer, K. Heim, and K. Adam, *Germany's New Religion: The German Faith Movement*, translated by T. Scott-Craig and R. Davies (London, 1937), 29–30.

[99] *Die kulturelle Bedeutung der komplexen Psychologie* (The cultural significance of complex psychology), edited by the Psychological Club, Zurich (Berlin, 1935).

[100] *CW*, vol. 12.

[101] Meier, letter to the editor, 25 October 1993. In his diary for 11 March, Hauer noted that the subject of his lecture that day was the spiritual and religious background of the political situation in Germany (cited in Dierks, *Jakob Wilhelm Hauer, 1881–1962*, 297). This presumably was the lecture that Meier is referring to.

the religio-political situation in Germany led to a break between Hauer and Jung and his circle.[102] Concerning Hauer's conduct during this period, Mircea Eliade recalled: "I heard from Scholem that Hauer was still a very good man because during the Nazi persecution, he adopted two or three Jewish children, or a Jewish girl. He said Hauer was one of the very few scholars in Germany sympathetic with the Nazi regime which Scholem said, 'I don't have anything against.'"[103]

Hauer carried on his half of his dialogue with Jung on the comparison between yoga and psychotherapy in his subsequent publications. In *Der Yoga: Ein Indischer Weg zum Selbst*[104] (Yoga: an Indian way to the self) he commenced by posing questions that have subsequently increased in pertinence with the advent of the new age movement and the popularity of alternative religions:

> This problem, whether and to what extent this Eastern "way to salvation" is also of value for Western people, remains in a state of flux, and has engaged me very seriously. Was it not a mistake or even a danger when for one's own "way of salvation" men of the West struggled with yoga? Why did these men not adhere to scientific research, philosophical reflections in the Western manner, life and deed, as the only ways to "salvation"? Did the West itself not also have in its mysticism a way to the inner, that was of better use to it than yoga? Why were the developing depth psychology and psychotherapy not enough for it? Did we actually need a new impulse from the East? These problems stem from the lectures and study seminars in C. G. Jung's "Psychological Club."[105]

In his view Jung's analytical psychology had become a method and hence had succumbed to the dangers of the psychotechnical externalization that had been a danger for yoga.[106] In *Der Yoga* he devoted a chapter to a critique of Jung's work. He wrote: "I myself stand critically opposed to the hypothesis of native and inherited 'Archetypes.' To say above all that the historico-religious empirical basis for the thesis of the 'archetypes' is extremely weak."[107] He had also come to a negative judgment on Jung's

[102] In his diary entry for 8 March Hauer wrote: "I am too 'German' for these people." Cited in Dierks, *Jakob Wilhelm Hauer, 1881–1962*, 297; my translation.

[103] Mircea Eliade interview, Jung Oral History Archive, 11.

[104] Hauer, *Der Yoga: Ein Indischer Weg zum Selbst* (Leipzig, 1958).

[105] Ibid., 5; my translation. There has been a great deal of literature comparing yoga and psychotherapy. For two early studies, see Geraldine Coster, *Yoga and Western Psychology: A Comparison* (London, 1934); and Alan Watts, *Psychotherapy East and West* (New York, 1961).

[106] Cited in Dierks, *Jakob Wilhelm Hauer, 1881–1962*, 298.

[107] Hauer, *Der Yoga*, 419; my translation.

interpretation of Kundalini yoga: "In my view in the Jungian circle the mythic images of tantric yoga are all too rapidly put together with the 'Archetypes,' which doesn't help the clear understanding of either."[108]

However, formidable problems confront any attempt to interpret tantric texts, because of the complexity of their composition. Eliade noted that "tantric texts are often composed in an 'intentional language' (*sandhā-bhāṣā*), a secret, dark and ambiguous language in which a state of consciousness is expressed by an erotic term and the vocabulary of mythology or cosmology is charged with Hatha-yogic or sexual meanings."[109] This leads to the situation that

> a tantric text can be read with a number of keys: liturgical, yogic, tantric, etc. . . . To read a text with the "yogic key" is to decipher the various stages of meditation to which it refers. The tantric meaning is usually erotic, but it is difficult to decide whether the reference is to a concrete act or to a sexual symbolism. More precisely, it is a delicate problem to distinguish between the "concrete" and the "symbolic," tantric *sādhana* having as its goal precisely the transubstantiation of every "concrete" experience, the transformation of physiology into liturgy.[110]

Subsequent evaluations of Jung's psychological interpretations have turned upon whether one can regard it as a valid additional "key." They have been criticized by both scholars and adepts of Kundalini yoga. Harold Coward concluded:

> With today's much better knowledge of Eastern thought, it is doubtful that Jung's "rope trick" of standing Kundalini yoga on its head and then lopping off the last two cakras as "superfluous speculations with no practical value" would be accepted. What Jung's "Commentary" accomplished then, and still does today, is to provide added insight into *his* understanding of the *process of Individuation*, not an accurate description of Kundalini.[111]

[108] Ibid., 421; my translation.

[109] Eliade, *Yoga: Immortality and Freedom*, 249.

[110] Ibid., 252. On the problems posed by intentional language, see Bharati, *The Tantric Tradition*, 164–88.

[111] Coward, *Jung and Eastern Thought*, 123. Coward is referring to Jung's statement that there was no need to elaborate upon the symbolism of the last two cakras, as they were beyond Western experience (see below, 57). One may add that their attainment is not exactly common in India. This text, which includes John Borelli's "Annotated Bibliography of Jung and Eastern Traditions," remains the most useful overall study of Jung and Indian thought, upon which it focuses. John Clarke's *Jung and Eastern Thought: A Dialogue with the Orient* is an unsuccessful attempt to subsume Jung's work on Eastern thought under the

If Jung's seminars are evaluated from the perspective of understanding Kundalini yoga within its own sociohistorical context this criticism is doubtless valid. However, within the context of Jung's collaboration with Hauer, this was the task of the latter; Jung's aim was to elucidate the psychological meaning of spontaneous symbolism that resembled that of Kundalini yoga. In this respect, Jung stated in a letter that "the entry of the East [into the West] is rather a psychological fact with a long history behind it. The first signs are found in Meister Eckhart, Leibniz, Kant, Hegel, Schopenhauer, and E. von Hartmann. But it is not at all the actual East we are dealing with but the fact of the collective unconscious, which is omnipresent."[112] Thus for Jung, the Western "discovery" of the East constituted a critical chapter in the "discovery" of the collective unconscious. Jung's psychological interpretation is predicated on the assumption that Kundalini yoga represented a systemization of inner experience that spontaneously presented itself in the West in a mode that resembled but was not necessarily identical with the way it did so in the East. This is borne out by an interchange shortly after the Kundalini seminars in the resumption of the seminar on visions:

> *Mrs. Sawyer:* But in the cakras we always had the Kundalini separate.
>
> *Dr. Jung:* Quite, and in this case they are apparently not separate, but that makes no difference. We must never forget that the Kundalini system is a specific Indian production, and we have to deal here with Western material; so we are probably wise to assume this is for us the real stuff, and not Indian material which has been differentiated and made abstract since thousands of years.[113]

---

rubric of Gadamerian hermeneutics. For a critique of Jung's approach to Eastern thought, see Richard Jones, "Jung and Eastern Religious Traditions," *Religion* 9 (1979): 141–55. For an appreciation, see F. Humphries, "Yoga Philosophy and Jung," in *The Yogi and the Mystic: Studies in Indian and Comparative Mysticism,* edited by Karl Werner (London, 1989), 140–48.

[112] Jung to A. Vetter, 25 January 1932, *Jung: Letters,* vol. 1, 87; translation modified. For Schopenhauer on India, see Schwab, *The Oriental Renaissance,* 427–35. Schopenhauer had compared Meister Eckhart's writings with the Vedanta (ibid., 428). Buddhism featured prominently in von Hartmann's *Philosophie des Unbewussten* (Philosophy of the unconscious) (Berlin, 1870).

[113] Jung, *The Visions Seminar,* vol. 7, 30–31. In his account of spontaneous Kundalini experiences in the West Lee Sannella also highlighted a notable divergence from the Eastern depictions: "According to the classical model, the Kundalini awakens, or is awakened, at the base of the spine, travels straight up the central axis of the body, and completes its journey when it reaches the crown of the head. . . . By contrast, the clinical picture is that the Kundalini energy travels up the legs and the back to the top of the head, then down the face, through the throat, to a terminal point in the abdominal area." *The Kundalini Experience: Psychosis or Transcendence?* 106.

It would also be a mistake to view Jung's commentary as consisting in the translation of the terms of Kundalini yoga into psychological concepts whose meaning had already been delimited in advance: for in the course of translating the terms of Kundalini yoga into those of analytical psychology, the latter became altered and extended. At base, the symbolism of the cakras enabled Jung to develop an archetypal regional topography of the psyche and to provide a narration of the process of individuation in terms of the imaginal transit between these regions.[114] It also led him to argue that for individual transformation to be possible, it required a concomitant transformation of ontology, to which his work was oriented. In his major works on Western religious traditions subsequent to his encounter with Kundalini yoga Jung presented his psychological interpretations of alchemy and Christianity.[115] In these his studies on yoga served as a vital orientation, both in his mode of understanding the practices of the alchemists—as evidenced by his stating that "every profound student of alchemy knows that the making of gold was not the real purpose and that the process was a Western form of yoga"[116]—and in his view of alchemy with its valuation of the body and the feminine—concerns that are preeminent in tantrism as representing the countercurrent to orthodox Christianity.

From the experiential viewpoint Gopi Krishna criticized Jung's exposition:

> C. G. Jung, in his commentary on the book [*The Secret of the Golden Flower*], entirely preoccupied with his own theories about the unconscious, despite the unambiguous nature of the statements in the work, finds in it only material for the corroboration of his own ideas, and nothing beyond that. The same thing happened in a seminar held by him on Kundalini, of which a written summary is available in the Jung Institute. None of the scholars present, as evident from the views expressed by them, displayed the least knowledge about the real significance of the ancient document they were discussing at the time.[117]

[114] On the issue of archetypal topography, see Edward Casey, "Toward an Archetypal Imagination," *Spring: An Annual for Archetypal Psychology and Jungian Thought* (1974): 1–33; and Peter Bishop, "Archetypal Topography: The Karma-Kargyuda Lineage Tree," ibid. (1981): 67–76.

[115] Jung, *CW*, vols. 11–14.

[116] Jung, *Modern Psychology 3*, 107.

[117] Gopi Krishna, *Kundalini for the New Age*, 43. For a critical appraisal of Jung's commentary on *The Secret of the Golden Flower*, see Thomas Cleary's new translation (together with commentary) of *The Secret of the Golden Flower: The Classic Chinese Book of Life* (San Francisco, 1991).

Fundamentally, the divergence between indigenous understandings of Kundalini yoga and Jung's interpretation of it is that for the former texts such as the *Ṣaṭ-cakra-nirūpaṇa* primarily depict the profound modifications of experience and embodiment occasioned by specific ritual practices rather than the symbolic depiction of a universal process of individuation. However, the problems that confront Jung's interpretations at a more general level apply to other attempts to translate the terms of Kundalini yoga into modern concepts.[118] In the course of such attempts the terms became hybridized, and the resultant blend is no longer distinctly "Eastern" or "Western."[119] Ultimately, Jung's seminars should be assessed in terms of the goal he set forward in the following statements:

> Western consciousness is by no means consciousness in general. It is rather a historically conditioned and geographically confined dimension, which represents only a part of mankind.[120]

> The knowledge of Eastern psychology namely forms the indispensable basis for a critique and an objective consideration of Western psychology.[121]

Thus in Jung's view the outcome of Western psychology's encounter with Eastern thought was by no means a small matter, for on this the very possibility of a psychology worthy of the name rested.[122] The continued relevance of this seminar today—in a vastly transformed historical clime—principally lies in the mode in which it highlights this capital question and attempts to establish it at the forefront of the psychological agenda, whether or not one accepts Jung's provisional solutions to it.

S.S.

[118] Such as Gopi Krishna's own theoretical attempts to transcribe it in contemporary post-Darwinian categories, as in the following statement: "In the language of science, Kundalini represents the mechanism of evolution in human beings." Gopi Krishna, *Kundalini for the New Age*, 87.

[119] On the contemporary significance of the notion of hybridity within the postcolonial context, see Homi Bhabha, *The Location of Culture* (London, 1993).

[120] Jung, "Commentary on the 'Secret of the Golden Flower'," in *CW*, vol. 13, §84; translation modified.

[121] Jung, "Foreword to Abegg: 'Ostasien Denkt Anders' " (East Asia thinks otherwise), in *CW*, vol. 18, §1483; translation modified.

[122] On the encounter of Western psychology and Eastern thought, see Eugene Taylor, "Contemporary Interest in Classical Eastern Psychology," in *Asian Contributions to Psychology*, edited by A. Paranjpe, D. Ho, and R. Rieber (New York, 1988), 79–119.

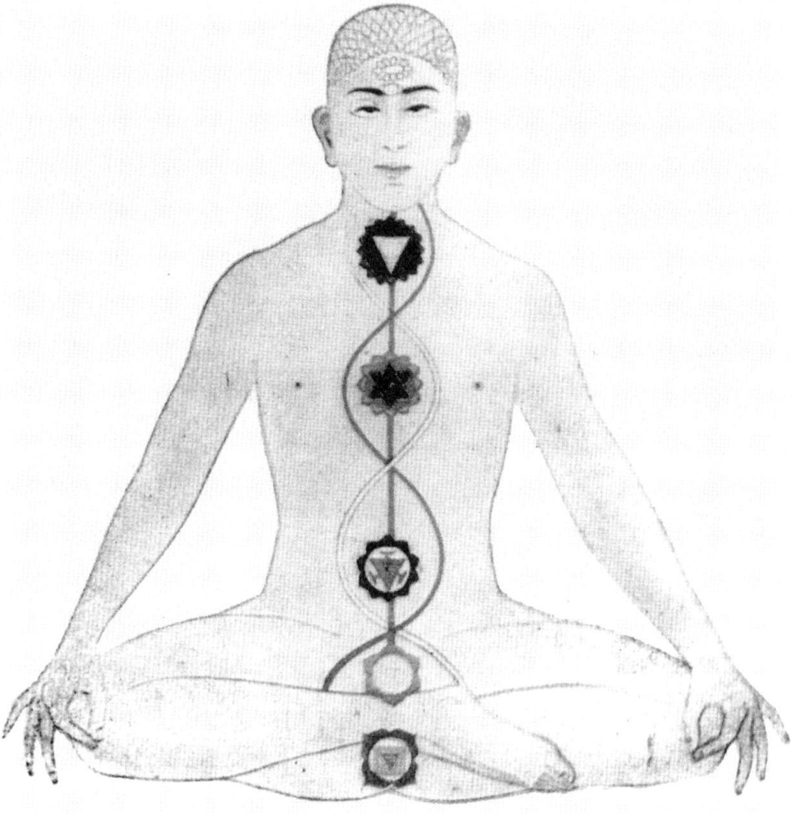

1. The cakras

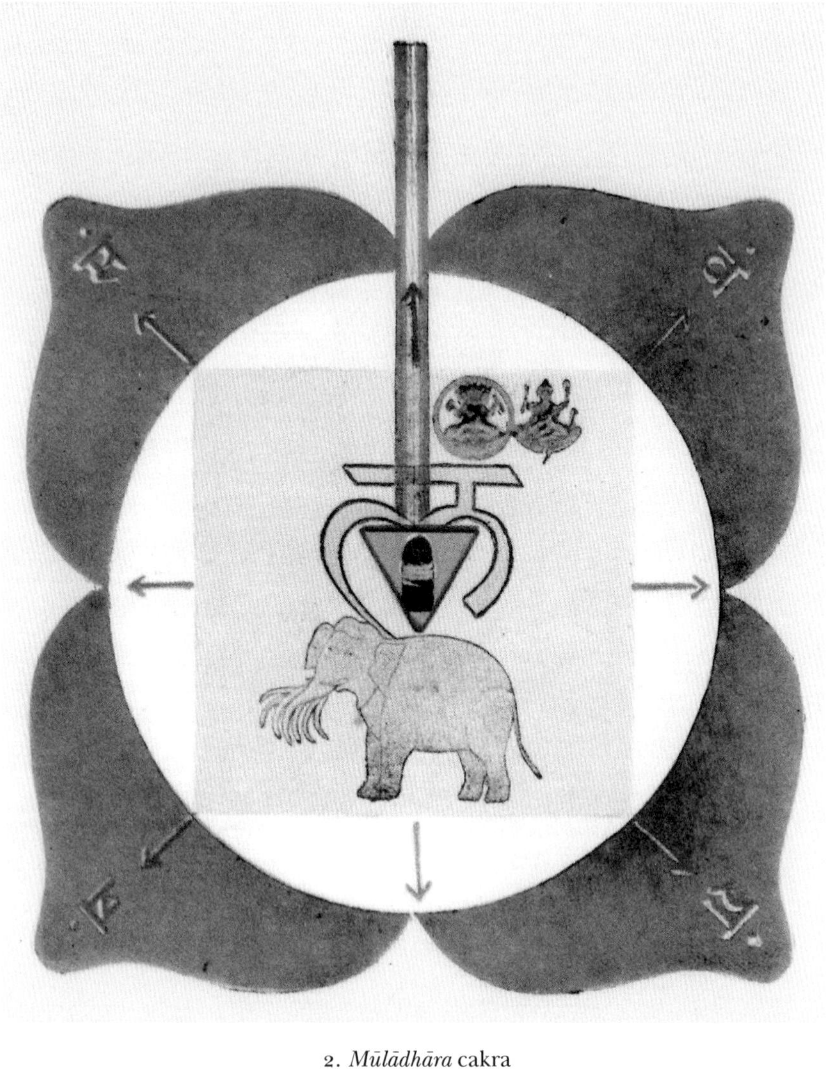

2. *Mūlādhāra* cakra

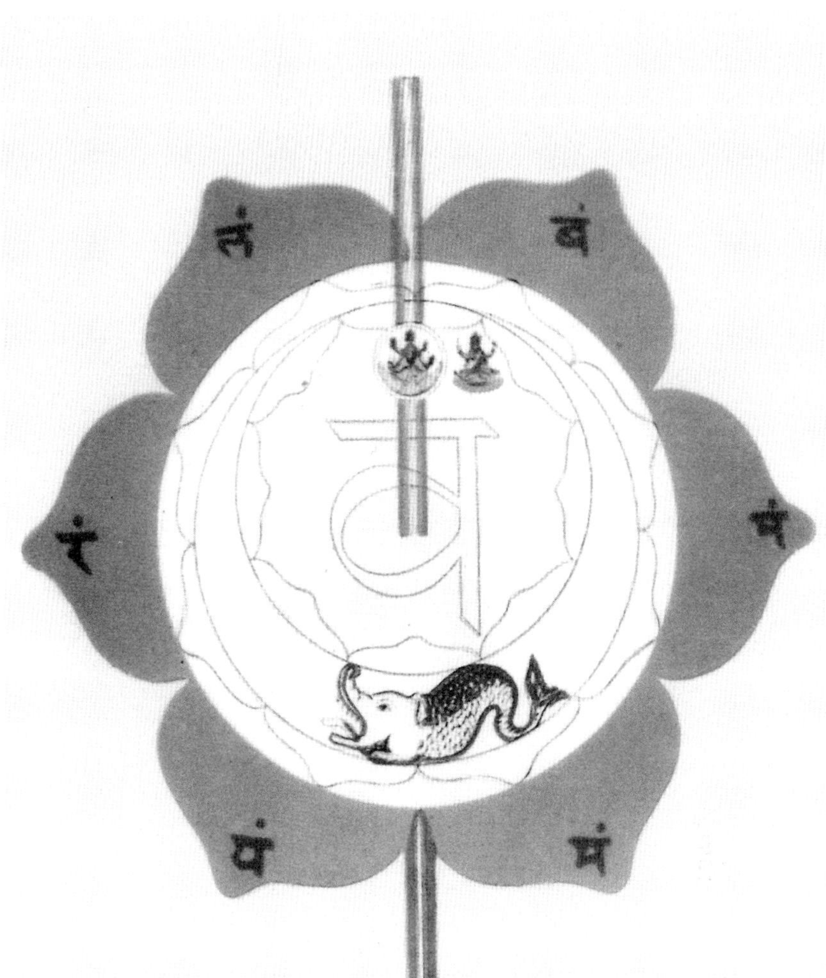

3. *Svādhiṣṭhana* cakra

4. *Maṇipūra* cakra

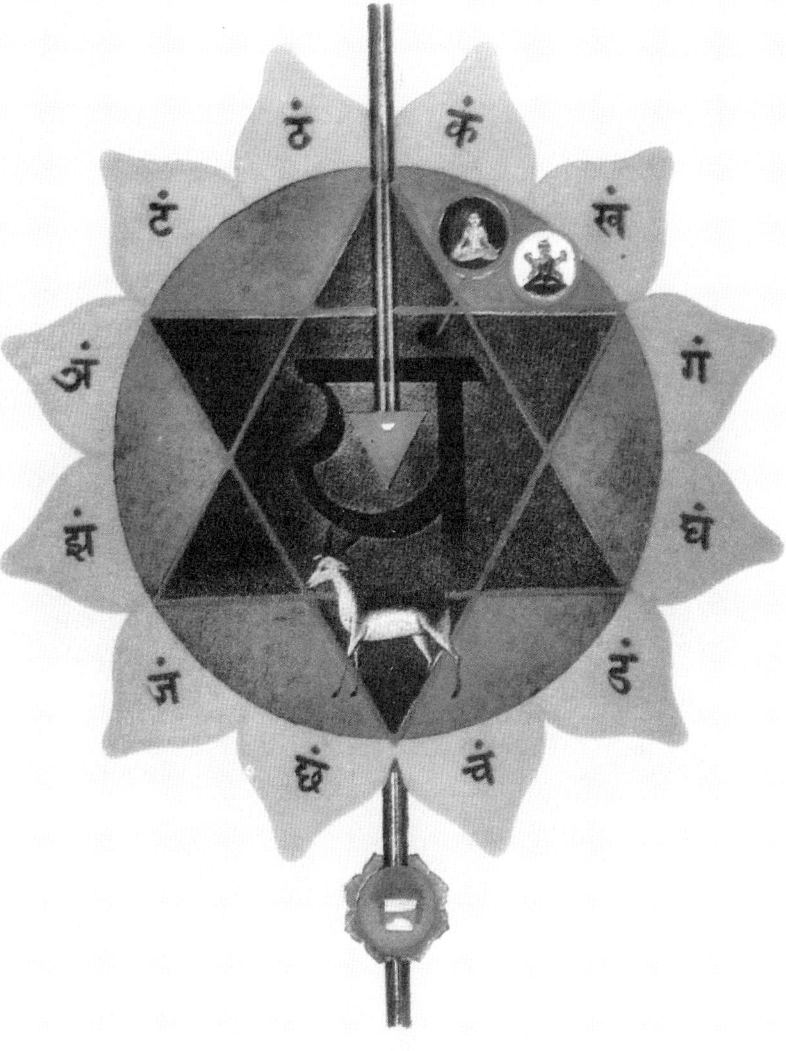

5. *Anāhata* cakra

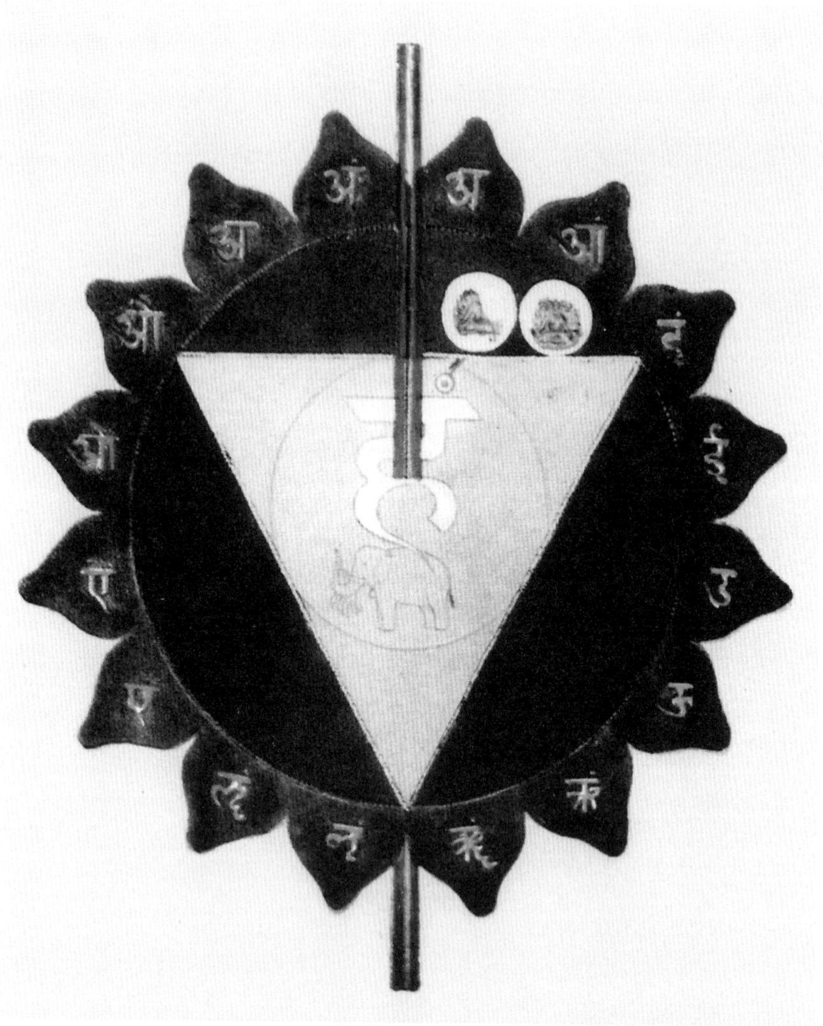

6. *Viśuddha* cakra

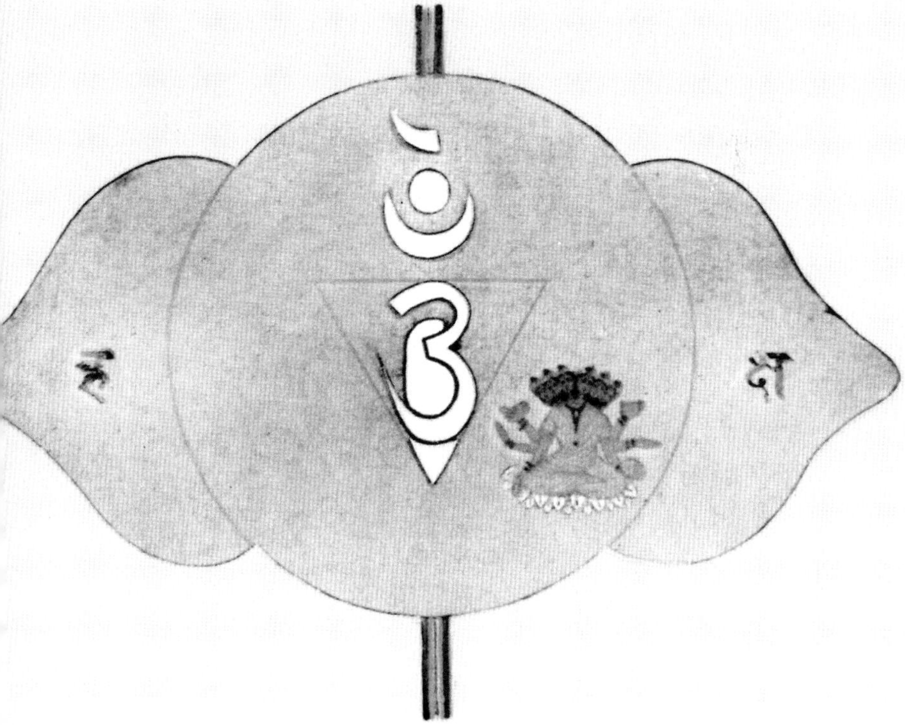

7. *Ājñā* cakra

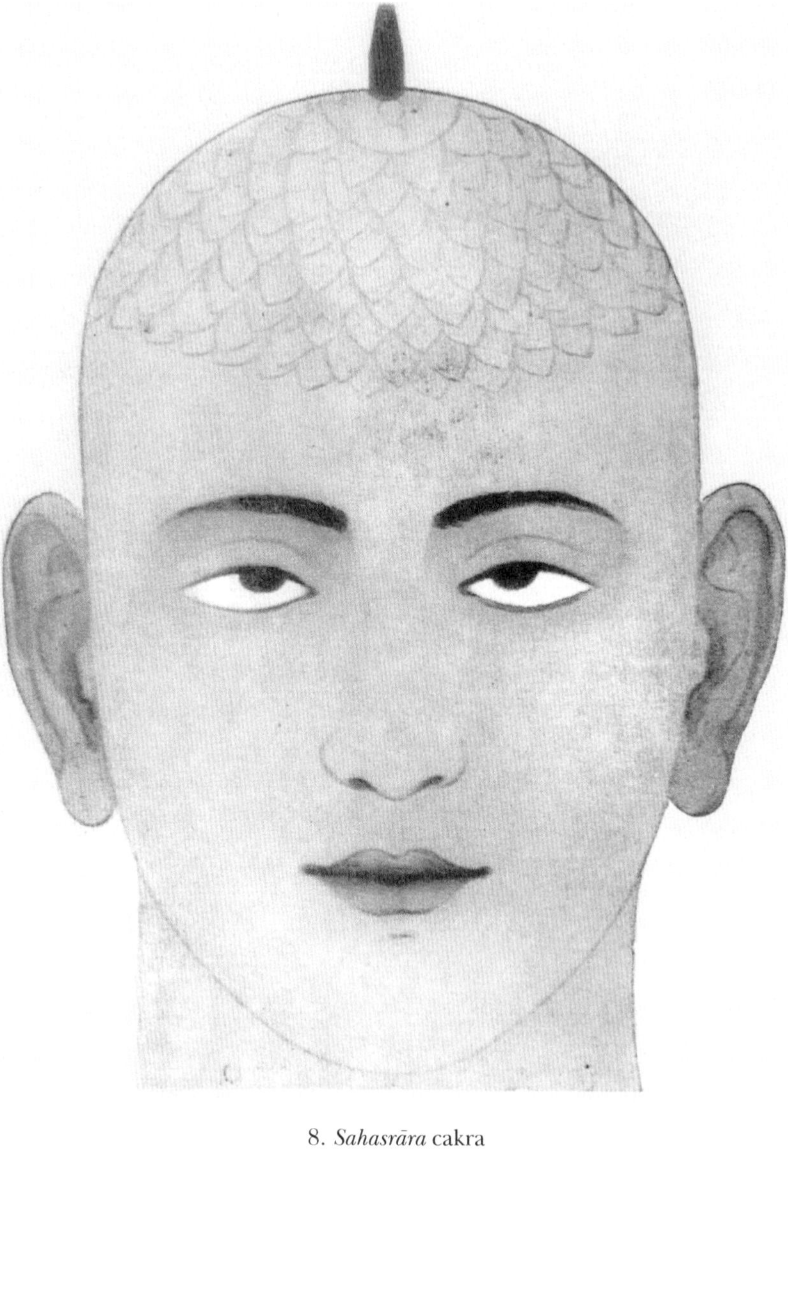

8. *Sahasrāra* cakra

THE PSYCHOLOGY OF KUNDALINI YOGA

LECTURE 1

12 October 1932

Dr. Jung: Ladies and gentlemen, we have just had a seminar about tantric yoga,[1] and as there are always misunderstandings in the wake of such an event, I am devoting some time to the discussion and elucidation of any questions that you may have. Even those who were not there will be interested, I suppose, because I have spoken of the cakras before.[2] Moreover, in the pursuit of our visions we have now reached the stage where symbols analogous to those of tantric yoga are beginning to operate. You remember, we have seen how our patient's visions in their natural and quite uninfluenced development brought the first mandala. In the last hour of our spring seminar I showed you a mandala that created itself, the mandala of the child within the circles, and the patient's attempts to unite with the child.[3] That is entering the mandala, and there already the symbolism of tantra yoga begins. So it is not irrelevant that we discuss this subject now; it fits in well with what we have done here. As a matter of fact, our former seminar has led us up to the psychology of tantric yoga, what I have hitherto called mandala psychology.

I shall take first this question by Mrs. Bailward: "I understand that the *kleśa asmitā* 'contains the germ of being a personality' and the *kleśa dveṣa*

[1] Concerning terminology, Hauer commenced his seminar by noting: "For Kundalini Yoga, I usually say Tantra Yoga, the word Tantra being the name for those works in which the Kundalini Yoga is expounded" (*HS*, 1).

[2] See appendix 1. Concerning the cakras, Woodroffe stated: "According to the Hindu doctrine, these Cakras are differing centres of consciousness, vitality and Tattvik energy." In Arthur Avalon (pseud. Sir John Woodroffe), *The Serpent Power* (London, 1919), 16. Hauer had defined them as "symbols of the experience of life, they show the real inner meaning of such an experience, to help you to understand and to interpret spiritually what you have lived" (*HS*, 58).

[3] The vision was as follows: "'I saw two rings of gold upon the black ground. One ring was smaller and was encircled by the larger ring. Within the small ring lay a male child as though in the womb.' (That is, in the centre.) 'It was surrounded by amniotic fluid. I wanted to get to the child which held out its arm toward me but I could not seem to step over the outer rim'"; to which Jung commented: "Here the mandala psychology begins." *Interpretation of Visions* vol. 6, 29 June 1932, 127–28.

'the wish to be two,' or hatred.[4] Does Professor Hauer mean personality or individuality here? When it has built up the individuality, how would hatred be torn out by the roots?"

Well, there is the *kleśa* of dividing and discrimination, of becoming a personality, an ego, where there is also the aspect of hatred. The *kleśas* are urges, a natural instinctive form in which libido first appears out of the unconscious; that is the psychological energy, or libido, in its simplest form of manifestation.[5] Now, according to tantric teaching, there is an urge to produce a personality, something that is centered, and divided from other beings, and that would be the *kleśa* of discrimination. It is what one would describe in Western philosophical terms as an urge or instinct of individuation.

The instinct of individuation is found everywhere in life, for there is no life on earth that is not individual. Each form of life is manifested in a differentiated being naturally, otherwise life could not exist. An innate urge of life is to produce an individual as complete as possible. For instance, a bird with all its feathers and colors and the size that belongs to that particular species. So the *entelechia*, the urge of realization, naturally pushes man to be himself. Given a chance to be himself, he would most certainly grow into his own form, if there were not obstacles and inhibi-

[4] Hauer defined the *kleśas* as follows: "The roots in the subconscious are called *kleśa* . . . and *kleśa* I translate as 'ailment, or the force that makes the ailment' " (*HS*, 37). He defines the *kleśa dveṣa* as "the wish to be two, that is, putting one's own being and personality up against another one, it is the power of being one's self" (ibid., 38), and the *kleśa asmitā* as "the character of being an ego. The way we assume that *I* think, that *I* feel, or *I* experience is a certain faculty in us which is called *asmitā*" (ibid., 40). Dasgupta defined the *kleśas* as afflictions. Surendranath Dasgupta, *Yoga as Philosophy and Religion* (London, 1924), 104. Zimmer defined *kleśa* as "anything which, adhering to man's nature, restricts or impairs its manifestation of its true essence." Heinrich Zimmer, *Philosophies of India*, edited by Joseph Campbell (London, Bollingen Series XXVI, 1953), 294. He defined the *kleśa asmitā* as "the sensation, and crude notion, 'I am I; *cogito ergo sum*; the obvious ego, supporting my experience, is the real essence and foundation of my being' " (Zimmer, *Philosophies of India*, 295). He defined the *kleśa dveṣa* as the feeling of "disinclination, distaste, dislike, repugnance, and hatred" (Zimmer, *Philosophies of India*). Feuerstein stated: "The *kleśas* provide the dynamic framework of the phenomenal consciousness. They urge the organism to burst into activity, to feel, to think, to want. As the basic emotional and motivational factors they lie at the root of all misery. . . . Thus the normal human situation can be characterized as the product of a cognitive error . . . for which there is one remedy: the recovery of the self as the true identity of man." *The Philosophy of Classical Yoga* (Manchester, 1980), 65–66.

[5] In his commentary on Patanjali's *Yoga Sutras*, Jung stated that the *kleśas* are "the instinctive urges and oppressions. These are the compulsive mechanisms which lie at the base of the human being. . . . Not knowing our true being is the foundation of all the other *kleśas*." *Modern Psychology 3*, 16.

tions of many descriptions that hinder him from becoming what he is really meant to be. So the *kleśa* that contains the germ of personality can be called just as well the *kleśa* of individuation, because what we call personality is an aspect of individuation. Even if you don't become a complete realization of yourself, you become at least a person; you have a certain conscious form. Of course, it is not a totality; it is only a part, perhaps, and your true individuality is still behind the screen—yet what is manifested on the surface is surely a unit. One is not necessarily conscious of the totality, and perhaps other people see more clearly who you are than you do yourself. So individuality is always. It is everywhere. Everything that has life is individual—a dog, a plant, everything living—but of course it is far from being conscious of its individuality. A dog has probably an exceedingly limited idea of himself as compared with the sum total of his individuality. As most people, no matter how much they think of themselves, are egos, yet at the same time they are individuals, almost as if they were individuated. For they are in a way individuated from the very beginning of their lives, yet they are not conscious of it. Individuation only takes place when you are conscious of it, but individuality is always there from the beginning of your existence.

Mrs. Baynes: I did not get where the hate, *dveṣa,* came in.

Dr. Jung: Hatred is the thing that divides, the force which discriminates. It is so when two people fall in love; they are at first almost identical. There is a great deal of *participation mystique,* so they need hatred in order to separate themselves. After a while the whole thing turns into a wild hatred; they get resistances against one another in order to force each other off—otherwise they remain in a common unconsciousness which they simply cannot stand. One sees that also in analysis. In the case of an exaggerated transference, after a while there are corresponding resistances. This too is a certain hatred.

The old Greek put *phobos,* fear, instead of hatred. They said that the firstborn thing was either Eros or *phobos;* some say Eros and others *phobos,* according to their temperaments. There are optimists who say the real thing is love, and pessimists who say the real thing is *phobos. Phobos* separates more than hatred, because fear causes one to run away, to remove oneself from the place of danger.

I was once asked a philosophical question by a Hindu: "Does a man who loves God need more or fewer incarnations to reach his final salvation than a man who hates God?" Now, what would you answer? I gave it up naturally. And he said: "A man who loves God will need seven incarnations to become perfect, and a man who hates God only three, because he certainly will think of him and cling to him very much more than the man who loves God." That, in a way, is true; hatred is a tremendous cement. So for us the Greek formulation *phobos* is perhaps better than hatred as the principle of separation. There has been, and is still, more *participation mystique* in India than in Greece, and the West has certainly a more discriminating mind than the East. Therefore, as our civilization largely depends upon the Greek genius, with us it would be fear and not hatred.

Mrs. Crowley: Yet in the cakras apparently the most important gesture is that of dispelling fear.

Dr. Jung: Yes, but the gods are always carrying weapons also, and weapons are not an expression of any particular love.

Miss Wolff: I have my notes here, and I think I see what caused Mrs. Bailward's confusion. Professor Hauer said in German *hasserfüllte Zweiung*, but it does not mean to become two, exactly; it means to become a subject against an object—there are two things.[6] The English translation is not so clear.

Dr. Jung: Entzweiung means separation. Now the rest of the question?

Mrs. Bailward: I mean, would the yogi consider the state of hatred a necessary condition in building up individuality?

Dr. Jung: Yes, he cannot help considering it so, for the whole yoga process, whether classical or Kundalini yoga, naturally has a tendency to make the individual one, even as the god is one, like brahman, an existing nonexisting oneness.

The question continues: "And when it had built up the individuality, how would hatred be torn out by the roots?"

Miss Wolff: Professor Hauer spoke of the two aspects of the *kleśa.*[7] In the imperfect condition—the *sthūla* aspect—the urge to be a subject over against an object is mingled with hatred. But in the *sūkṣma* aspect the same urge is the power to become a personality.

Dr. Jung: Yes, it is an important and very bewildering thing in this whole terminology that one always must make the distinction between the *sthūla* and *sūkṣma* aspects.[8] I do not speak of the *parā* aspect because

[6] See n. 4.

[7] Hauer stated: "The *kleśa* are in *citta* in two forms or aspects, the *sthūla*, meaning the rough coarse aspect . . . and the *sūkṣma*, or subtle aspect" (*HS*, 37), and "the subtle or *sūkṣma* aspect of *dveṣa* is the power to be a separate personality; that is the metapsychic force that creates or makes possible the personality. But the *sthūla* aspect is the one we experience in ordinary life, that is mixed with hatred" (ibid., 38).

[8] Hauer stated that according to tantric yoga, there were three aspects of reality—*sthūla*, *sūkṣma*, and *parā*: "The *sthūla* aspect means reality as it appears to our senses. . . . Behind this, or working as the dynamic force within this *sthūla* aspect, we have the *sūkṣma* aspect, which, literally translated, means the subtle, fine aspect" (ibid., 26). He defined the *parā*

that is what Professor Hauer calls the metaphysical. I must confess that there the mist begins for me—I do not risk myself there. The *sthūla* aspect is simply things as we see them. The *sūkṣma* aspect is what we guess about them, or the abstractions or philosophical conclusions we draw from observed facts. When we see people who make efforts to consolidate themselves, to be egos, and therefore resist and hate one another, we see the *sthūla* aspect, and we are only aware of the *kleśa* of hatred, called *dveṣa*. But if we go a step higher, we suddenly understand that this foolish kind of hatred, all these personal resistances, are merely external aspects of very important and profound things.

To quote a practical case: when a person complains that he is always on bad terms with his wife or the people whom he loves, and that there are terrible scenes or resistances between them, you will see when you analyze this person that he has an attack of hatred. He has been living in *participation mystique* with those he loves. He has spread himself over other people until he has become identical with them, which is a violation of the principle of individuality. Then they have resistances naturally, in order to keep themselves apart. I say:

> Of course, it is most regrettable that you always get into trouble, but don't you see what you are doing? You love somebody, you identify with them, and of course you prevail against the objects of your love and repress them by your very self-evident identity. You handle them as if they were yourself, and naturally there will be resistances. It is a violation of the individuality of those people, and it is a sin against your own individuality. Those resistances are a most useful and important instinct: you have resistances, scenes, and disappointments so that you may become finally conscious of yourself, and then hatred is no more.

That is the *sūkṣma* aspect.

If a person thoroughly understands this, he will agree and not worry. In other words, he knows when he loves that soon he will hate. Therefore he will laugh when he is going uphill and weep when he is going downhill, like Till Eulenspiegel.[9] He will realize the paradox of life—that he

aspect as "the causes and the real character of those centres of energy. For beyond those dynamic forces of the subtle kind . . . there is a power which can no longer be conceived in mere terms of cosmic energies. . . . There we get into the religious sphere, which is connected with the godhead as it is in its inner nature" (ibid., 26–27).

[9] This was an analogy that Jung used on several occasions; cf. *CW*, vol. 7, §47; and *Nietzsche's "Zarathustra": Notes of the Seminar Given in 1934–1939*, edited by James Jarrett (Princeton, Bollingen Series XCIX, and London, 1988), vol. 1, 226. The editors of Jung's letters

cannot be perfect, and he cannot always be one with himself. It is our idea to be one, to have absolutely clear situations in life. But it is all impossible—it is all too one-sided, and we are not one-sided. You see, the analytical process tears up hatred by the roots by explaining the *sūkṣma* aspect, namely, the aspect on the level of understanding, of abstraction, theory, wisdom. And so we learn that what is a regrettable habit, for instance, or impossible moods or inexplicable disagreements in the *sthūla* aspect, is something quite different in the *sūkṣma* aspect.

Then a second question: "Is there a psychological equivalent to the *tattva*,[10] and the *saṃskāra*?"[11] Well, the *tattva*, being the essence of things, is psychologically again a *sūkṣma* aspect of things. The term *libido*, or energy, is a good example of a *tattva*. It is not a substance but an abstraction. Energy is not to be observed in nature; it does not exist. What exists in nature is natural force, like a waterfall, or a light, or a fire, or a chemical process. There we apply the term *energy*, but energy in itself does not exist, despite the fact that you can buy it at the electrical works. But that is merely a metaphorical energy. Energy proper is an abstraction of a physical force, a certain amount of intensity. It is a concept of the natural forces in their *sūkṣma* aspect, where they are no longer manifestations but *tattva*, essence, abstraction. You see the Eastern mind is concretistic—when it arrives at a conclusion or builds up an abstraction, the latter is already a substance; it is almost visible or audible—one can almost touch it. Whereas with us this process is rather spurious, as when a concept like energy becomes fairly well known, so that any workman speaks of it. Then naturally people assume that this energy must be something one can put into a bottle—one can buy it and sell it, so it must be something tangible. There that concretistic quality of the Eastern mind comes in with us. For in reality energy is not substantial: it is a conformity of things, say, or the intensity of various physical or material processes. In the East, when anybody speaks of *tattva*, they conceive of it

provide the following note: "A popular figure in German folklore, representing the superiority of the wily peasant over the town dwellers and tradesmen. The first collection of his jests and practical jokes was published in 1515. In one story Till Eulenspiegel, unlike his companions, rejoices when walking uphill in anticipation of the coming descent." *C. G. Jung: Letters*, vol. 2, 603.

[10] Hauer translated *tattva* "literally as thatness, or in German *Dasheit*. Thatness means that hidden power in the whole universe which has a certain tendency to create and move in a specific way—that and that" (*HS*, 31).

[11] Hauer translated *saṃskāra* as "the maker who makes things so that they are really a working compound, a working whole" (*HS*, 41). He commented: "At this moment, what we think, how we sit, how we talk, is all caused by *saṃskāra*. If we think we are now talking freely, if we experience it as that in our consciousness . . . that is illusion" (ibid., 42).

as already in existence, and, mind you, a complete existence—as if a *tattva* really could become visible to them. I don't know whether anybody has had a vision of *tattva*, but that might be, for they can visualize any concept, no matter how abstract. So the *tattva*, which is a concrete thing in the East, has with us a *sūkṣma* aspect—it is an abstraction, an idea. The concept of energy is a very suitable example, but there are of course other ideas of the sort, such as the principles of gravity, or the idea of an atom, or of electrons—these are the equivalents of *tattvas*. In psychology, as I say, it would be libido, which is also a concept.

Then the *saṃskāra*, if understood as something concrete, has really no analogy with us. We are unable to concretize these things. That is an entirely philosophical teaching, which for us has only a certain validity inasmuch as we believe in the migration of souls, reincarnation, or any pre-existing conditions. Our idea of heredity would be similar to the idea of *saṃskāra*, as well as our hypothesis of the collective unconscious. For the mind in a child is by no means *tabula rasa*. The unconscious mind is full of a rich world of archetypal images. The archetypes are conditions, laws or categories of creative fantasy, and therefore the psychological equivalent of the *saṃskāra*. But mind you, in the Eastern mind the doctrine of the *saṃskāra* is so different from that definition that perhaps a Hindu would object to my attempt at a comparison. But the archetypal images are really the nearest thing we can see.

Dr. Reichstein: I want to ask about the *sthūla* aspect. I thought *sthūla* was the more physical aspect, and *sūkṣma* more the psychological, not only the abstract, aspect. For it cannot be perceived by intellect only; it is a peculiar kind of being connected with things.

Dr. Jung: You are quite right, but the psychological aspect of things implies also a philosophy about them. For instance, take the psychological aspect of a chair: it has both a *sthūla* and a *sūkṣma* aspect. It is a physical phenomenon and as such it is obvious in its *sthūla* aspect. But in its *sūkṣma* aspect it is not so obvious—the *sūkṣma* aspect is the idea. As in the Platonic teaching of the *eidolon*, the *eidos* of a thing is the *sūkṣma* aspect. But in Plato we can still see concretizations: he says that all things are derivatives, or incomplete imitations of the *eidola* that are conserved in a sort of heavenly storehouse, in which are the models of every existing thing. So all the forms of our empirical world would derive from these *eidola*. This idea is the *sūkṣma* aspect, or you can say the psychology of things. But for us, the Platonic ideas, which Plato understood to be really existing, are psychological concepts, or even mere illusions or assumptions. For even if we assume that there is such a heavenly storehouse where models of things really do exist, we are not a bit sure of it; thinking like that does not produce the thing. If the primitive mind thinks a thing, it *is*. A dream, for instance, is to them as real as this chair. They must be very careful not to think certain things, as the thought easily might become reality. We are still like that—we say a mouthful, and at the same time we touch wood.

Mrs. Diebold: Would the *sūkṣma* aspect correspond to Kant's thing in itself [*das Ding an sich*]?

Dr. Jung: Yes, as would also his use of the term *noumenon*. The *noumenon* is the idea, the spiritual essence of a thing. You see, Kant was already a very critical man, and in his *Critique of Pure Reason*[12] he says that the thing in itself, *das Ding an sich*, is a purely negative borderline concept, which does not guarantee that such a thing exists at all. He simply makes such a concept to express the fact that behind the world of phenomena, there is something about which we can say nothing. Yet in his psychological lectures he spoke of a plurality of *noumena*—that there are many things in themselves—which is a contradiction of his *Critique of Pure Reason*.[13]

Mrs. Crowley: Is that not really an archetype?

Dr. Jung: Yes, the *eidos* in Plato is of course the archetype. The term archetype comes from St. Augustine, who used it in that Platonic sense. He was in that respect a neoplatonist, like so many other philosophers in those days. But with them it was not a psychological concept; the ideas were concretized—that means hypostatized, which is a very good word. You see, hypostasis is not a hypothesis. A hypothesis is an assumption I make, an idea I have formed, in order to attempt an explanation of facts. But I know all the time that I have only assumed it, and that my idea still needs proof. Hypothesis means to put something which isn't there under something; *Unterstellung* is the German term for it. There is no English term, as far as I am aware, with exactly that sense. It might be an assumption, or it could also have an unfavorable nuance of insinuation. Now, hypostasis means that there is something below which *is* substantial, upon which something else rests.

Mr. Dell: From what root does hypostasis come?

[12] Immanuel Kant, *Critique of Pure Reason*, 2d ed., translated by Norman Kemp Smith (London, 1929), 266ff.

[13] In his 1898 lecture before the Zofingia Society, "Thoughts on Speculative Inquiry," Jung critiqued Kant's concept of the *Ding an sich*, arguing against Kant's rigid distinction between the knowable, phenoumenal realm and the unknowable phenoumenal realm, arguing that science progressively made the noumenal known. *Zofingia Lectures*, in *CW* A, §§195–99. He also commented on Kant's lectures on psychology (*Vorlesungen über Psychologie* [Leipzig, 1889]) in "The Relations between the Ego and the Unconscious," in *CW* 7, §260, note 7.

Dr. Jung: Histemi is the Greek verb, to be standing, and *hypo* means below. The same root is in the Greek word *ikonostasis,* which, in the Greek Orthodox church, is the background behind the altar where the statues of the saints stand. The image or picture of a saint is called an *ikon,* and *ikonostasis* is the place upon which it stands, usually a pedestal, or a wall upon which are placed such images or pictures. To make a hypostasis means to invent a subject which is hanging in the air. It has no basis, but you assume that it has, and say it is a real thing. For instance, you invent the idea of a *tattva* and say it is by no means a mere word, a breath of air with nothing underneath it. You say *tattva* is an essence; it is something substantial—something is standing underneath that holds it up. A hypostasis contains always the assumption that a thing really is, and the natural primitive mind is always hypostatizing. In our better moments, when we are a bit superstitious, we also have hypostases.

Mr. Dell: The hypostasis of gravity makes the apple fall.

Dr. Jung: Yes, you assume the thing is, and that makes the apple fall. Or, for instance, Kant says, in his famous discussion of the assumption of God, that "God is, God is not"—that when anybody says God is, he just says so, but his saying so does not mean that he is. He can say God is, but perhaps he is not. But when you hypostatize, then by saying God is, you assume that God really exists. You have made God, so that he is in reality. One can bring about most unfortunate situations by simply declaring that a thing is so. That is what the animus does and what one always objects to in the animus. "Oh, I thought . . ."—and then the house burns down because you thought you had put the fire out. But unfortunately the house has burned down.

Mrs. Baynes: Don't all heuristic principles tend to run into hypostases?

Dr. Jung: They run a risk, sure enough. As soon as a hypothesis has given evidence of its applicability, it tends to become a truth, to become a hypostasis—and we forget entirely that it is only a hypothesis, an intentional, arbitrary theory on our part.

Dr. Kranefeldt: The sexual theory of Freud could be called a hypothesis, which then became a hypostasis.

Dr. Jung: Exactly: it proves its evidence by a certain amount of facts, and then one assumes it must be a truth. Well now, this is merely about concepts, and in tantric yoga there were things which needed further explanation from the psychological side.

Mrs. Sawyer: When Professor Hauer spoke of the cakras, he called only the picture inside each a mandala. Could we not call the total cakra a mandala?

Dr. Jung: Yes, the cakras are also occasionally called mandalas. Naturally

Professor Hauer does not attach such a technical meaning to the mandala as we do. He called the total picture *padma,* the lotus, or cakra.[14] Mandala means ring, or circle. It can be a magic circle, for example, or it can be a cycle. There are Vedic *sutras* in which the series of chapters makes a cycle that is called a mandala; for instance, the third mandala, chapter 10, verse 15—the mandala is simply the name of the cycle.

Mrs. Sawyer: But he called a square a mandala.[15]

Dr. Jung: Yes, he calls that a mandala, and naturally anything within is a mandala too, and this is exactly what you see in the Lamaistic pictures:[16] the mandala, the lotus, is inside, as well as the temple, and the cloister with the square walls, the whole surrounded by the magic circle; then above are the gods, and mountains below. The term mandala with us has taken on an importance which it does not possess in India, where it is merely one of the Yantras,[17] an instrument of worship in the Lamaistic cult and in tantric yoga. And mind you, the tantric school is little known in India—you could ask millions of Hindus, and they would not have the faintest idea of what it was. It would be as if you asked the honorable citizens of Zurich what they had to tell you of scholasticism; they would know about as much as the Hindu knows about tantric yoga. And if you asked a Hindu what a mandala was, he would say that a round table, or anything circular, was a mandala. But to us it is a specific term. Even within the frame of the tantric school the mandala has not the importance that it has with us. Our idea of it would come nearest to Lamaism, the Tibetan religion, but this is hardly known, and its textbooks have been translated only very recently, hardly ten years ago. One of the fundamental sources is the *Shrichakrasambhara,* a tantric text translated by Sir John Woodroffe.[18]

[14] Hauer stated: "Cakra means circle, but it is also called *padma,* meaning lotus-flower" (*HS,* 61).

[15] In his description of the *mūlādhāra* cakra, Hauer referred to the "square or mandala of the earth" (*HS,* 71).

[16] [Note to the 1932 edition: See the frontispiece of the *Golden Flower.*] Jung and Wilhelm, *The Secret of the Golden Flower* (London and New York, 1931). This illustration is also reproduced in "Concerning Mandala Symbolism," in *CW,* vol. 9, part 1, fig. 1, and *Psychology and Alchemy,* in *CW,* vol. 12, fig. 43.

[17] Zimmer stated that "the figurative sacred image (*pratimā*) [under which he included the mandala] is just one member of an entire family of representational sacred images (*yantras*)." *Artistic Form and Yoga in the Sacred Images of India,* translated by G. Chapple and J. Lawson (Princeton, 1984), 29.

[18] This text was actually edited and translated by Kazi Dawa-Samdap: *Shrichakrasambhara: A Buddhist Tantra, Tantrik Texts,* vol. 7 (London, 1919). The series was under the general editorship of Woodroffe, who wrote a foreword to this volume. Jung's library contained six

Dr. Barker: Professor Hauer said that in the second cakra of the water region, one plunges into life without any reservations.[19] But that region is still far above us. It is difficult to believe this interpretation, because when the adolescent goes into life without reserves, it is as if he were going from the higher to the lower.

Dr. Jung: You are playing the role of the world bewilderer[20] in asking such questions. Here you touch upon something really most bewildering, for when you try to translate that material into psychological language, you reach amazing conclusions. Take the *mūlādhāra* cakra,[21] which seems very simple. Its psychological location is in the perineum. You assume you know all about it, but psychologically what is *mūlādhāra*? You think of it as that region down below in the abdomen, having to do with sexuality and all sorts of unsavory things. But that is not *mūlādhāra*; *mūlādhāra* is something quite different. Perhaps we should look at the second cakra[22] first.

The ocean with the sea monster is above in the system of the cakras, but in reality we find always that it is below in our psychology—we always descend into the unconscious. Therefore *mūlādhāra* must be something quite different from what we would conclude. Have you ever been in *mūlādhāra*? Some of you could say you have been in the unconscious, in the ocean, and there you had seen the leviathan. Let us assume that you have really done the night sea journey, have wrestled with the great monster. That would mean you had been in *svadhiṣṭhana*, the second center, the water region. But then, have you been in *mūlādhāra*, too? Here is a great difficulty. You will probably be puzzled when I tell you my conception of *mūlādhāra*. You see, *mūlādhāra* is a whole world; each cakra[23] is a whole world. Perhaps you remember the picture which I showed of a patient, where she was entangled in the roots of a tree, and then above

volumes from this series, published between 1914 and 1924. Jung provided an extended commentary on this text in his Eidgenössische Technische Hochschule lectures in 1938–39, in *Modern Psychology* 3, 42–120.

19 Hauer described the second cakra, *svādhiṣṭhāna*, as "the life we live freely and thoughtlessly, just throwing ourselves into the stream of life and letting ourselves be carried, floating on to all that comes to us" (*HS*, 75).

20 A term by which the Kundalini is described in the *Ṣaṭ-cakra-nirūpaṇa*; see appendix 4, 112.

21 Hauer described *mulĀdhĀra* as "the cakra that holds the root of things. It is the region of the earth, of the creative man and woman power . . . the foundation of the world" (*HS*, p. 68).

22 The representation of the *svādhiṣṭhana cakra* shows a *makara*, a mythological sea monster, on water. See figure 3.

23 Hauer defined the cakras as "symbols of the experience of life" (*HS*, 58).

she was stretching up toward the light.[24] Now, where was that woman when she was in the roots?

Answer: In *mūlādhāra.*

Dr. Jung: Yes, and in what condition would that be in reality?

Miss Hannah: Was it the self sleeping?

Dr. Jung: Of course, the self is then asleep. And in which stage is the self asleep and the ego conscious? *Here,* of course, in this conscious world where we are all reasonable and respectable people, adapted individuals as one says. Everything runs smoothly; we are going to have lunch, we have appointments, we are perfectly normal citizens of certain states. We are under certain obligations and cannot run away easily without getting neurotic; we have to look after our duties. So we are all in the roots, we are upon our root support. ("Root support" is the literal translation of *mūlādhāra.*) We are in our roots right in this world—when you buy your ticket from the streetcar conductor, for instance, or for the theater, or pay the waiter—that is reality as you touch it. And then the self is asleep, which means that all things concerning the gods are asleep.

Now, after this startling statement we have to find out whether such an interpretation is really justifiable. I am by no means sure. I am even convinced that Professor Hauer would not agree with me right on the spot. In these matters one needs a great deal of psychology in order to make it palatable to the Western mind. If we do not try hard and dare to commit many errors in assimilating it to our Western mentality, we simply get poisoned. For these symbols have a terribly clinging tendency. They catch the unconscious somehow and cling to us. But they are a foreign body in our system—*corpus alienum*—and they inhibit the natural growth and development of our own psychology. It is like a secondary growth or a poison. Therefore one has to make almost heroic attempts to master these things, to do something against those symbols in order to deprive them of their influence. Perhaps you cannot fully realize what I say, but take it as a hypothesis. It is more than a hypothesis, it is even a truth. I have seen too often how dangerous their influence may be.

If we assume that *mūlādhāra,* being the roots, is the earth upon which we stand, it necessarily must be our conscious world, because here we are, standing upon this earth, and here are the four corners of this earth. We are in the earth mandala. And whatever we say of *mūlādhāra* is true

[24] [Note to the 1932 edition: See the *Golden Flower,* no. 5.] In *CW,* vol. 13, figure A5. This illustration was also reproduced in "Concerning Mandala Symbolism," in *CW,* vol. 9, part 1, figure 25. However, the description seems to correspond more closely to a vision of Christiana Morgan that Jung discussed on 25 February 1931. See *The Visions Seminar,* vol. 2, 77.

of this world. It is a place where mankind is a victim of impulses, instincts, unconsciousness, of *participation mystique,* where we are in a dark and unconscious place. We are hapless victims of circumstances, our reason practically can do very little. Yes, when times are quiet, if there is no important psychological storm, we can do something with the help of technique. But then comes a storm, say, a war or a revolution, and the whole thing is destroyed and we are nowhere.

Moreover, when we are in this three-dimensional space, talking sense and doing apparently meaningful things, we are nonindividual—we are just fish in the sea. Only at times have we an inkling of the next cakra. Something works in certain people on Sunday mornings, or perhaps one day in the year, say Good Friday—they feel a gentle urge to go to church. Many people instead have an urge to go to the mountains, into nature, where they have another sort of emotion. Now, that is a faint stirring of the sleeping beauty; something which is not to be accounted for starts in the unconscious. Some strange urge underneath forces them to do something which is not just the ordinary thing. So we may assume that the place where the self, the psychological non-ego, is asleep is the most banal place in the world—a railway station, a theater, the family, the professional situation—there the gods are sleeping; there we are just reasonable, or as unreasonable, as unconscious animals. And this is *mūlādhāra.*

If that is so, then the next cakra, *svādhiṣṭhāna,* must be the unconscious, symbolized by the sea, and in the sea is a huge leviathan which threatens one with annihilation. Moreover, we must remember that men have made these symbols. Tantric yoga in its old form is surely the work of men, so we can expect a good deal of masculine psychology. Therefore no wonder that in the second cakra is the great half-moon, which is of course a female symbol. Also, the whole thing is in the form of the *padma* or lotus, and the lotus is the *yoni.*[25] (*Padma* is simply the hieratic name, the metaphor for the *yoni,* the female organ.)

Mrs. Sawyer: Professor Hauer said that the crescent was not a female symbol; it belonged to Śiva.[26]

Dr. Jung: That is so for the East, and if you ask a Hindu about these things he would never admit that you could put *mūlādhāra* above *svādhiṣṭhāna.* Their point of view is absolutely different. If you ask them

[25] Hauer described the representation of this cakra as follows: "Inside is a circle, the pericarp, containing a white lotus mandala. . . . There is a half moon, also white" (*HS,* 74).

[26] Hauer had stated: "The crescent in *svādhiṣthana* stands for Śiva," to which Mrs. Sawyer asked: "Is not the crescent usually a feminine symbol?" Hauer replied: "Not in India. There the crescent is always the sign of Śiva" (*HS,* 84).

about the sun analogy they would equally deny it, yet one can show that the symbolism of the sun myth is there too.

Mrs. Crowley: Their symbolism can't be the same as ours; their gods are in the earth.

Dr. Jung: Naturally. You see, a Hindu is normal when he is not in this world. Therefore if you assimilate these symbols, if you get into the Hindu mentality, you are just upside-down, you are all wrong. They have the unconscious above, we have it below. Everything is just the opposite. The south on all our maps is below, but in the East the south is above and the north below, and east and west are exchanged. It is quite the other way around.

Now, the second center has all the attributes that characterize the unconscious. Therefore we may assume that the way out of our *mūlādhāra* existence leads into the water. A man I know who is not in analysis has had interesting dreams representing this quite frequently, and they were all identical. He found himself moving along a certain road, or a little street or path, either in a vehicle or on foot—the dream always began with such a movement—and then, to his great amazement, all these roads inevitably led into water, the second cakra.

Therefore, the very first demand of a mystery cult always has been to go into water, into the baptismal fount. The way into any higher development leads through water, with the danger of being swallowed by the monster. We would say today that is not the case with the Christian baptism—there is no danger in being baptized. But if you study the beautiful mosaic pictures in the Baptistry of the Orthodox in Ravenna (which dates from the fourth or the beginning of the fifth century, when the baptism was still a mystery cult), you see four scenes depicted on the wall: two describe the baptism of Christ in the Jordan; and the fourth is St. Peter drowning in a lake during a storm, and the Saviour is rescuing him.[27] Baptism is a symbolical drowning. There are certain sects in Russia that, in order to make it real, put people under the water until they occasionally do get drowned. It is a symbolic death out of which new life comes, a newborn babe. The initiates are often fed with milk after-

[27] Jung provides an account of this experience in *MDR*, 314–18. There he stated that he had asked an acquaintance who was going to Ravenna to obtain pictures for him, and his acquaintance learned that the mosaics did not exist (ibid., 315). Aniela Jaffé noted that Jung explained this as a "momentary new creation by the unconscious, arising out of his thoughts about archetypal initiation. The immediate cause of the concretisation lay, in his opinion, in a projection of his anima upon Galla Placida" (ibid., 316). Jung's recollections in *MDR* of the mosaics differ somewhat from that given here; these differences are noted in Dan Noel's "A Viewpoint on Jung's Ravenna Vision," *Harvest: Journal for Jungian Studies* 39 (1993): 159–63, which forms a reappraisal of this whole episode.

ward, as in the cult of Attis, where after the baptism people were fed with milk for eight days as if they were little babies, and they got a new name.[28]

So the symbolism in the *svādhiṣṭhāna* cakra is the worldwide idea of the baptism by water with all its dangers of being drowned or devoured by the makara. Today, instead of the sea or leviathan we say analysis, which is equally dangerous. One goes under the water, makes the acquaintance of the leviathan there, and that is either the source of regeneration or destruction. And if that analogy holds true, then the analogy of the sun myth must hold true too, for the whole baptismal story is in the sun myth. You see that the sun in the afternoon is getting old and weak, and therefore he is drowned; he goes down into the Western sea, travels underneath the waters (the night sea journey), and comes up in the morning reborn in the East. So one would call the second cakra the cakra or mandala of baptism, or of rebirth, or of destruction—whatever the consequence of the baptism may be.

We also can say something about the details of this cakra. The fiery red is understandable. *mūlādhāra* is darker, the color of blood, of dark passion. But this vermilion of *svādhiṣṭhāna* contains far more light, and if you assume that this has really also something to do with the sun's course, it might be the sun's rays while setting or rising—the color of the dawn or the last rays of the sun are a rather humid kind of red. Then after the second center we could expect the manifestation of newborn life, a manifestation of light, intensity, of high activity, and that would be *maṇipūra*.[29] But before we speak of that center we should exhaust this second cakra. It is a peculiar fact that in the East they put these cakras not below our feet but above. We would put *mūlādhāra* above because this is our conscious world, and the next cakra would be underneath—that is our feeling, because we really begin above. It is all exchanged; we begin in our conscious world, so we can say our *mūlādhāra* might be not down below in the belly but up in the head. You see, that puts everything upside-down.

Mrs. Sawyer: But in the unconscious it is the same.

Dr. Jung: Ah, now comes the unconscious where *les extrêmes se touchent.* There everything is yea and nay, and there *mūlādhāra* is above as well as below. We have an analogy in the tantric system of cakras. What is

[28] Jung provided an interpretation of the Attis myth in *Symbols of Transformation,* in *CW,* vol. 5, §§659–62.

[29] Hauer defined the *maṇipūra* cakra as follows: "*Maṇi* means the pearl or the jewel, and the *pūra* meaning fullness or richness, one might call it the treasure of the pearl, or the treasure of the jewels" (*HS,* 68).

the analogy between *ājñā*,[30] the highest center, and *mūlādhāra*? It is very important.

Mrs. Fierz: The uniting of Śakti and Śiva.[31]

Dr. Jung: Yes, Kundalini is united with the *liṅga* in *mūlādhāra*[32] in the state of the sleeping beauty, and the same condition prevails up above in the *ājñā* center where the *devī* has returned to the god and they are one again. Again they are in the creative condition, but in an entirely different form. As they are united below so they are united above. So the two centers can be exchanged.

You see, in adapting that system to ourselves, we must realize where we stand before we can assimilate such a thing. With us it is apparently the other way around; we do not go up to the unconscious, we go down—it is a *katabasis*. This was always so. The old mystery cults often took place underground. One sees that in old Christian churches in the crypt below the altar—the underchurch. It is the same idea as the Mithraic *spelaeum*, which was the cave or the room where the cult of Mithras took place. It was always a place under the earth, or it was a real grotto. The cult of Attis also took place in grottos. The grotto in which Christ was born in Bethlehem is said to have been a *spelaeum*.[33] Then you remember that St. Peter's in Rome now stands where the *taurobolia*, the blood baptisms in the cult of Attis, had taken place before. Also, the high priests of the cult of Attis had the title Papas, and the pope, who before was simply a bishop of Rome, took on that title. Attis himself is a dying and resurrecting god—showing the continuity of true history.

Mr. Baumann: Professor Hauer mentioned that man can go two ways to the unconscious—either to the left or to the right. In one way he faces the monster and is swallowed by it, and in the other way he comes from behind and can attack the sea monster.[34]

[30] Hauer defined the *ājñā* cakra as meaning "'command'; it is something that one knows one ought to do, it has to do with *Erkenntnis*, knowledge. . . . You might call it, in English, acknowledgement. It is a command, or an acknowledgement to oneself, as if told that something was one's duty" (*HS*, 69).

[31] Hauer described the *ājñā* cakra as follows: "The *yoni* and the *liṅga*, woman power and man power, are united, they are not apart" (*HS*, 90).

[32] Hauer described the *muladhāra* cakra as follows: "Here are again the *yoni* and the *liṅga*, and here Kundalini sleeps. This *yoni* is red and the *liṅga* dark brown, which is the symbol of the erotic life in its fullness. It is quite a different red from that in the heart [*ājñā*] centre where it is the erotic life in the higher sense, where whilst here it is in the real earthly sense" (*HS*, 92).

[33] In "Visions of Zosimos" (1937), Jung noted: "Attis has close affinities with Christ. According to tradition, the birthplace at Bethlehem was once an Attis sanctuary. This tradition has been confirmed by recent excavations." *CW*, vol. 13, §92, n. 6.

[34] See appendix 3, n. 5, 93.

Dr. Jung: Those are finesses in the Hindu system. We must be quite satisfied if we succeed in digesting and assimilating this material in a rough outline. Well, I have explained why in the East the unconscious is above whereas with us it is below. So we can reverse the whole thing, as if we were coming down from *mūlādhāra,* as if that were the highest center. Of course, we can put it like that. But then, we can also say we are going up.

Mrs. Sawyer: In all the visions we have been dealing with in the English seminar, first one goes down and then up. I don't see how you can change that.

Dr. Jung: When you start in *mūlādhāra* you go down, for *mūlādhāra* is then on top.

Mrs. Sawyer: But *mūlādhāra* is underground.

Dr. Jung: No, it is not necessarily underground, it is of earth. This is a *façon de parler.* We are on the earth or in the earth. That woman entangled in the roots is just entangled in her personal life. As a matter of fact, she happens to have been particularly so, and therefore she represented herself as entangled in the duties of life, in her relations with her family, and so on. For her, going to analysis was surely going up. And going through the Christian baptism is going up, but that does not hinder its being represented by going down into the water. Christ doesn't climb up into the Jordan.

Mrs. Crowley: Don't you think the Eastern idea of the unconscious is different from ours? It is a different kind of unconscious.

Dr. Jung: Yes, they have an entirely different idea, but it is no use discussing what their idea is because we don't know it.

Mrs. Crowley: But you can get it from reading the Sanskrit things—the Vedic things.

Dr. Jung: I have read a good deal but it is not clear. I know only that they see these things very differently. For instance, I had some correspondence with a Hindu pundit about the mandala cakras. He informed me that they had to do with medicine, that they were anatomical and had nothing like a philosophical meaning. Such an idea did not enter his horizon. He was a man who had read the Sanskrit texts. I don't know him personally; he is a university professor at Dacca.

Mrs. Crowley: They are just as divided in their types over there as here.

Dr. Jung: Naturally—they have many different views, and the whole East has very different views from ours about these matters. They don't recognize the unconscious, and just as little do they know what we mean by consciousness. Their picture of the world is entirely different from ours, so we can understand it only inasmuch as we try to understand it in our own terms. Therefore, I make the attempt to approach the thing from the psychological point of view. I am sorry to have bewildered you, but you will be more bewildered if you take these things literally. (You had better not.) If you think in those terms, you build up an apparent Hindu system with the psychology of the Western mind, and you cannot do that—you simply poison yourself. So if we deal with it all—and I am afraid we have to because of similar structures in our own unconscious—we must do it in this way. We must realize, or take into consideration at least, that *mūlādhāra* is here, the life of this earth, and here the god is asleep. And then you go to the *krater*[35]—to use that old quotation from Zosimos—or to the unconscious, and that is understood to be a higher condition than before, because there you approach another kind of life. And you move there only through the Kundalini that has been aroused.[36]

Now, here we have to speak of Kundalini and what she is, or how she can be awakened.[37] You remember that Professor Hauer said that some instigation from above arouses Kundalini, and he also said one must have a purified *buddhi*,[38] or a purified spirit, in order to arouse her. So the progress into the second cakra is possible only if you have aroused the serpent, and the serpent can only be aroused by the right attitude. Expressed in psychological terms, that would mean that you can approach the unconscious in only one way, namely, by a purified mind, by a right attitude, and by the grace of heaven, which is the Kundalini. Something in you, an urge in you, must lead you to it. If that does not

[35] In "Visions of Zosimos" Jung wrote of the *krater*: "The *krater* is obviously a wonder-working vessel, a font or piscina, in which the immersion takes place and transformation into a spiritual being is effected." *CW*, vol. 13, §97.

[36] In the manuscript "Die Beschreibung der beiden Centren Shat-chakra Nirupana," Jung wrote: "In Mula dhara Kundalini sleeps. It is latent activity, which shows outside. Through it man is bound to the world of appearance and believes that his ego is identical with his self. Kundalini is concealed cit (consciousness), and when it awakes it turns back to its master. It is 'world-consciousness,' in contrast to civ-atma = individual consciousness" (2; my translation).

[37] Hauer defined the Kundalini as follows: "Kundalini as understood here is not in any way an erotic power of man, but a form of woman power which is nothing but pure knowledge; there is in woman power a certain power of knowledge, a force, which has nothing to do with the erotic, and this has to be set free and united with the knowledge force of man power at its highest point of development" (*HS*, 97).

[38] Hauer described *buddhi* as follows: "*Buddhi* means the organ of intuition that is composed of pure *sattva*, that light-world-substance which is at the base of cognition or knowledge, insight" (*HS*, 96). Eliade stated that *buddhi* was the term in Samkhya yoga for the intellect. Mircea Eliade, *Yoga: Immortality and Freedom*, translated by Willard R. Trask (Bollingen Series LVI; reprint, London, 1989), 18.

exist, then it is only artificial. So there must be something peculiar in you, a leading spark, some incentive, that forces you on through the water and toward the next center. And that is the Kundalini, something absolutely unrecognizable, which can show, say, as fear, as a neurosis, or apparently also as vivid interest; but it must be something which is superior to your will. Otherwise you don't go through it. You will turn back when you meet the first obstacle; as soon as you see the leviathan you will run away. But if that living spark, that urge, that need, gets you by the neck, then you cannot turn back; you have to face the music.

I will give you an example from a medieval book, that famous *Hypnerotomachia*, or *Le Songe de Poliphile*,[39] which I have quoted here before. It was written in the fifteenth century by a Christian monk of a famous Roman family. He got into the unconscious, as we say. It is like the beginning of Dante's *Inferno* but expressed in entirely different terms. He depicts himself as traveling in the Black Forest, which in those days, especially to Italians, was still the *ultima Thule* where the unicorn still lived, as wild and unknown as the forests of central Africa to us. And there he loses his way, and then a wolf appears. At first he is afraid, but afterward he follows the wolf to a spring where he drinks of the water—an allusion to baptism. Then he comes to the ruins of an ancient Roman town, and he goes in through the gate and sees statues and peculiar symbolic inscriptions, which he quotes, and which are most interesting from a psychological point of view. Then suddenly he is afraid; it becomes uncanny. He wants to go back, and he turns to go out through the gate again, but now there is a dragon sitting behind him that bars the way, and he cannot go back; he simply must go forward. The dragon is Kundalini. You see, the Kundalini in psychological terms is that which makes you go on the greatest adventures. I say, "Oh, damn, why did I ever try such a thing?" But if I turn back, then the whole adventure goes out of my life, and my life is nothing any longer; it has lost its flavor. It is this quest that makes life livable, and this is Kundalini; this is the divine urge. For instance, when a knight in the Middle Ages did marvelous works, like the great labors of Hercules, when he fought dragons and liberated virgins, it was all for his Lady—she was Kundalini. And when Leo and Holly go to Africa to seek She,[40] and She urges them on to the most incredible adventures, that is Kundalini.

[39] *The Dream of Poliphio*, related and interpreted by Linda Fierz-David, translated by Mary Hottinger (Bollingen Series XXV; reprint, Dallas, 1987). Jung wrote an introduction to this volume, which is also reproduced in *CW*, vol. 18, §§1749–52.

[40] For Jung's discussion of Rider Haggard's *She* (London, 1887), see his *Analytical Psychology*, 136–44.

Mrs. Crowley: The anima?

Dr. Jung: Yes, the anima is the Kundalini.[41] That is the very reason why I hold that this second center, despite the Hindu interpretation of the crescent being male, is intensely female, for the water is the womb of rebirth, the baptismal fount. The moon is of course a female symbol; and, moreover, I have a Tibetan picture at home in which Śiva is depicted in the female form, dancing on the corpses in the burial ground. At all events, the moon is always understood as the receptacle of the souls of the dead. They migrate to the moon after death, and the moon gives birth to the souls in the sun. She first gets quite full of dead souls—that is the pregnant full moon—and then she gives them to the sun, where the souls attain new life (a Manichean myth). So the moon is a symbol of rebirth. Then the moon in this cakra is not above—it is below, like a cup from which flows the offering of souls to the cakras above, *maṇipura* and *anāhata*. You see, there is the sun myth again.

[41] Jung's interpretation of the Kundalini as the anima may in part have been suggested by the following description of her cited in *The Serpent Power*: "She . . . is the 'Inner Woman' to whom reference was made when it was said, 'What need have I of outer women? I have an Inner Woman within myself' " (1st ed., 272). This sentence is heavily marked in Jung's copy of the book; the whole phrase is cited in his "Die Beschreibung der beiden Centren Shat-chakra Nirupana" (2), and the last phrase, "I have an Inner Woman within myself," is cited again in his "Avalon Serpent" manuscript (1). In "Concerning Mandala Symbolism" (1950), while commenting on a mandala painted by a young woman in which a coiled snake appeared, Jung said of the snake: "It is trying to get out: it is the awakening of Kundalini, meaning that the patient's chthonic nature is becoming active. . . . In practice it means becoming conscious of one's instinctual nature." *CW*, vol. 9, part 1, §667.

LECTURE 2

19 October 1932

Dr. Jung: We will go on with further information about the cakras. You remember, I told you last time that I would analyze the meaning of the symbolic attributes of the *mūlādhāra.* You probably have noticed that in analyzing these symbols we have followed very much the same method that we use in dream analysis: we look at all the symbols and try to construct the meaning which seems to be indicated by the totality of the attributes. In that way we reached the conclusion that *mūlādhāra* was a symbol of our conscious earthly personal existence.

To repeat in a few words the argument: *mūlādhāra* is characterized as being the sign of the earth; the square in the center is the earth, the elephant being the carrying power, the psychical energy or the libido. Then the name *mūlādhāra,* meaning the root support, also shows that we are in the region of the roots of our existence, which would be our personal bodily existence on this earth. Another very important attribute is that the gods are asleep; the *liṅga* is a mere germ, and the Kundalini, the sleeping beauty, is the possibility of a world which has not yet come off. So that indicates a condition in which man seems to be the only active power, and the gods, or the impersonal, non-ego powers, are inefficient—they are doing practically nothing. And that is very much the situation of our modern European consciousness. Then we have still another attribute which is not shown in that symbol itself but which is given in the Hindu commentaries—namely, that this cakra is located, as it were, in the lower basin, which at once gives an entirely different meaning to the thing. For it is then something that is within our body, whereas we had reached the conclusion that it was without—that is, our conscious world. That the Hindu commentaries put the conscious world inside the body is to us a very astonishing fact.

We can take this commentary exactly like a patient's association in a dream or vision, and according to his idea, the association would be: it was something in his belly. Now, why does he say so? Perhaps our existence here in the flesh, in the three-dimensional space, really has something to do with the symbol in question. Perhaps it is a condition that could be expressed by the allegory of an abdomen—as if we were in an abdomen. And to be in an abdomen would mean most probably that we were in the mother, in a condition of development or beginning. That point of view would throw a peculiar light on our symbolism. It would convey the idea that our actual existence, this world, is a sort of womb; we are mere beginnings, less than embryos; we are just germs that have still to become, like an egg in the womb. Of course, this is simply a commentary, showing how the Hindu would look upon our world as it is—he perhaps understands his conscious world as being merely a nursery.

Now, that is a piece of philosophy. As you see, it is an analogy with Christian philosophy according to which this actual personal existence is only transitory. We are not meant to stay in this condition; we are planted on this earth for the purpose of becoming better and better, and when we die we shall become angels. In the Islamic world there is very much the same idea. I remember talking to an Arab in the tombs of the Caliphs in Cairo. I was admiring a tomb that was made in a wonderful style, really a very beautiful thing. He noticed my admiration and said:

> You Europeans are funny people. To admire this house is what *we* do, that is what we believe. You believe in dollars and automobiles and railways. But which is wiser, to build a house for a short time or for a long time? If you know that you will be in a place only for a few years, and that you will later stay in another place for fifty years, will you build your house for those few years, or for the fifty years?

I said, sure enough, "For the fifty years." And he said: "That is what we do—we build our houses for eternity, where we shall stay the longest."[1] That is the point of view of many peoples, whether they are Hindus or Christians or Mohammedans. According to their idea *mūlādhāra* is a transitory thing, the sprouting condition in which things begin. Of course, that is very much in opposition to what people of today believe. We read our papers, we look into the political and economic world, believing this to be the definite thing, as if all depended on what we were going to do about the currency, the general economic conditions, and so on. We are all quite crazy about it, as if it were particularly right to be concerned with it. But those other people are countless; we are few in number compared with the people who have an entirely different point

[1] Jung was in Cairo in 1926, and his account of his trip is found in *MDR*, 282–304, where this anecdote doesn't appear.

of view as to the meaning of the world. To them, we are just ridiculous; we are living in a sort of illusion about our world. So this standpoint of the yoga philosophy is thus far a part of the general tendency of the philosophic and religious world. It is very general to look at the *mūlādhāra* as a transitory phenomenon.

For our purpose we can leave aside this particular philosophic comment. It is quite interesting, yet it should not disturb us. For we have to take for granted that this is the world where the real things happen, that it is the only world, and perhaps there is nothing beyond—at least, we have no experiences that would prove it to us. We have to be concerned with the immediate reality, and we must say, as it is shown in the *mūlādhāra* symbol, that the gods which would stand for that other eternal order of things are asleep. They are inefficient, they mean nothing. Yet we are allowed to admit that in the very center of this field of consciousness are germs of something that point to a different kind of consciousness, though for the time being they are inactive. So, to put it on a psychological level, it seems evident that even in our consciousness, of which we believe that it is "nothing but," and perfectly clear and self-evident and banal—even in that field there is the spark of something that points to another conception of life.

This is merely a statement about a generally prevailing condition, namely, through the *consensus gentium*, the harmony of opinion in the whole world, among men, it is understood that somewhere in the interior of our normal consciousness, there is such a thing. There are sleeping gods, or a germ, that might enable us, as it has enabled people at all times, to look at the *mūlādhāra* world from an entirely different point of view, that allows them even to put *mūlādhāra* right down into the bottom of the trunk where things start—meaning that in the great body of the cosmic world, this world holds the lowest place, the place of the beginning. So what we take to be the culmination of a long history and a long evolution would be really a nursery, and the great, important things are high above it and are still to come—exactly as the unconscious contents which we feel down below in our abdomen are slowly rising to the surface and becoming conscious, so that we begin to have the conviction: this is definite, this is clear, this is really what we are after. As long as it was down below in the abdomen it simply disturbed our functions; it was a small germ. But now it is an embryo, or as it reaches the conscious, it is slowly seen as a full-grown tree.

If you look at the symbol of the *mūlādhāra* in such a way, you understand the purpose of the yoga in the awakening of Kundalini. It means to separate the gods from the world so that they become active, and with that one starts the other order of things. From the standpoint of the gods this world is less than child's play; it is a seed in the earth, a mere potentiality. Our whole world of consciousness is only a seed of the future. And when you succeed in the awakening of Kundalini, so that she begins to move out of her mere potentiality, you necessarily start a world which is a world of eternity, totally different from our world.

Here it will become clear why I speak at length about this whole problem.

You remember that in our former seminars I always tried to point out to you that the series of visions was an experience of a nonpersonal or impersonal kind, and to explain to you why I was so particularly reticent in speaking about the personal side of our patient; the personal side is really perfectly negligible in comparison with her visions. Her visions could be the visions of anybody, because they are impersonal, they correspond to the world of Kundalini and not to the world of *mūlādhāra*. They are experiences which really mean the development of Kundalini and not of Mrs. So-and-So. Sure enough, a very clever analyst would be able to analyze out of that material a series of personal incidents in her life, but it would be from only the *mūlādhāra* point of view, that is, our rational point of view of this world as the definite world. But from the standpoint of the Kundalini yoga, that aspect is not interesting, because it is merely accidental.[2] *mūlādhāra* is the world of illusion from that other point of view—as the world of the gods, the impersonal experience, is naturally an illusion from the *mūlādhāra* psychology, the rational viewpoint of our world.

I insist upon this particular symbolism because it really can give you an incomparable opportunity to understand what is meant by the impersonal experience, and by the peculiar duality, even duplicity, of the human psychology, where two aspects form a bewildering crisscross. On the one side the personal aspect, in which all the personal things are the only meaningful things; and another psychology in which the personal things are utterly uninteresting and valueless, futile, illusory. You owe it to the existence of these two aspects that you have fundamental conflicts at all, that you have the possibility of another point of view, so that you

[2] When the seminar on visions resumed on 2 November, Jung reiterated this statement: "You know I must refrain entirely from speaking of the personal life of our patient because it leads nowhere; if you begin to think of her as a personal being it will lead you astray. These visions are not to be understood in a personal way, for then it would be nothing but the subjective foolishness of one person." *The Visions Seminar*, vol. 7, 7. Clearly, the excursus on the psychology of Kundalini yoga was pedagogically intended to drive home this point.

can criticize and judge, recognize and understand. For when you are just one with a thing you are completely identical—you cannot compare it, you cannot discriminate, you cannot recognize it. You must always have a point outside if you want to understand. So people who have problematic natures with many conflicts are the people who can produce the greatest understanding, because from their own problematical natures they are enabled to see other sides and to judge by comparison. We could not possibly judge this world if we had not also a standpoint outside, and that is given by the symbolism of religious experiences.

Now, if the yogin or the Western person succeeds in awakening Kundalini, what starts is not in any way a personal development, though of course an impersonal development can influence the personal status, as it does very often and very favorably. But it is not always so. What starts are the impersonal happenings with which you should not identify. If you do, you will soon feel obnoxious consequences—you will get an inflation, you will get all wrong. That is one of the great difficulties in experiencing the unconscious—that one identifies with it and becomes a fool. You must not identify with the unconscious; you must keep outside, detached, and observe objectively what happens. But you then see that all the events that happen in the impersonal, nonhuman order of things have the very disagreeable quality that they cling to us, or we cling to them. It is as if the Kundalini in its movement upward were pulling us up with it, as if we were part of that movement, particularly in the beginning.

It is true that we *are* a part, because we are then that which contains the gods; they are germs in us, germs in the *mūlādhāra*, and when they begin to move they have the effect of an earthquake which naturally shakes us, and even shakes our houses down. When that upheaval comes, we are carried with it, and naturally we might think we were moving upward. But it makes, of course, a tremendous difference whether one flies, or whether it is a wave or a great wind that lifts one. For to fly is one's own activity, and one can safely come down again, but when one is carried upward, it is not under one's control, and one will be put down after a while in a most disagreeable way—then it means a catastrophe. So, you see, it is wise not to identify with these experiences but to handle them as if they were outside the human realm. That is the safest thing to do—and really absolutely necessary. Otherwise you get an inflation, and inflation is just a minor form of lunacy, a mitigated term for it. And if you get so absolutely inflated that you burst, it is schizophrenia.

Of course the idea of an impersonal, psychical experience is very strange to us, and it is exceedingly difficult to accept such a thing, because we are so imbued with the fact that our unconscious is our own—my unconscious, his unconscious, her unconscious—and our prejudice is so strong that we have the greatest trouble disidentifying. Even if we must recognize that there is a non-ego experience, it is a long way until we realize what it might be. That is the reason why these experiences are secret; they are called mystical because the ordinary world cannot understand them, and what they cannot understand they call mystical—that covers everything. But the point is that what they call mystical is simply not the obvious. Therefore the yoga way or the yoga philosophy has always been a secret, but not because people have *kept* it secret. For as soon as you *keep* a secret it is already an open secret; you know about it and other people know about it, and then it is no longer a secret. The real secrets are secrets because nobody understands them. One cannot even talk about them, and of such a kind are the experiences of the Kundalini yoga. That tendency to keep things secret is merely a natural consequence when the experience is of such a peculiar kind that you had better not talk about it, for you expose yourself to the greatest misunderstanding and misinterpretation. Even if it is a matter of dogmatized experience of things that already have a certain form, you still feel, as long as the original fresh impression of such an experience is alive, that you had better continue to cover it up. You feel that these things will not fit in, that they may have an almost destructive influence upon the convictions of the *mūlādhāra* world.

For the convictions of the *mūlādhāra* world are very necessary. It is exceedingly important that you are rational, that you believe in the definiteness of our world, that this world is the culmination of history, the most desirable thing. Such a conviction is absolutely vital. Otherwise you remain detached from the *mūlādhāra*—you never get there, you are never born, even. There are plenty of people who are not yet born. They seem to be all here, they walk about—but as a matter of fact, they are not yet born, because they are behind a glass wall, they are in the womb. They are in the world only on parole and are soon to be returned to the pleroma where they started originally. They have not formed a connection with this world; they are suspended in the air; they are neurotic, living the provisional life. They say: "I am now living on such-and-such a condition. If my parents behave according to my wishes, I stay. But if it should happen that they do something I don't like, I pop off." You see, that is the provisional life, a conditioned life, the life of somebody who is still connected by an umbilical cord as thick as a ship's rope to the pleroma, the archetypal world of splendor. Now, it is most important that you should be born; you ought to come into this world—otherwise you cannot realize the self, and the purpose of this world has been missed. Then you must simply be thrown back into the melting pot and be born again.

The Hindus have an extremely interesting theory about that. I am not strong on metaphysics, but I must admit that in metaphysics there is a great deal of psychology. You see, it is utterly important that one should be in this world, that one really fulfills one's *entelechia,* the germ of life which one is. Otherwise you can never start Kundalini; you can never detach. You simply are thrown back, and nothing has happened; it is an absolutely valueless experience. You must believe in this world, make roots, do the best you can, even if you have to believe in the most absurd things—to believe, for instance, that this world is very definite, that it matters absolutely whether such-and-such a treaty is made or not. It may be completely futile, but you have to believe in it, have to make it almost a religious conviction, merely for the purpose of putting your signature under the treaty, so that trace is left of you. For you should leave some trace in this world which notifies that you have been here, that something has happened. If nothing happens of this kind you have not realized yourself; the germ of life has fallen, say, into a thick layer of air that kept it suspended. It never touched the ground, and so never could produce the plant. But if you touch the reality in which you live, and stay for several decades if you leave your trace, then the impersonal process can begin. You see, the shoot must come out of the ground, and if the personal spark has never gotten into the ground, nothing will come out of it; no *liṅga* or Kundalini will be there, because you are still staying in the infinity that was before.

Now if, as I say, you succeed in completing your *entelechia,* that shoot will come up from the ground; namely, that possibility of a detachment from this world—from the world of *Māyā,* as the Hindu would say—which is a sort of depersonalization. For in *mūlādhāra* we are just identical. We are entangled in the roots, and we ourselves are the roots. We make roots, we cause roots to be, we are rooted in the soil, and there is no getting away for us, because we must be there as long as we live. That idea, that we can sublimate ourselves and become entirely spiritual and no hair left, is an inflation. I am sorry, that is impossible; it makes no sense. Therefore we must invent a new scheme, and we speak of the impersonal. Other times may invent other terms for the same thing.

You know, in India they do not say "personal" and "impersonal," "subjective" and "objective," "ego" and "non-ego." They speak of *buddhi,* personal consciousness, and Kundalini, which is the other thing; and they never dream of identifying the two. They never think, "I myself am Kundalini." Quite the contrary, they can experience the divine because they are so deeply conscious of the utter difference of God and man. We are identical with it from the beginning because our gods, inasmuch as they are not just conscious abstractions, are mere germs, or functions, let us say. The divine thing in us functions as neuroses of the stomach, or of the colon, or bladder—simply disturbances of the underworld. Our gods have gone to sleep, and they stir only in the bowels of the earth.[3] For our conscious idea of God is abstract and remote. One hardly dares to speak of it. It has become taboo, or it is such a worn-out coin that one can hardly exchange it.

Well now, Kundalini yoga in its system of cakras symbolizes the development of that impersonal life. Therefore it is at the same time an initiation symbolism, and it is the cosmogonic myth. I will tell you one example. There is a Pueblo myth according to which man was generated far down in the earth in a pitch-black cave. Then, after untold time of a dormant and absolutely dark wormlike existence, two heavenly messengers came down and planted all the plants. Finally they found a cane which was long enough to go through the opening in the roof and was jointed like a ladder, so mankind could climb up and reach the floor of the next cave; but it was still dark. Then, after a long time, they again placed the cane under the roof and again climbed up and reached the third cave. And so again, until finally they came to the fourth cave where there was light, but an incomplete and ghostly light. That cave opened out upon the surface of the earth, and for the first time they reached the surface; but it was still dark. Then they learned to make a brilliant light, out of which finally the sun and the moon were made.

You see, this myth depicts very beautifully how consciousness came to pass, how it rises from level to level. Those were cakras, new worlds of consciousness of natural growths, one above the other. And this is the symbolism of all initiation cults: the awakening out of *mūlādhāra*, and the going into the water, the baptismal fount with the danger of the makara, the devouring quality or attribute of the sea.

Then, if you pass through that danger you reach the next center, *maṇipūra*, which means the fullness of jewels. It is the fire center, really the place where the sun rises. The sun now appears; the first light comes after the baptism. This is like the initiation rites in the Isis mysteries,

[3] In his "Commentary on 'The Secret of the Golden Flower' " (1929) Jung wrote: "The gods have become diseases; Zeus no longer rules Olympus but rather the solar plexus and produces curious specimens for the doctor's consulting room" (*CW*, vol. 13, §54). For a reevaluation of this often-cited notion, see Wolfgang Giegerich, "Killings," *Spring: A Journal of Archetype and Culture* 54 (1993): 9–18.

according to Apuleius, where the initiate at the end of the ceremony was put upon the pedestal and worshiped as the god Helios, the deification that always follows the baptismal rite.[4] You are born into a new existence; you are a very different being and have a different name.

One sees all that very beautifully in the Catholic rite of baptism when the godfather holds the child and the priest approaches with the burning candle and says: *Dono tibi lucem eternam*" (I give thee the eternal light)—which means, I give you relatedness to the sun, to the God. You receive the immortal soul, which you did not possess before; you are then a "twice-born." Christ receives his mission and the spirit of God in his baptism in the Jordan. He is only a Christus after baptism because Christus meant the anointed one. He too is "twice-born." He is now above the ordinary mortal that he was as Jesus, the son of the carpenter. He is now a Christus, a nonpersonal or symbolic personality, no longer a mere person belonging to this or that family. He belongs to the whole world, and in his life it becomes evident that this is a very much more important role than if he were the son of Joseph and Mary.

So *maṇipūra* is the center of the identification with the god, where one becomes part of the divine substance, having an immortal soul. You are already part of that which is no longer in time, in three-dimensional space; you belong now to a fourth-dimensional order of things where time is an extension, where space does not exist and time is not, where there is only infinite duration—eternity.

This is a worldwide and ancient symbolism, not only in the Christian baptism and the initiation in the Isis mysteries. For instance, in the religious symbolism of ancient Egypt, the dead Pharaoh goes to the underworld and embarks in the ship of the sun. You see, to approach divinity means the escape from the futility of the personal existence and the achieving of the eternal existence, the escape to a nontemporal form of existence. The Pharaoh climbs into the sun bark and travels through the night and conquers the serpent, and then rises again with the god, and is riding over the heavens for all eternity. That idea spread in the later centuries, so that even the nobles who were particularly friendly with the Pharaoh succeeded in climbing into the ship of Ra. Therefore one finds so many mummies buried in the tomb of the Pharaohs, the hope being that all the bodies in the tombs would rise with him. I saw something very touching in a newly excavated tomb in Egypt. Just before they had locked up the tomb of this particular noble, one of the workmen had put a little baby that had recently died, in a miserable little basket of reeds

[4] Lucius Apuleius, *The Golden Ass*, translated by Robert Graves (London, 1950), 286.

with a few poor little pieces of cloth, right inside the door, so that the baby—who was probably his child—would rise with the noble on the great day of judgment. He was quite satisfied with his own futility, but his baby, at least, should reach the sun. So this third center is rightly called the fullness of jewels. It is the great wealth of the sun, the never-ending abundance of divine power to which man attains through baptism.

But of course, that is all symbolism. We come now to the psychological interpretation, which is not as easy as the symbolic or comparative method.[5] It is far less easy to understand *maṇipūra* from a psychological point of view. If one dreams of baptism, of going into the bath or into the water, you know what it means when people are in actual analysis: that they are being pushed into the unconscious to be cleansed; they must get into the water for the sake of renewal. But it remains dark what follows after the bath. It is very difficult to explain in psychological terms what will follow when you have made your acquaintance with the unconscious. Have you an idea? Mind you, this question is not easy to answer, because you will be inclined to give an abstract answer, for a psychological reason.

Dr. Reichstein: You could say that the old world is burning down.

Dr. Jung: That is not just abstract, but it is very universal and at a safe distance.

Dr. Reichstein: The old conventional forms and ideas are breaking down.

Dr. Jung: Oh yes, our philosophy of the world may be changed tremendously, but that is no proof that you have reached *maṇipūra.*

Dr. Reichstein: But is not *maṇipūra* a symbol of fire, of things burned?

Dr. Jung: Well, it is not just a destructive symbol; it means more a source of energy. But you are quite right—there is always a note of destruction when one speaks of fire; the mere mention of fire is enough to rouse the idea of destruction. And there you touch upon that fear that causes abstraction; we easily get abstract when we do not want to touch a thing that is too hot.

Miss Hannah: Is one not able, then, to see the opposites at the same time?

Dr. Jung: Yes, that is nicely put, very abstract, but you could designate it more completely.

Mrs. Sawyer: In the visions, the patient came to the place where she had to stand the fire, and then the stars fell down.[6] So the impersonal things began.

[5] The contrast is to Hauer's method of interpretation.

[6] See *The Visions Seminar,* vol. 5, 9 March 1932, 114.

Dr. Jung: Quite so—there we have a connection.

Dr. Bertine: Is it not a capacity for living more fully? A greater intensity of conscious living?

Dr. Jung: We think we are living quite consciously and with great intensity. What is the next effect when you become acquainted with the unconscious and take it seriously? You see you are inclined not to take it seriously and to invent an apotropaic theory that is "nothing but"—nothing but infantile memories or inhibited wishes, for instance. Why do you accept such a theory? In reality it is something quite different.

Mrs. Crowley: It is becoming acquainted with the shadow part.

Dr. Jung: That is also conveniently put, but what does it mean?

Mrs. Sigg: Isolation.

Dr. Jung: That might be the consequence of it, but first of all it is just the horrible thing that leads into isolation, just the opposite.

Mrs. Crowley: Desirousness, all that shadow part of yourself.

Dr. Jung: Yes, desire, passions, the whole emotional world breaks loose. Sex, power, and every devil in our nature gets loose when we become acquainted with the unconscious. Then you will suddenly see a new picture of yourself. That is why people are afraid and say there is no unconscious, like children playing hide-and-seek. A child goes behind a door and says, "Nobody is behind this door; don't look here!" And so we have two marvelous psychological theories that nothing is behind this door, don't look here, this is nothing important.[7] Those are apotropaic theories. But you will see that there is something, you must admit that there are such powers. Then you make an abstraction, you make marvelous abstract signs of it, and talk of it with only a sort of shy hinting. You speak euphemistically. As sailors never dared to say, "This damned hell of a sea, this black sea that is always so stormy and smashes our ships!" They said, "The welcoming benevolent sea . . ."—in order not to arouse those alarming impressions, or to irritate those dark wind demons. Instead of saying the archbishop of Canterbury, you say His Grace. You don't say the pope has issued a very foolish encyclica, you say the Vatican. Or instead of speaking of those hellish liars, you say Wilhelmstraße, or Downing Street, or the Quai d'Orsay. That is the euphemistic abstract way of putting things. Our science has the same purpose in using Latin or Greek words. It is a marvelous shield against the demons—the demons are afraid of Greek because they do not understand it. And therefore we talk, as you have just demonstrated, in such an abstract way.

So it is just that—you get into the world of fire, where things become red-hot. After baptism you get right into hell—that is the enantiodromia.

[7] The reference is to Freud's psychoanalysis and Adler's individual psychology.

And now comes the paradox of the East: it is also the fullness of jewels. But what is passion, what are emotions? There is the source of fire, there is the fullness of energy. A man who is not on fire is nothing: he is ridiculous, he is two-dimensional. He must be on fire even if he does make a fool of himself. A flame must burn somewhere, otherwise no light shines; there is no warmth, nothing. It is terribly awkward, sure enough; it is painful, full of conflict, apparently a mere waste of time—at all events, it is against reason. But that accursed Kundalini says, "It is the fullness of jewels; there is the source of energy." As Heraclitus aptly said: war is the father of all things.

Now this third center, the center of emotions, is localized in the *plexus solaris*, or the center of the abdomen. I have told you that my first discovery about the Kundalini yoga was that these cakras really are concerned with what are called psychical localizations. This center then would be the first psychical localization that is within our conscious psychical experience. I must refer again to the story of my friend, the Pueblo chief, who thought that all Americans were crazy because they were convinced that they thought in the head. He said: "But we think in the heart." That is *anāhata*.[8] Then there are primitive tribes who have their psychical localization in the abdomen. And that is true of us as well; there is a certain category of psychical events that take place in the stomach. Therefore one says, "Something weighs on my stomach." And if one is very angry, one gets jaundice; if one is afraid, one has diarrhea; or if in a particularly obstinate mood, one is constipated. You see, that shows what psychical localization means.

Thinking in the abdomen means that there was once a time when consciousness was so dim that people noticed only the things that disturbed their intestinal functions, and everything else simply passed by the board; it did not exist because it had no effect upon them. There are still traces of that among the central Australian aborigines, who have the funniest ceremonies in order to make them realize a thing. I told you about the ceremony of making a man angry; and one sees other forms of the same thing in all primitive tribes. Before they can make up their minds to go hunting, for instance, there must be a whole ceremonial by which they are put into the mood of hunting; otherwise they don't do it. They must be excited by something. It has to do not only with the intestines, then, but with the whole body.

Therefore that primitive method of the schoolmasters fifty years ago,

[8] Hauer described the *anāhata* cakra as "the heart lotus, which means the one that has not or cannot be hurt" (*HS*, 69).

which I myself have experienced. We were taught the ABCs with a whip. We were eight boys sitting on one bench, and the schoolmaster had a whip of three willow wands, just long enough to touch all the backs at once. He said, "This is A" (bang), "This is B" (bang). You see, causing a physical sensation was the old method of teaching. It was not very painful, because when he beat on eight backs at the same time you just cringed and didn't feel it very much. But it makes an impression; the boys were actually sitting up and listening. That was instead of "Will you be kind enough to pay attention, please?" Then nobody listens; they think he is a damned fool. But when he cracks the whip over them and says, "*That* is A," then they get it.

It is for the same reason that primitives inflict wounds in initiations when they hand over the secrets, the mystical teaching of the tribe. At the same time they cause intense pain: they make cuts and rub ashes into them, or they starve the initiants, they don't let them sleep, or frighten them out of their wits. Then they give the teaching, and it catches hold of them because it has gone in with physical discomfort or pain.

Now, as I said, the first psychical localization that is conscious to us is the abdomen; we are not conscious of anything deeper. I don't know of a trace in primitive psychology where people would locate their psyche in their bladder. Then the next is the heart, which is a very definite center that still functions with us. For instance we say, "You know it in the head, but you don't know it in the heart." There is an extraordinary distance from the head to the heart, a distance of ten, twenty, thirty years, or a whole lifetime. For you can know something in the head for forty years and it may never have touched the heart. But only when you have realized it in the heart do you begin to take notice of it. And from the heart it is an equally long distance down to the *plexus solaris*, and then you are caught. For there you have no freedom at all. There is no air substance: you are just bones and blood and muscles; you are in the intestines; you are functioning there like a worm with no head. But in the heart you are on the surface. The diaphragm would be about the surface of the earth. As long as you are in *maṇipūra* you are in the terrible heat of the center of the earth, as it were. There is only the fire of passion, of wishes, of illusions. It is the fire of which Buddha speaks in his sermon in Benares where he says, The whole world is in flames, your ears, your eyes, everywhere you pour out the fire of desire, and that is the fire of illusion because you desire things which are futile. Yet there is the great treasure of the released emotional energy.

So when people become acquainted with the unconscious they often get into an extraordinary state—they flare up, they explode, old buried emotions come up, they begin to weep about things which happened forty years ago. That simply means that they were prematurely detached from that stage of life; they have forgotten that there are buried fires still burning. Then they were unconscious, but when they touch the lower centers, they get back into that world and become aware that it is still hot, like a fire that has been left forgotten under the ashes. But take away the ashes and there are still the glowing embers underneath, as it is said of pilgrims going to Mecca: they leave their fires buried under the ashes, and when they return the following year the embers are still glowing.

Now, in *maṇipūra* you have reached an upper layer where there comes a definite change.[9] The bodily localization of this cakra under the diaphragm is the symbol for the peculiar change that now takes place. Above the diaphragm you come into *anāhata*, the heart or air center, because the heart is embedded in the lungs and the whole activity of the heart is closely associated with the lungs. One must be naive to understand these things. In primitive experience, it is the same thing. In fact, it is a physiological truth. We understand more or less what *maṇipūra* means psychologically, but now we come to the great leap, *anāhata*. What follows psychologically after you have fallen into hell? When you have come into the whirlpool of passions, of instincts, of desires and so on, what follows after?

Mrs. Crowley: Usually an enantiodromia; some opposite will now be constellated. Some vision perhaps, or something more impersonal will follow.

Dr. Jung: An enantiodromia, which would be the discovery of something impersonal? In other words, that one no longer identifies with one's desires. Now, one must consider the fact that it is hard to talk of these things, because most people are still identical with *maṇipūra*. It is exceedingly difficult to find out what is beyond. Therefore we must remain a bit in the symbolism first. The next center, as I told you, has to do with the air. The diaphragm would correspond to the surface of the earth, and apparently in getting into *anāhata* we reach the condition where we are lifted up from the earth. What has happened? How do we get there at all? You see in *maṇipūra* we still don't know where we are; we are in *mūlādhāra* just as well, at least our feet are still standing in *mūlādhāra*: but in *anāhata* they are lifted up above the surface of the earth. Now, what could literally lift one above the earth?

Dr. Meier: The wind.

[9] In the manuscript "Die Beschreibung der beidem Centrem Shat-chakra Nirupana" Jung described *maṇipūra* as "center of corporeal men, carnivores" (2; my translation).

Dr. Jung: Yes, that would be within the symbolism, but there is another thing that would make it a bit plainer.

Dr. Bertine: A sort of distillation?

Dr. Jung: That is a good idea, which leads us right away into alchemistic symbolism. The alchemist calls this process sublimation. But to remain in the symbolism of which we were speaking today?

Mr. Allemann: The sun rises above the horizon.

Dr. Jung: Yes, you rise above the horizon according to the Egyptian symbolism. If you are identical with the sun, you rise above the horizon with the sun ship and travel over the heavens. The sun is a superior power. If you are an appendix of the Pharaoh, the sun can lift you up to almost a divine position. And the contact with the sun in *maṇipūra* lifts you up off your feet into the sphere above the earth. The wind also can do it, because in primitive beliefs the spirit is a kind of wind.

Therefore in many languages there is the same word for wind and spirit, *spiritus* for instance, and *spirare* means to blow or breathe. *Animus*, spirit, comes from the Greek *anemos*, wind; and *pneuma*, spirit, is also a Greek word for wind. In Arabic *ruch* is the wind or soul of the spirit; and in Hebrew *ruach* means spirit and wind. The connection between wind and spirit is due to the fact that the spirit was thought originally to be the breath, the air one breathes out or expires. With a person's last breath his spirit leaves the body. So it would be either a magic wind or the sun that lifts you up. And where do we find the two things coming together? Perhaps you still remember in analytical literature that very interesting case.

Mrs. Sawyer: Is it the primitives blowing on their hands and worshiping the sunrise?

Dr. Jung: That is identification with the sun. It is not the same, you see, but I have published an example of the wind and the sun being the same.

Mr. Baumann: The sun is sometimes the origin of the wind.

Dr. Jung: Yes. You remember the case of the insane man who saw a sort of tube hanging down from the sun. He called it the "sun phallus," and it caused the wind. That shows that the sun and the wind are the same.[10]

[10] In *Transformations and Symbols of the Libido* (1912), Jung cited his pupil Johann Honegger's discovery of a patient's hallucination: "The patient sees in the sun a so-called 'upright tail' (i.e., much like an erect penis). When the patient moves his head back and forth, the sun's penis also moves back and forth, and from this the wind arises. This strange delusionary idea remained unintelligible to us for a long time, until I became acquainted with the visions of the Mithraic liturgy." *Psychology of the Unconscious*, in *CW* B, §173; translation modified. In 1927 Jung stated that he made this observation in 1906 and came across Albrecht Dietrich's *Eine Mithrasliturgie* (A Mithras liturgy) (Leipzig, 1903) in 1910, which ruled out the possibility of cryptomnesia (the revival of forgotten memories) or telepathy

Mr. Baumann: I think there is a Greek myth, where you hear voices before the sun has risen.

Dr. Jung: That is the figure of Memnon in Egypt, which was said to produce a peculiar sound when the sun rises, because according to the Greek legend Memnon is the son of Aurora, the dawn, so when dawn appears he greets his mother. But that is not exactly the wind and the sun. You see, the symbolism tells us what happens in *anāhata.* But that is not psychological; we are really in mythology so far, and we ought to know what it means psychologically. How do you get lifted up above the *maṇipūra* center, above the world of your mere emotions?

Miss Hannah: You get an inflation, and you identify with the god.

Dr. Jung: That might be, it is very inflating, but we are speaking here of the normal case. We are supposing that sequence of the Kundalini is a normal sequence, because it is the condensation of the experiences of perhaps thousands of years.

Mr. Baumann: When you are very emotional you try to express yourself, for instance, by music or poetry.

Dr. Jung: You mean it produces a certain utterance. But emotions always produce utterances. You can manifest all sorts of things when you are still caught in your emotions. It must be something above the emotions.

Mrs. Mehlich: Is it that one begins to think?

Dr. Jung: Exactly.

Dr. Reichstein: It is said that here the *puruṣa*[11] is born, so it would be here that the first idea of the self is seen more completely.

Dr. Jung: Yes, but how would that show in psychology? We must try now to bring the thing down to psychological facts.

Dr. Reichstein: That we become conscious of something which is not personal at this point.

Dr. Jung: Yes, you begin to reason, to think, to reflect about things, and so it is the beginning of a sort of contraction or withdrawal from the mere emotional function. Instead of following your impulses wildly, you

---

and hence provided evidence for the collective unconscious. The editors noted that Jung subsequently learned that the 1910 edition was the second edition, and that the original had actually been published in 1903. They added that the patient had been committed prior to 1903. *CW*, vol. 8, §§319–21.

[11] Woodroffe defined *puruṣa* as "a center of limited consciousness—limited by the associated Prakṛti and its products of Mind and Matter. Popularly by Puruṣa . . . is meant sentient being with body and senses—that is, organic life." Arthur Avalon (pseud. Sir John Woodroffe), *The Serpent Power* (London, 1919), 49. Surendranath Dasgupta defined *puruṣa* as spirit (*Yoga as Philosophy and Religion* [London, 1924], 3) and as "consciousness itself" (ibid., 173).

begin to invent a certain ceremony that allows you to disidentify yourself from your emotions, or to overcome your emotions actually. You stop yourself in your wild mood and suddenly ask, "Why am I behaving like this?"

We find the symbolism for that in this center. In *anāhata* you behold the *puruṣa*, a small figure that is the divine self, namely, that which is not identical with mere causality, mere nature, a mere release of energy that runs down blindly with no purpose.[12] People lose themselves completely in their emotions and deplete themselves, and finally they are burned to bits and nothing remains—just a heap of ashes, that is all. The same thing occurs in lunacy: people get into a certain state and cannot get out of it. They burn up in their emotions and explode. There is a possibility that one detaches from it, however, and when a man discovers this, he really becomes a man. Through *maṇipūra* he is in the womb of nature, extraordinarily automatic; it is merely a process. But in *anāhata* a new thing comes up, the possibility of lifting himself above the emotional happenings and beholding them. He discovers the *puruṣa* in his heart, the thumbling, "Smaller than small, and greater than great."[13] In the center of *anāhata* there is again Śiva in the form of the *liṅga*, and the small flame means the first germlike appearance of the self.

Mr. Dell: Is the process you describe the beginning of individuation in psychological terms?

Dr. Jung: Yes. It is the withdrawal from the emotions; you are no longer identical with them. If you succeed in remembering yourself, if you succeed in making a difference between yourself and that outburst of passion, then you discover the self; you begin to individuate. So in *anāhata* individuation begins. But here again you are likely to get an inflation. Individuation is not that you become an ego—you would then become an individualist. You know, an individualist is a man who did not succeed in individuating; he is a philosophically distilled egotist. Individuation is becoming that thing which is not the ego, and that is very strange. Therefore nobody understands what the self is, because the self is just the thing which you are not, which is not the ego. The ego discovers itself as being a mere appendix of the self in a sort of loose connection. For the ego is

[12] In his commentary on Patanjali's *Yoga Sutras*, Jung stated, concerning the translation of the term *puruṣa*, "Deussen designates [it] as 'das von allem Objectiven freie Subject des Erkennens' [the subject of knowledge freed from everything objective]. I doubt this definition—it is too logical, and the East is not logical; it is observant and intuitive. So it is better to describe the *puruṣa* as primeval man or as the luminous man." *Modern Psychology 3*, 121.

[13] *Katha Upanisad* 2.20–21; cited also in *CW*, vol. 6, §329, where *puruṣa* is rendered as "Self."

always far down in *mūlādhāra* and suddenly becomes aware of something up above in the fourth story, in *anāhata*, and that is the self.

Now, if anybody makes the mistake of thinking that he lives at the same time in the basement and on the fourth story, that he is the *puruṣa* himself, he is crazy. He is what the German very aptly call *verrückt*, carried off his feet up to somewhere else. He just sits up there and spins. We are allowed to behold only the *puruṣa*, to behold his feet up there. But we are not the *puruṣa*; that is a symbol that expresses the impersonal process. The self is something exceedingly impersonal, exceedingly objective. If you function in your self you are not yourself—that is what you feel. You have to do it as if you were a stranger: you will buy as if you did not buy; you will sell as if you did not sell. Or, as St. Paul expresses it, "But it is not I that lives, it is Christ that liveth in me," meaning that his life had become an objective life, not his own life but the life of a greater one, the *puruṣa*.

All the primitive tribes that are on a somewhat higher level of civilization usually have discovered *anāhata*. That is, they begin to reason, and to judge; they are no longer quite wild. They have elaborate ceremonies—the more primitive they are the more elaborate are the ceremonies. They need them in order to prevent *maṇipūra* psychology. They have invented all sorts of things, magic circles, forms for the palavers, for the intercourse of people; all those peculiar ceremonials are special psychological techniques to prevent an explosion of *maṇipūra*. In a palaver with primitives it is simply *de rigueur* that you do certain things—to us, perfectly superfluous things—but you can do nothing with the primitives unless you observe the rules.

For instance, there must be an unmistakable hierarchy; therefore the man who calls the palaver must be a man of power. If I call a palaver, I must have a stool, and the other people are on the ground; they must sit down immediately. The chief has men with whips who whip everybody down if they don't sit down at once. And then one does not begin to talk. One first hands around presents—matches, cigarettes—and the chief necessarily must have many more cigarettes than his subjects, because the hierarchy of that moment must be emphasized to show that there is authority on top.[14] That is all ceremony against *maṇipūra*, and only when that is silently done can the man who calls the palaver begin to speak. I say that I have a *shauri*, a business. That is the beginning. You see, I must speak a mantra by which everybody is caught—nobody is allowed to talk; everybody listens. Then I say my *shauri*, after which my partner, with

[14] For Jung's account of his palavers among the Elgonyi in Kenya in 1925–26, which overlaps with his description here, see *MDR*, 293–97.

whom I have to deal, talks too, but in a very low voice, hardly audible, and he shall not get up. If a man speaks too loudly, somebody comes with a whip. He may not speak loudly, because that would show emotion, and as soon as there is emotion, there is danger of fighting and killing. Therefore no weapons are allowed. Also, when the palaver ends one must say *shauri kisha*, meaning, "Now the palaver is finished."

I once got up before I had said that, and my headman came quite excitedly to me and said, "Now, don't get up!" And then I said *shauri kisha*, and everything was all right. If I said a mantra, I could go. I must say that the whole magic circle is now dissolved, and then I can go without rousing the suspicion that somebody is offended or in a wild mood. Otherwise it is dangerous, then there might be anything, perhaps murder, for one is getting up obviously because one is crazy. It sometimes happens that they get so excited in their dances that they begin to kill. For instance, those two cousins Sarasin, who made the exploration in Celebes, were almost killed by men who were really very friendly with them.[15] They were showing them the war dances, and they got so much in the mood of war, so frenzied, that they threw their spears at them. It was sheer luck that they escaped.

You see, *anāhata* is still very feeble, and *maṇipūra* psychology is quite close to us. We still have to be polite to people to avoid the explosions of *maṇipūra*.

[15] Paul and Fritz Sarasin published an account of their anthropological expeditions in *Reisen in Celebes ausgeführt in den Jahren 1893–1896 und 1902–1903* (Travels in Celebes taken in the years 1893–1896 and 1902–1903), 2 vols. (Wiesbaden, 1905).

LECTURE 3

26 October 1932

Dr. Jung: I will continue our discussion of the cakras. You remember, we were speaking chiefly of the transformation from *maṇipūra* to *anāhata.* In *anāhata* something is attained which was begun in *mulādhāra,* through a series of four stages. How might these four stages also be designated?

Dr. Reichstein: They are the four elements.

Dr. Jung: Exactly. Each of the four lower centers has an element belonging to it—*mūlādhāra,* the earth, *svādhiṣṭhāna,* the water, then comes fire in *maṇipūra,* and finally air in *anāhata.* So one can see the whole thing as a sort of transformation of elements, with the increase of volatility—of volatile substance. And the next form we reach is *viśuddha,*[1] which is the ether center. Now, what is ether? Do you know anything about it from the physical point of view?

Remark: It penetrates everything.

Mrs. Sawyer: You cannot catch it.

Dr. Jung: Why not? Since it penetrates everywhere, why can it not be found everywhere?

Mr. Dell: It cannot be measured; it is a thought.

Dr. Jung: Yes, one finds it only within one's brain, nowhere else; it is a concept of substance that has none of the qualities that matter should have. It is matter that is not matter, and such a thing must necessarily be a concept. Now, in the *viśuddha* center—beyond the four elements—one reaches what stage?

Mrs. Crowley: A more conscious state, abstract thought perhaps?

Dr. Jung: Yes, one reaches a sphere of abstraction. There one steps beyond the empirical world, as it were, and lands in a world of concepts. And what are concepts? What do we call the substance of concepts?

Mrs. Crowley: Psychology?

Dr. Jung: Or say psychical psychology; that would express the science

[1] Hauer described the *viśuddha* cakra as "the cleansed one, or cleansing" (*HS,* 69).

of psychical things. The reality we reach there is a psychical reality; it is a world of psychical substance, if we can apply such a term. I think we get nearest to it when we say it is a world of psychical reality. So another point of view to explain the series of the cakras would be a climbing up from gross matter to the subtle, psychical matter. Now, the idea of this transformation from earth to ether is one of the oldest constituents of Hindu philosophy. The concept of the five elements is a part of the Samkhya philosophy, which is pre-Buddhistic, belonging to the seventh century B.C. at the latest. All subsequent Hindu philosophies, like the Upanisads, took their origin in the Samkhya philosophy. So this concept of the five elements dates back endlessly—there is no way of telling its age. One sees from the age of that component that the fundamental ideas of tantric yoga reach back into a dim past. Also the idea of the transformation of the elements shows the analogy of tantric yoga with our medieval alchemistic philosophy. There one finds exactly the same ideas, the transformation of the gross matter into the subtle matter of the mind—the sublimation of man, as it was then understood.

Speaking of this alchemistic aspect of the cakras, I want to call your attention to the symbol of *maṇipūra*, the fire center. You remember, perhaps, that in the fire center there are those peculiar handles, one could call them, which Professor Hauer hypothetically explained as parts of the swastika.[2] Now, I must confess that I never have seen a swastika symbol that had only three feet. There is the Greek form of the *triskelos*, but I don't know whether that existed in India. It was found on Greek coins in Sicily, from a period between four hundred and about two hundred B.C.—when Sicily belonged to Graecia Magna and was a large and flourishing Greek colony. The *triskelos* is like this: the three-legged being. But the swastika is like this: running on four feet. So I suggest that these might be handles attached to the triangle of *maṇipūra*. I rather think that they are handles of a pot—to lift the pot—and there is a lid on top which has also a handle. I think that is probably to be explained from the alchemistic aspect, because *maṇipūra* is the fire region, and that is the kitchen, or the stomach, where the food is cooked. One stuffs the food into the pot, or into the belly, and there it is heated by the blood. In that way food is prepared so that one can digest it.

Cooking is an anticipation of digestion, a sort of predigestion. For example, in Africa the papaya tree has the very peculiar quality that its fruit and leaves are full of pepsin, the same stuff which is found in the juice of the stomach, the digestive stuff par excellence. The Negroes wrap up

[2] Ibid., 75.

their meat for two or three hours in papaya leaves instead of cooking it—it thus becomes partially digested; it is predigested. And so the whole art of cooking is predigestion. We have transferred part of our digestive ability into the kitchen, so the kitchen is the stomach of every house, and the labor of preparing the food is then taken away from our stomachs. Our mouth is also a predigestive organ, because the saliva contains a digestive substance. The mechanical action of the teeth is predigestive, because we cut up the food, which is what we also do in the kitchen in cutting up the vegetables, and so on. So you could really say that the kitchen is a digestive tract projected from the human body. And it is the alchemistic place where things are transformed.

Therefore *maṇipūra* would be a center in which substances are digested, transformed. The next thing one would expect would be the transformation shown as completed. As a matter of fact, this center is right below the diaphragm, which marks the dividing line between *anāhata* and the centers of the abdomen.

For after *maṇipūra* follows *anāhata*,[3] in which entirely new things occur; a new element is there, air, no longer gross matter. Even fire is understood to be in a way gross matter. It is thicker, denser than air, and it is quite visible, whereas air is invisible. Fire is exceedingly movable, yet perfectly well defined, and also in a way tangible, whereas air is exceedingly light and almost intangible—unless you feel it as a wind. It is relatively gentle in comparison with fire, which moves and burns.

So at the diaphragm you cross the threshold from the visible tangible things to the almost invisible intangible things. And these invisible things in *anāhata* are the psychical things, for this is the region of what is called feeling and mind. The heart is characteristic of feeling, and air is characteristic of thought. It is the breath-being; therefore one has always identified the soul and thought with breath.

For instance, it is the custom in India, when the father dies, that the oldest son must watch during the last moments in order to inhale the last breath of his father, which is the soul, in order to continue his life. The Swahili word *roho* means the stertorous breathing of a dying man, which we call in German *röcheln*; and *roho* also means the soul. It is no doubt taken from the Arabic word *ruch*, which means wind, breath, spirit, with probably the same original idea of stertorous breathing. So the original idea of spirit or of psychical things is the idea of breath or air. And I told you that the mind in Latin is *animus*, which is identical with the Greek word *ánemos* meaning wind.

[3] Hauer stated of the *anāhata* cakra: "This heart lotus is the cakra of the fundamental insights into life; it is what we call the creative life in the highest sense" (*HS*, 90–91).

The heart is always characteristic of feeling because feeling conditions influence the heart. Everywhere in the world feelings are associated with the heart. If you have no feelings, you have no heart; if you have no courage, you have no heart, because courage is a definite feeling condition. And you say, "Take it to heart." Or you learn something "by heart." You learn it, of course, by the head but you won't keep it in mind unless you take it to heart. Only if you learn a thing by heart do you really get it. In other words, if it is not associated with your feelings, if it has not sunk into your body until it reaches the *anāhata* center, it is so volatile that it flies away. It must be associated with the lower center in order to be kept. Therefore that method of teaching pupils that I described to you last week, where the teacher used the whip, in order that their feelings of anger and suffering would make the pupils remember the letters. If they were not associated with pain, they would not keep them. That is particularly true for the primitive man: he learns nothing if not in such a way.

The real importance of thoughts and values becomes clear to us only when we consider them as compelling forces in our lives. The beginning of such a recognition of such values and thoughts in primitives would be embodied in the secret teaching of the tribe, which is given at the time of the puberty initiations together with pain and torture to make them remember it. At the same time they are taught certain moral values, which prevent the mere blind action of the *maṇipūra* fires of passion.

So *anāhata* is really the center where psychical things begin, the recognition of values and ideas. When man has reached that level in civilization or in his individual development one could say he was in *anāhata*, and there he gets the first inkling of the power and substantiality, or the real existence, of psychical things.

For instance, take a patient in analysis who has reached the stage of *maṇipūra*, where he is an absolute prey to his emotions and passions. I say: "But you really ought to be a bit reasonable; don't you see what you do? You cause no end of trouble to your relations." And it makes no impression whatever. But then these arguments begin to have a pull; one knows that the threshold of the diaphragm is crossed—he has reached *anāhata*. You see, values, convictions, general ideas are psychical facts that are nowhere to be met with in natural science. One cannot catch them with a butterfly net, nor can one find them under microscopes. They become visible only in *anāhata*. Now according to tantric yoga, the *puruṣa* is first seen in *anāhata*: the essence of man, the supreme man, the so-called primordial man then becomes visible. So *puruṣa* is identical with the psychical substance of thought and value, feeling. In the recognition of feelings and of ideas one sees the *puruṣa*. That is the first inkling of a being within your psychological or psychical existence that is not yourself—a being in which you are contained, which is greater and more important than you but which has an entirely psychical existence.

You see, we could finish here; we could say that about covers the growth of humanity. As we are all convinced that psychical things have a certain weight, mankind as a whole has about reached *anāhata*. For instance, the great war has taught practically everybody that the things that have the greatest weight are the *imponderabilia*, the things you cannot possibly weigh, like public opinion or psychical infection. The whole war was a psychical phenomenon. If you are looking for the causal root of it, it could not possibly be explained as arising out of the reason of man or out of economic necessity. One could say that Germany needed a greater expansion and had to go to war, or that France felt threatened and had to crush Germany. But nobody was threatened—everybody had enough money, the German exports were increasing from year to year, Germany had all the expansion she needed. All the economic reasons you mention are no good at all; they don't explain that phenomenon. It was simply the time when that thing had to happen from unknown psychical reasons. Any great movement of man has always started from psychical reasons; so it is our experience that has taught us to believe in the psychical. Therefore we are rightly afraid of mob psychology, for instance. Every man of today will take that into account. And formerly man did not believe in the value of advertising; now look what is done with it! Or would anybody have believed that the little sheets which appeared every fortnight—gazettes, which we now call newspapers—would be a world power? The press is recognized as a world power today; it is a psychical fact.

So we can say that our civilization has reached the state of *anāhata*—we have overcome the diaphragm. We no longer locate the mind in the diaphragm, as the Old Greeks did in Homeric times. We are convinced that the seat of consciousness must be somewhere up in the head. We already have a more farsighted view in *anāhata*; we become aware of the *puruṣa*. But we do not yet trust the security of psychical existence, so we have not reached *viśuddha*. We still believe in a material world built of matter and psychical force. And we cannot connect the psychical existence or substance with the idea of anything cosmic or physical. We have not yet found the bridge between the ideas of physics and psychology.[4]

Therefore collectively we have not crossed the distance between

[4] Jung attempted such a bridge in his collaboration with the physicist Wolfgang Pauli in *The Interpretation of Nature and the Psyche* (Bollingen Series LI, 1955). On this issue, see especially *Wolfgang Pauli und C. G. Jung: Ein Briefwechsel 1932–1958*, edited by C. A. Meier (Berlin, 1992).

anāhata and *viśuddha.* So if one speaks of *viśuddha,* it is of course with a certain hesitation. We are stepping into the slippery future right away when we try to understand what that might mean. For in *viśuddha* we reach beyond our actual conception of the world, in a way we reach the ether region. We are trying something that would be more than Professor Piccard achieved![5] He was only in the stratosphere—he reached something exceedingly thin, I admit, but it was not yet ether. So we have to construct a sort of skyrocket of very large dimensions which shoots us up into space. It is the world of abstract ideas and values, the world where the psyche is in itself, where the psychical reality is the only reality, or where matter is a thin skin around an enormous cosmos of psychical realities, really the illusory fringe around the real existence, which is psychical.

The concept of the atom, for instance, might be considered as corresponding to the abstract thinking of the *viśuddha* center. Moreover, if our experience should reach such a level, we would get an extraordinary vista of the *puruṣa.* For then the *puruṣa* becomes really the center of things; it is no longer a pale vision, it is the ultimate reality, as it were. You see, that world will be reached when we succeed in finding a symbolical bridge between the most abstract ideas of physics and the most abstract ideas of analytical psychology. If we can construct that bridge then we will have reached at least the outer gate of *viśuddha.* That is the condition. I mean, we will then have reached it collectively; the way will then be opened. But we are still a long distance from that goal. For *viśuddha* means just what I said: a full recognition of the psychical essences or substances as the fundamental essences of the world, and by virtue not of speculation but of fact, namely as *experience.* It does not help to speculate about *ājñā* and *sahasrāra*[6] and God knows what; you can reflect upon those things, but you are not there if you have not had the experience.

I will give you an example of the transition from one state to another.

[5] Auguste Piccard was a Swiss professor of physics at the University of Brussels. Commencing on 27 May 1931, he ascended for the first time into the stratosphere by means of a special balloon to make scientific observations. His second flight was from the Dübendorf aerodrome near Zurich on 18 August 1932. See his *Au dessus des nuages* (Above the clouds) (Paris, 1933) and *Between Earth and Sky,* translated by C. Apcher (London, 1950).

[6] Hauer stated that the *sahasrāra* cakra "is the thousand-spoked or the thousand-petaled cakra" (*HS,* 69). Eliade noted that "it is here that the final union (*unmanī*) of Śiva and Śakti, the final goal of tantric *sādhana,* is realized, and here the *kuṇḍalinī* ends its journey after traversing the six *cakras.* We should note that the *sahasrāra* no longer belongs to the plane of the body, that it already designates the plane of transcendence—and this explains why writers usually speak of the 'six' *cakras.*" In Mircea Eliade, *Yoga: Immortality and Freedom,* translated by Willard R. Trask (Bollingen Series LVI; reprint, London, 1989), 243.

I remember the case of a man who was an extrovert in the most exaggerated sense of the word. He was always convinced that the world was best wherever he was not; there was the real bliss, and he must make for it. Naturally he was after women all the time, because always the women whom he did not yet know contained the secret of life and bliss. He could never see a woman in the street talking to another man without being envious, because that might be the woman. Of course, he never succeeded, as you can imagine. He succeeded less and less, and he made a perfect fool of himself. He grew older, and the chances of meeting the ultimate woman became exceedingly small. So the time came for a new realization. He got into analysis, but nothing changed until the following thing happened: he was walking in the street and a young couple came along talking intimately, and instantly there was pain in his heart—that was the woman! Then suddenly the pain vanished, and for a moment he had an absolutely clear vision. He realized: "Well, they will do it, they are going on, the thing is taken care of, I have not to take care of it any longer, thank heaven!"

Now, what happened? Simply that he crossed the threshold of the diaphragm, for in *maṇipūra* one is blind in passion. Of course, when he sees such a couple he thinks, "I want it, I am identical with that man." And he *is* identical in *maṇipūra.* He is identical with every buffalo, and naturally he complains when he cannot jump out of his skin and into the skin of somebody else. But here he suddenly realizes that he is not that man; he breaks through the veil of illusion, that mystical identity, and knows that he is not that fellow. Yet he has an inkling that he is in a peculiar way identical with him, that man is himself continuing life; he is not cast aside. For his substance is not only his personal self but the substance of that young man, too. He himself lives on, and the thing is taken care of. And he is in it, he is not out of it.

You see, that is a picture of psychical existence over or beyond the *maṇipūra* form. It is nothing but a thought—nothing has changed in the visible world; not one atom is in a different place from before. But one thing has changed: the psychical substance has entered the game. You see, a mere thought, or almost an indescribable feeling, a *psychical fact,* changes his whole situation, his whole life, and he can step across to *anāhata,* to the world where psychical things begin.

Now, going from *anāhata* to *viśuddha* is quite analogous, but it goes very much further. You see, in *anāhata* thought and feeling are identical with objects. For a man, feeling is identical with a certain woman, for instance, and for a woman with that particular man. The thought of a scientist is identical with such-and-such a book. It is such a book. So there are always external conditions, either for the feeling or for the mind. Thought is always specific—scientific, philosophic, or aesthetic, for example—because it is always identical with a particular object. And so feeling is identical with certain people or things. It is because somebody has done so-and-so that one is angry, because there are such-and-such conditions. Therefore our emotions, our values, our thoughts, our convictions are interdependent with facts, with what we call objects. They are not in themselves or through themselves. They are, as I say, interwoven with concrete facts.

You know, it is sometimes an ideal not to have any kind of convictions or feelings that are not based upon reality. One must even educate people, when they have to cross from *maṇipūra* to *anāhata*, that their emotions ought to have a real basis, that they cannot swear hell and damnation at somebody on a mere assumption, and that there are absolute reasons why they are not justified in doing such a thing. They really have to learn that their feelings should be based on facts.

But to cross from *anāhata* to *viśuddha* one should unlearn all that. One should even admit that all one's psychical facts have nothing to do with material facts. For instance, the anger which you feel for somebody or something, no matter how justified it is, is not caused by those external things. It is a phenomenon all by itself. That is what we call taking a thing on its subjective level. Say somebody has offended you, and you dream of that person and feel again the same anger in the dream. Then I say, "That dream tells me just what the anger means, what it is in reality." But you contend that the person had said such-and-such a thing, so you are perfectly justified in feeling such anger and assuming such an attitude toward him. Well, I must admit all that to be perfectly true, and then I humbly say, "Now, when you have had your anger and are reasonable again, let us consider this dream, for there is a subjective stage of interpretation. You consider that man to be your specific *bête noire*, but he is really yourself. You project yourself into him, your shadow appears in him, and that makes you angry. Naturally one is not inclined to admit such a possibility, but after a while, when the process of analysis is effective, it dawns upon one that it is most probably true. We are perhaps identical even with our own worst enemy. In other words, our worst enemy is perhaps within ourselves.

If you have reached that stage, you begin to leave *anāhata*, because you have succeeded in dissolving the absolute union of material external facts with internal or psychical facts. You begin to consider the game of the world as your game, the people that appear outside as exponents of your psychical condition. Whatever befalls you, whatever experience or adventure you have in the external world, is your own experience.

For instance, an analysis does not depend upon what the analyst is. It is your own experience. What you experience in analysis is not due to me; it is what you are. You will have exactly that experience with me which is your own experience. Not everybody falls in love with me, not everybody takes offense when I make a caustic remark, and not everybody admires a very drastic expression I use. The experience in analysis, in which I am always the same Dr. Jung, is a very different procedure with different people. Individuals are very different, and on account of that, analysis is always a different experience, even to myself. I am the one who is equal to myself in all such conditions, but the patients vary, and accordingly the experience of analysis varies to me all the time. But naturally the patient believes that his analysis is so-and-so because I am in it. He does not see that it is also his subjective experience. As long as the patient looks at analysis in such a way—that it is merely a personal flirtation or a personal discussion—he has not gained what he ought to have gained out of it, because he has not seen himself. When he really begins to see it as his own experience, then he realizes that Dr. Jung, the partner in the game, is only relative. He is what the patient thinks of him. He is simply a hook on which you are hanging your garment; he is not so substantial as he seems to be. He is also your subjective experience.

If you can see that, you are on your way to *viśuddha,* because in *viśuddha* the whole game of the world becomes your subjective experience. The world itself becomes a reflection of the psyche. For instance, when I say that the world consists of psychical images only—that whatever you touch, whatever you experience, is imaged because you cannot perceive anything else; that if you touch this table, you might think it substantial, but what you really experience is a peculiar message from the tactile nerves to your brain; and even this you may not experience because I can cut off your fingers, you still experience your fingers only because the cut-off nerves cannot function in any other way; and your brain even is also only an image up here—when I say such a heretical thing I am on the way to *viśuddha.* If I should succeed—and I hope I shall not—in taking all of you up to *viśuddha,* you would certainly complain; you would stifle, you would not be able to breathe any longer, because there is nothing you could possibly breathe. It is ether. In reaching *viśuddha,* you reach the airless space, where there is no earthly chance for the ordinary individual to breathe. So it seems to be a very critical kind of adventure.

Now, in talking about these centers, we must never omit the actual symbols; they teach us a great deal. I want to call your attention to the animal symbolism of which I have not yet spoken. You know that the series of animals begins in *mūlādhāra* with the elephant that supports the earth, meaning that tremendous urge which supports human consciousness, the power that forces us to build such a conscious world. To the Hindu the elephant functions as the symbol of the domesticated libido, parallel to the image of the horse with us. It means the force of consciousness, the power of will, the ability to do what one wants to do.

In the next center is the makara, the leviathan. So in crossing from *mūlādhāra* to *svādhiṣṭhāna*, the power that has nourished you hitherto shows now an entirely different quality: what is the elephant on the surface of the world is the leviathan in the depths. The elephant is the biggest, strongest animal upon the surface of the earth, and the leviathan is the biggest and most terrible animal down in the waters. But it is one and the same animal: the power that forces you into consciousness and that sustains you in your conscious world proves to be the worst enemy when you come to the next center. For there you are really going out of this world, and everything that makes you cling to it is your worst enemy. The greatest blessing in this world is the greatest curse in the unconscious. So the makara is just the reverse: the water elephant, the whale dragon that devours you, is the thing that has nourished and supported you hitherto—just as the benevolent mother that brought you up becomes in later life a devouring mother that swallows you again. If you cannot give her up she becomes an absolutely negative factor—she supports the life of your childhood and youth, but to become adult you must leave all that, and then the mother force is against you. So anyone attempting to leave this world for another kind of consciousness, the water world or the unconscious, has the elephant against him; then the elephant becomes the monster of the underworld.

In *maṇipūra* the ram is the symbolic animal, and the ram is the sacred animal of Agni, the god of fire. That is astrological. The ram, Aries, is the domicilium of Mars, the fiery planet of passions, impulsiveness, rashness, violence, and so on. Agni is an apt symbol. It is again the elephant, but in a new form. And it is no longer an insurmountable power—the sacred power of the elephant. It is now a sacrificial animal, and it is a relatively small sacrifice—not the great sacrifice of the bull but the smaller sacrifice of the passions. That is, to sacrifice the passions is not so terribly expensive. The small black animal that is against you is no longer like the leviathan of the depths in the cakra before; the danger has already diminished. Your own passions are really less a danger than to be drowned in unconsciousness; to be unconscious of one's passion is much worse than to suffer from passion. And that is expressed by Aries, the ram; it is a small sacrificial animal of which you don't need to be afraid, for it is no longer equipped with the strength of the elephant or the leviathan. You have overcome the worst danger when you are aware of your fundamental desires or passions.

The next animal is the gazelle, again a transformation of the original force. The gazelle or antelope is not unlike the ram, living upon the surface of the earth—the difference being that it is not a domesticated animal like the male sheep, nor is it a sacrificial animal. It is not at all offensive; it is exceedingly shy and elusive, on the contrary, and very fleet of foot—it vanishes in no time. When you come upon a herd of gazelles, you are always amazed at the way they disappear. They just fly into space with great leaps. There are antelopes in Africa that take leaps of six to ten meters—something amazing; it is as if they had wings. And they are also graceful and tender, and have exceedingly slender legs and feet. They hardly touch the ground, and the least stirring of the air is sufficient to make them fly away, like birds. So there is a birdlike quality in the gazelle. It is as light as air; it touches the earth only here and there. It is an animal of earth, but it is almost liberated from the power of gravity. Such an animal would be apt to symbolize the force, the efficiency, and the lightness of psychical substance—thought and feeling. It has already lost a part of the heaviness of the earth. Also, it denotes that in *anāhata* the psychical thing is an elusive factor, hardly to be caught. It has exactly the quality that we doctors would mean when we say that it is exceedingly difficult to discover the psychogenic factor in a disease.

Mr. Dell: Would you compare it also to the unicorn?

Dr. Jung: I would say it is a close analogy, and you know the unicorn is a symbol of the Holy Ghost—that would be a Western equivalent.[7]

Mrs. Sawyer: The unicorn derives from the rhinoceros, so that would also be an analogy.

Dr. Jung: Yes, the rhinoceros has survived in the legend of the unicorn. The unicorn is not a real animal, but the rhinoceros has been a very real animal in this country. For instance, one half of a rhinoceros has been found, well preserved, in an oil pit somewhere in Eastern Europe—I think in Poland. It was of the glacial period, a European rhinoceros. So the unicorn is most probably a faint echo of those days when man saw the actual rhinoceros here. Of course, one cannot prove it, but it is at least

[7] Jung gave an extended commentary on the symbolic significance of the unicorn in *Psychology and Alchemy*, in *CW*, vol. 12, §§518–54.

a very nice analogy to our process here—the transformation of the elephant into this tender, gentle, light-footed gazelle.

Now, that is a very apt symbol of the psychogenic factor. And the discovery of the psychogenic factor in medicine was really something you could compare with the crossing from *maṇipūra* to *anāhata*. I remember very well the time when professors said: "Well, there is some psychic disturbance too, naturally imagination has something to do with it, and an upset psychology can produce all sorts of symptoms," and so on. It was thought originally that the psyche was some sort of foam or essence, produced by the body, and nothing in itself, and that so-called psychological causality did not really exist, that it was more symptomatic. Not even Freud takes the psychogenic factor as substantial. The psyche for him is something rather physiological, a sort of byplay in the life of the body. He is convinced that there is a lot of chemistry in it, or ought to be—that the whole thing goes back to the chemistry of the body, that it is hormones or God knows what. So the discovery of a real psychogenic factor (which is not yet realized in medicine, please!) is a great and taletelling event. It would be the recognition of the psyche itself as something that of course functions together with the body, but which has the dignity of a cause. You see, if a doctor admits such a thing he is going really a long way. If he puts the psychogenic factor, as causal, among microbes, colds, unfavorable social conditions, heredity, and so on, with that he recognizes the psyche as something that does exist and has actual effect. The logical medical mind does not quite trust whether it is really something you could lay hands on, for it has that elusive quality of the gazelle. And you know that when the psyche manifests itself in reality, it is usually against us. For inasmuch as it is not against us, it is simply identical with our consciousness. Our consciousness is not against us, and we consider everything to be our own conscious doing, but the psychic factor is always something that we assume to be not our doing. We try to deny it and to repress it. Say I want to write a letter that is disagreeable to me. Then immediately I have the psychic factor against me. I am not able to find that letter—it has been spirited away; I discover that I have mislaid it unconsciously. I wanted to take particular care of that letter, but because I have resistances against it I put it in the wrong pocket or in a corner where I shall not find it for months. One is inclined to speak of an imp that has busied himself with it. One feels something demoniacal in the way just the things one painfully needs are spirited away. The same thing occurs in hysteria: just where it would matter, things take a queer course. Where it is very important that one should say the right thing, one says just the wrong thing; one's words are turned in one's mouth. So one cannot help recognizing the fact that some living devil is against one. Thus the old idea that such people were possessed by devils, were the victims of witches, and so forth.

Mr. Baumann: There is a very good book by Friedrich Theodor Vischer, *Auch Einer* (Also one).[8]

Dr. Jung: Yes, a German book about one of those who know about things, that is, the imp in objects. For instance, when you lose your spectacles you will always lose them in an unlikely place, perhaps upon a chair of such a design that the spectacles fit in perfectly. And you can be absolutely sure that when you drop a piece of buttered toast on the floor it will always fall on the buttered side. Or when you are putting your coffeepot upon the table, it will try by all means to put its spout through the handle of the milk pot, so that you spill the milk when you lift the pot.

Mr. Dell: Die Tücke des Objekts (the malice of objects).

Dr. Jung: Yes, the devilish cunning of objects, and Vischer made a whole system of that in *Auch Einer.* It is exceedingly quixotic naturally, but he gets the psychic factor all right, because it is in a way our doing, and yet it is not our doing; it happens in an impish way. The elusiveness of the psychogenic factor is amazing. In analysis also it is always escaping, because wherever you try to attack it the patient denies it and says, "But that is what I wanted to do; that is myself." He keeps it out of the way all the time because he himself is afraid to discover it. He is afraid that a screw is loose somewhere in his head; he thinks it would mean that he was mad.

So the crossing-over from *maṇipūra* to *anāhata* is really very difficult. The recognition that the psyche is a self-moving thing, something genuine and not yourself, is exceedingly difficult to see and to admit. For it means that the consciousness which you call yourself is at an end. In your consciousness everything is as you have put it, but then you discover that you are not master in your own house, you are not living alone in your own room, and there are spooks about that play havoc with your realities, and that is the end of your monarchy. But if you understand it rightly, and as tantric yoga shows you, this recognition of the psychogenic factor is merely the first recognition of the *puruṣa.* It is the beginning of the great recognition appearing in the most grotesque and ridiculous forms. You see, that is what the gazelle signifies.

Now you remember the elephant appears in *viśuddha* again. So here we encounter the full power, the insurmountable sacred strength of the

[8] Friedrich Theodor Vischer, *Auch Einer,* (Stuttgart and Leipzig, 1884).

animal as it was in *mūlādhāra*. That is, we meet there all the power which led us into life, into this conscious reality. But here it is not supporting *mūlādhāra*, this earth. It is supporting those things which we assume to be the most airy, the most unreal, and the most volatile, namely, human thoughts. It is as if the elephant were now making realities out of concepts. We admit that our concepts are nothing but our imagination, products of our feeling or of our intellect—abstractions or analogies, sustained by no physical phenomena.

The thing that unites them all, that expresses them all, is the concept of energy. In philosophy, for instance, take the example of Plato in his parable of the cave.[9] He tries by that rather clumsy parable to explain the subjectivity of our judgment, which is really the same idea which was called later on in the history of philosophy the theory of cognition. He describes people sitting in a cave with their backs against the light, looking at the shadows on the wall, cast by the moving figures outside. Now, this is an exceedingly apt parable to explain the problem, but it needed more than two thousand years until that problem was formulated in a philosophically abstract way in Kant's *Critique of Pure Reason*.

We always have the impression that such philosophical or scientific concepts as energy—call them theories or hypotheses—are perfectly futile things that change tomorrow, like a breath of air that has no existence whatever. Yet these are apparently the things sustained and pushed by the elephant, as if the elephant were making a reality of such concepts which are really the mere products of our mind. That is our prejudice—to *think* that those products are not also realities.

But here is the hitch in the whole thing, this is not so simple. Your speculations lead to abstractions, and these abstractions you very clearly feel to be merely your conclusions. They are artificial; you are never sure that they do exist in reality. But if perchance you should experience in reality what you have concluded, then you say, "Now this is real, insofar as my thought is real." For example, you say, "Tomorrow we shall have a thunderstorm." It is not very likely at this time of the year, but from all the meteorological data you make that conclusion though you yourself think it rather improbable. And tomorrow we do actually have a thunderstorm, and then you say, "Is it not marvelous that I came to such a conclusion? My feeling must be right." So you substantiate your thinking in reality, and this reality affects the whole man. It affects you through and through—you get drenched by the rain, you hear the thunder, and you may be struck by the lightning—you get the whole thing.

9 Plato, *The Republic*, book 7, translated by D. Lee (London, 1955), 514ff.

Now, according to the symbolism of the cakras something similar happens in *viśuddha*. The power of the elephant is lent to psychic realities, which our reason would like to consider as mere abstractions. But the power of the elephant is never lent to products of the mere intellect because they are never convincing; they always need physical evidence. And for purely psychical things, there is no possibility of anything like physical evidence. For instance, you know that it is impossible in physical fact ever to make a concept of God, because it is not a physical concept. It has nothing to do with an experience in space and time. It has simply no connection with space and time, and therefore you cannot expect any such subsequent effect. But if you have the psychical *experience*, if the psychical fact forces itself upon you, then you understand it, and you can then make a concept of it. The abstraction, or the concept of God, has come out of experience. It is not your intellectual concept, though it can be intellectual too. But the main thing in such an experience is that it is a psychical fact. And psychical facts are the reality in *viśuddha*. Therefore the insurmountable force of reality is sustaining no longer the data of this earth but psychical data.

For example, you know that you would like to do something very much, but you feel it is simply not to be, as if there were an absolute interdiction. Or you feel very strongly that you don't want to do a certain thing, yet the psychical factor demands it, and you know there is no defense—you must go that way; there is no hesitation about it. That is the power of the elephant, which you feel perhaps even in what you would call absurdities. Those are the experiences of the reality of *viśuddha* as expressed by the symbolism.

That is only the fifth cakra, and we are already out of breath—literally so—we are beyond the air we breathe; we are reaching, say, into the remote future of mankind, or of ourselves. For any man has at least the potential faculty to experience that which will be the collective experience in two thousand years, perhaps in ten thousand years. What we are dealing with today has already been we don't know how many millions of times before in dim ages of the past by primitive medicine men, or by old Romans or Greeks—it has all been anticipated. And we anticipate thousands of years to come, so we really reach out into a future which we do not yet possess. Therefore it is rather bold to speak of the sixth cakra,[10] which is naturally completely beyond our reach, because we have not

[10] Of the *ājñā* cakra, Hauer stated: "The god, man power, has disappeared at this stage, but a differentiated woman power is still working, and disappears only in the last cakra. I am not sure whether you will find psychological parallels for that" (*HS*, 90).

even arrived at *viśuddha*. But since we have that symbolism we can at least construct something theoretical about it.

The *ājñā* center, you remember, looks like a winged seed, and it contains no animal. That means there is no psychical factor, nothing against us whose power we might feel. The original symbol, the *liṅga*, is here repeated in a new form, the white state. Instead of the dark germinating condition, it is now in the full blazing white light, fully conscious. In other words, the God that has been dormant in *mūlādhāra* is here fully awake, the only reality; and therefore this center has been called the condition in which one unites with Śiva. One could say it was the center of the *unio mystica* with the power of God, meaning that absolute reality where one is nothing but psychic reality, yet confronted with the psychic reality that one is not. And that is God. God is the eternal psychical object. God is simply a word for the non-ego. In *viśuddha* psychical reality was still opposed to physical reality. Therefore one still used the support of the white elephant to sustain the reality of the psyche. Psychical facts still took place within us, although they had a life of their own.

But in the *ājñā* center the psyche gets wings—here you know you are nothing but psyche. And yet there is another psyche, a counterpart to your psychical reality, the non-ego reality, the thing that is not even to be called self, and you know that you are going to disappear into it. The ego disappears completely; the psychical is no longer a content in us, but we become contents of it. You see that this condition in which the white elephant has disappeared into the self is almost unimaginable. He is no longer perceptible even in his strength because he is no longer against you. You are absolutely identical with him. You are not even dreaming of doing anything other than what the force is demanding, and the force is not demanding it since you are already doing it—since you are the force. And the force returns to the origin, God.

To speak about the lotus of the thousand petals above, the *sahasrāra* center, is quite superfluous because that is merely a philosophical concept with no substance to us whatever; it is beyond any possible experience. In *ājñā* there is still the experience of the self that is apparently different from the object, God. But in *sahasrāra* one understands that it is not different, and so the next conclusion would be that there is no object, no God, nothing but brahman. There is no experience because it is one, it is without a second. It is dormant, it is not, and therefore it is *nirvāṇa*. This is an entirely philosophical concept, a mere logical conclusion from the premises before. It is without practical value for us.

Mrs. Sawyer: I would like to ask you if the Eastern idea of going up through the cakras means that each time you have reached a new center you have to return to *mūlādhāra*?

Dr. Jung: As long as you live you are in *mūlādhāra* naturally. It is quite self-evident that you cannot always live in meditation, or in a trance condition. You have to go about in this world; you have to be conscious and let the gods sleep.

Mrs. Sawyer: Yes, but you could think of it in two ways: as doing all these things together, or as making a trip up and down.

Dr. Jung: The cakra symbolism has the same meaning that is expressed in our metaphors of the night sea-journey, or climbing a sacred mountain, or initiation. It is really a continuous development. It is not leaping up and down, for what you have arrived at is never lost. Say you have been in *mūlādhāra* and then you reach the water center, and afterward you return apparently. But you do not return; it is an illusion that you return—you have left something of yourself in the unconscious. Nobody touches the unconscious without leaving something of himself there. You may forget or repress it, but then you are no longer whole. When you have learned that two times two makes four, it will be so in all eternity—it will never be five. Only those people return who thought they touched it but were only full of illusions about it. If you have really experienced it, you cannot lose this experience. It is as if so much of your substance had remained, so much of your blood and weight. You can return to the previous condition, forgetting that you have lost a leg, but your leg has been bitten off by the leviathan. Many people who got into the water say, "Never shall I go there again!" But they left something, something has stayed there. And if you get through the water and into the fire of passion, you never can really turn back, because you cannot lose the connection with your passion that you have gained in *maṇipūra*.

Question: Is it like Wotan, who loses one eye?

Dr. Jung: Exactly. And like Osiris, the god of the underworld, who also loses one eye. Wotan has to sacrifice his one eye to the well of Mimir, the well of wisdom, which is the unconscious. You see, one eye will remain in the depths or turned toward it.[11] Thus Jakob Boehme, when he was "enchanted into the center of nature," as he says, wrote his book about the "reversed eye." One of his eyes was turned inward; it kept on looking into the underworld—which amounts to the loss of one eye. He had no longer two eyes for this world. So when you have actually entered a higher cakra you never really turn back; you remain there. Part of you

[11] For Jung's analysis of Wotan, in which he does not specifically deal with this motif, see "Wotan" (1936), in *CW*, vol. 10.

can split off, but the farther you have reached into the series of the cakras, the more expensive will be the apparent return. Or if you return, having lost the memory of the connection with that center, then you are like a wraith. In reality you are just nothing, a mere shadow, and your experiences remain empty.

Mrs. Crowley: Do you think the idea is to experience those cakras, which one has gone through, simultaneously?

Dr. Jung: Certainly. As I told you, in our actual historical psychological development we have about reached *anāhata* and from there we can experience *mūlādhāra,* and all the subsequent centers of the past, by knowledge of records, and tradition, and also through our unconscious. Suppose somebody reached the *ājñā* center, the state of complete consciousness, not only self-consciousness. That would be an exceedingly extended consciousness which includes everything—energy itself—a consciousness which knows not only "That is Thou" but more than that—every tree, every stone, every breath of air, every rat's tail—all that is yourself; there is nothing that is not yourself. In such an extended consciousness all the cakras would be simultaneously experienced, because it is the highest state of consciousness, and it would not be the highest if it did not include all the former experiences.

LECTURE 4[1]

2 November 1932

Dr. Jung: We have here a question from Mr. Allemann:

> I do not understand why our daily life should be thought of as taking place solely in *mūlādhāra.* Would not *mūlādhāra* apply more to the life of animals and primitives who live in complete harmony with nature? Should we not rather consider our cultivated life under the *sthūla* aspect of the higher cakras? The awakening of the Kundalini would then be similar to the conscious understanding of the *sūkṣma* aspect. That would mean: in order to awaken Kundalini we must go down to the roots of things, to the "mothers," and first of all understand consciously the sūkṣma aspect of *mūlādhāra,* the earth.

Mr. Allemann has brought up a very complicated problem. I understand his difficulties because they represent the difficulties of our Western standpoint when it is confronted with Eastern ideas. We are confronted with a paradox: for us consciousness is located high up, in the *ājñā* cakra, so to speak, and yet *mūlādhāra,* our reality, lies in the lowest cakra. Besides this, another apparent contradiction strikes us: *mūlādhāra* is, as we have seen, our world. How can it then be located in the pelvis as it is in the cakra system?

I will try once again to give a general explanation of how we are to understand this, but for the moment we must keep quite separate the *symbolism* of the cakras and the *philosophy* of the *sthūla-sūkṣma* aspect of things. The three aspects covered by the terms *sthūla, sūkṣma,* and *parā* are a philosophical way of looking at things. From the standpoint of theory, each cakra can be regarded from all three aspects. The cakras however, are *symbols.* They bring together in image form complex and manifold ideas of ideas and facts.

The word symbol comes from the Greek word *symballein,* to throw together. It has to do, then, with things gathered together, or with a heap of

[1] [Note to the 1932 edition: This lecture was arranged by Miss Wolff for the report of the German seminar, with additional material from Dr. Jung. It is translated by Mrs. Baynes.]

material thrown together, which we, as the expression shows, take as a whole. We could translate the word symbol as "something viewed as a totality," or as "the vision of things brought into a whole." We must always have recourse to a symbol when we are dealing with a great variety of aspects or with a multiplicity of things which form a connected unit and which are so closely woven together in all their separate parts that we cannot separate or take away any parts without destroying the connections and losing the meaning of the totality. Modern philosophy has formulated this way of looking at things under what is known as *Gestalt* theory.[2] A symbol, then, is a living *Gestalt*, or form—the sum total of a highly complex set of facts which our intellect cannot master conceptually, and which therefore cannot be expressed in any way other than by the use of an image.

Take, for example, the problem of knowledge, which has presented difficulties so great and so manifold as to occupy thinkers from the time when philosophy first developed down to the present moment. Plato, for instance, never got as far as formulating an adequate theory of the problem of knowledge; he could not go beyond the image of the cave, and had to describe the problem in terms of a vision or concrete image. Two thousand years had to pass before Kant could formulate a theory of knowledge.

So, too, the cakras are symbols. They symbolize highly complex psychic facts which at the present moment we could not possibly express except in images. The cakras are therefore of great value to us because they represent a real effort to give a symbolic theory of the psyche. The psyche is something so highly complicated, so vast in extent, and so rich in elements unknown to us, and its aspects overlap and interweave with one another in such an amazing degree, that we always turn to symbols in order to try to represent what we know about it. Any theory about it would be premature because it would become entangled in particularities and would lose sight of the totality we set out to envisage.

You have seen from my attempt at an analysis of the cakras how difficult it is to reach their content, and with what complex conditions we have to deal when we are studying not just consciousness but the totality of the psyche. The cakras, then, become a valuable guide for us in this obscure field because the East, and India especially, has always tried to understand the psyche as a whole. It has an intuition of the self, and therefore it sees the ego and consciousness as only more or less unessential parts of the self. All this seems very strange to us: it appears to us as though India were fascinated by the background of consciousness, because we ourselves are entirely identified with our foreground, with the

[2] See Kurt Koffka, *Principles of Gestalt Psychology* (New York, 1935).

conscious. But now, among us, too, the background, or hinterland, of the psyche has come to life, and since it is so obscure and so difficult to access, we are at first forced to represent it symbolically. Thus, for example, there comes to our notice the paradoxical situation in which *mūlādhāra* is localized in the pelvis and at the same time represents our world, and this paradox can be expressed only by a symbol. It is the same with the apparent contradiction contained in the fact that we think of consciousness as located in our heads, and nonetheless we live in the lowest cakra, in *mūlādhāra.*

As we have seen in the first English seminar of this autumn, *mūlādhāra* is the symbol of our present psychic situation, because we live entangled in earthly causalities.[3] It represents the entanglement and dependence of our conscious life *as it actually is. mūlādhāra* is not just the outer world as we live in it; it is our total consciousness of all outer and inner personal experiences. In our conscious life of everyday we are like highly developed animals, tied down by our environment and entangled and conditioned by it. But our Western consciousness does not look at it this way at all. In our world, on the contrary, we are living in the upper centers. Our consciousness is localized in the head; we feel it to be there; we think and will in our heads. We are the lords of nature, and we have command over the environmental conditions and the blind laws that bind primitive man hand and foot. In our consciousness we sit enthroned on high and look down upon nature and animals. To us archaic man is Neanderthal man, little better than an animal. We do not see in the very least that God appears as an animal also. To us animal means "bestial." What should really seem above us seems to be below us and is taken as something regressive and degraded. Therefore we "go down into" *svādhiṣṭhāna* or "fall into" the emotionality of *maṇipūra.* Because we are identified with the consciousness we talk about the subconscious. When we go into the unconscious we descend to a lower level. Therefore we can say that humanity in general has reached the level of the *anāhata* cakra insofar as it feels itself bound by the suprapersonal values of *anāhata.* All culture creates suprapersonal values. A thinker whose ideas show an activity that is independent of the events of daily life could say that he is in the *viśuddha*, or almost in the *ājñā* center.

But all that is only the *sthūla* aspect of the problem. The *sthūla* aspect is the personal aspect. To us personally, it seems as if we were in the higher centers. We think that because our consciousness and the collective suprapersonal culture in which we live are in the *anāhata* center, we

[3] The seminar on visions had resumed earlier the same day. For Jung's comments on *mulādhāra*, see *The Visions Seminar* vol. 7, 10.

are there in all respects. Being identified with the conscious, we do not see that there exists something outside it and that this something is not above but below.

But by means of psychology or tantric philosophy we can achieve a standpoint from which we can observe that suprapersonal events do take place within our own psyche. To look at things from a suprapersonal standpoint is to arrive at the *sūkṣma* aspect. We can attain this standpoint because inasmuch as we create culture, we create suprapersonal values, and when we do this, we begin to see the *sūkṣma* aspect. Through culture we get an intuition of the other than personal psychological possibilities because the suprapersonal appears in it. The cakra system manifests itself in culture, and culture can therefore be divided into various levels such as that of the belly, heart, and head centers. Therefore we can experience and demonstrate the various centers as they appear in the life of the individual, or in the evolution of humanity. We begin in the head; we identify with our eyes and our consciousness: quite detached and objective, we survey the world. That is *ājñā*. But we cannot linger forever in the pure spheres of detached observation, we must bring our thoughts into reality. We voice them and so trust them to the air. When we clothe our knowledge in words, we are in the region of *viśuddha*, or the throat center. But as soon as we say something that is especially difficult, or that causes us positive or negative feelings, we have a throbbing of the heart, and then the *anāhata* center begins to be activated. And still another step further, when for example a dispute with someone starts up, when we have become irritable and angry and get beside ourselves, then we are in *maṇipūra*.

If we go lower still, the situation becomes impossible, because then the *body* begins to speak. For this reason, in England, everything below the diaphragm is taboo. Germans always go a little below it and hence easily become emotional. Russians live altogether below the diaphragm—they consist of emotions. French and Italians *behave* as if they were below it but they know perfectly well, and so does everyone else, that they are not.

It is a rather delicate and painful matter to speak of what happens in *svādhiṣṭhāna*. When for example, an emotion reaches a point of great intensity, it no longer expresses itself in words, but in a physiological way. It does not leave the body by way of the mouth, but in other ways—as, for instance, the bladder. *Svādhiṣṭhāna* represents the level where psychic life may be said to begin. Only when this level became activated did mankind awaken from the sleep of *mūlādhāra* and learn the first rules of bodily decency. The beginning of moral education consisted in attending to our needs in the places suitable for them, just as still happens in the education of a small child. Dogs too have learned this; they are already living in *svādhiṣṭhāna* inasmuch as they deposit their visiting cards at trees and corners. The dogs that come after read the messages and know from them how the land lies, whether the preceding dog was fed or empty, whether it was a large or a small dog—an important difference in the breeding season. Thus dogs can give all sorts of news about one another and can direct themselves accordingly.

This first and lowest means of expressing psychic life is also still used by human beings, for instance by very primitive criminals. You know what is meant by *grumus merdae* (mound of excrement). The thief deposits his excrement in the place he has looted and says in this way: "This is my signature; this belongs to me; woe to him who crosses my path." Thus it becomes a sort of apotropaic charm—a relic of archaic times. For in primitive conditions this sign language actually has a great, even a vital, importance. A person can tell by it whether dangerous or useful animals have made a given track and whether the track is fresh or not. Naturally the same thing is true of human tracks; if hostile tribes are in the neighborhood, fresh human excrement is a sign of alarm. The more primitive the conditions of life, the more valuable the psychic manifestations of this level. We could say it is the first speech of nature. Psychic manifestations belonging to *svādhiṣṭhāna* are therefore often present in our dreams, and certain witticisms and the broad jokes of the Middle Ages are full of them.

As to *mūlādhāra*, we know nothing about it because at this level psychic life is dormant. Mr. Allemann is therefore quite correct in saying that *mūlādhāra* is the life of animals and primitives who live in complete harmony with nature. Our cultivated life, on the other hand, is to be looked at as the *sthūla* aspect of the higher cakras. The awakening of Kundalini would then be similar to the conscious understanding of the *sūkṣma* aspect. That is quite true. But what must we do in order to understand consciously the *sūkṣma* aspect of *mūlādhāra*, or of the earth?

Here we meet again the great paradox. In consciousness we are in *ājñā*, and yet we actually live in *mūlādhāra*. That is the *sthūla* aspect. But can we win another aspect? As we know, we cannot understand a thing if we are still immersed in it and identified with it. Only when we reach a standpoint that is "outside" the experience in question, can we wholly understand what we were experiencing before. Thus, for example, we can form an objective judgment of the nation, race, or continent to which we belong only when we have lived for a time in a foreign country and so are able to look at our own country from without.

How, then, can we put aside our personal standpoint, which represents the *sthūla* aspect, and take another, a suprapersonal one which will show us where we actually are in this world? How can we find out that we are in *mūlādhāra*? *Mūlādhāra* is a condition of psychic sleep, we have said;

we have then no consciousness there and can say nothing about it. I began by saying that by means of culture we create suprapersonal values and that by this means we can get an inkling of other psychological possibilities and can reach another state of mind. In the creation of suprapersonal values we begin with the *sūkṣma* aspect. We see things from the *sūkṣma* aspect when we create symbols. We can also see our psyche under the *sūkṣma* aspect, and this is just what the symbols of the cakras are. Nor can I describe this standpoint to you in any way except by means of a symbol. It is as if we viewed our psychology and the psychology of mankind from the standpoint of a fourth dimension, unlimited by space or time. The cakra system is created from this standpoint. It is a standpoint that transcends time and the individual.

The spiritual point of view of India in general is a standpoint of this sort. Hindus do not begin as we do to explain the world by taking the hydrogen atom as the starting point, nor do they describe the evolution of mankind or of the individual from lower to higher, from deep unconsciousness to the highest consciousness. They do not see humanity under the *sthūla* aspect. They speak only of the *sūkṣma* aspect and therefore say: "In the beginning was the one brahman without a second. It is the one indubitable reality, being and not-being."[4] They begin in *sahasrāra*; they speak the language of the gods and think of man from above down, taking him from the *sūkṣma* or *parā* aspect. Inner experience is to them revelation; they would never say about this experience "I thought it."

Naturally we see the East quite differently. In comparison with our conscious *anāhata* culture, we can truthfully say that the collective culture of India is in *mūlādhāra*. For proof of this we need only think of the actual conditions of life in India, its poverty, its dirt, its lack of hygiene, its ignorance of scientific and technical achievements. Looked at from the *sthūla* aspect the collective culture of India really is in *mūlādhāra*, whereas ours has reached *anāhata*. But the Indian concept of life understands humanity under the *sūkṣma* aspect, and looked at from that standpoint everything becomes completely reversed. Our personal consciousness can indeed be located in *anāhata* or even in *ājñā*, but nonetheless our psychic situation as a whole is undoubtedly in *mūlādhāra*.

Suppose we begin to explain the world in terms of *sahasrāra* and started off a lecture, for instance, with the words of the Vedanta: "This world in the beginning was brahman solely; since brahman was alone it was not unfolded. It knew itself only, and it realized: I am brahman. In this way it became the universe." We would rightly be taken for mad, or

[4] Jung provided an extended commentary on brahman in *Psychological Types*, in *CW*, vol. 6, §§326–47.

at least it would be thought that we were holding a revival meeting. So if we are wise and live in reality, when we want to describe something we always begin with everyday banal events, and with the practical and concrete. In a word, we begin with the *sthūla* aspect. To us the things that are real beyond question are our professions, the places where we live, our bank accounts, our families and our social connections. We are forced to take these realities as our premises if we want to live at all. Without personal life, without the here and now, we cannot attain to the suprapersonal. Personal life must first be fulfilled in order that the process of the suprapersonal side of the psyche can be introduced.

What is suprapersonal in us is shown us again and again in the visions of our seminar: it is an event outside of the ego and of consciousness. In the fantasies of our patient we are always dealing with symbols and experiences which have nothing to do with her as Mrs. So-and-So but which arise from the collective human soul in her and which are therefore collective contents. In analysis the suprapersonal process can begin only when all the personal life has been assimilated to consciousness. In this way psychology opens up a standpoint and types of experience that lie beyond ego consciousness. (The same thing happens in tantric philosophy, but with this difference: there the ego plays no role at all.) This standpoint and this experience answer the question as to how we can free ourselves from the overwhelming realities of the world, that is, how to disentangle our consciousness from the world. You remember, for example, the symbol of water and fire, a picture in which the patient stood in flames.[5] That represents the diving down into the unconscious, into the baptismal font of *svādhiṣṭhāna*, and the suffering of the fire of *maṇipūra*. We now understand that the diving into the water and the enduring of the flames is not a descent, not a fall into the lower levels, but an ascent. It is a development beyond the conscious ego, an experience of the personal way into the suprapersonal—a widening of the psychic horizons of the individual so as to include what is common to all mankind. When we assimilate the collective unconscious we are not dissolving but creating it.

Only after having reached this standpoint—only after having touched the baptismal waters of *svādhiṣṭhāna*—can we realize that our conscious culture, despite all its heights, is still in *mūlādhāra*. We may have reached *ājñā* in our personal consciousness, our race in general can still be in *anāhata*, but that is all on the personal side still—it is still the *sthūla* aspect, because it is valid only for our consciousness. And as long as the ego is identified with consciousness, it is caught up in this world, the world of

[5] [Note to the 1932 edition: English seminar print no. 27.] Jung had commented on this image earlier that day (*The Visions Seminar* vol. 7, 11).

the *mūlādhāra* cakra. But we see that it is so only when we have an experience and achieve a standpoint that transcends consciousness. Only when we have become acquainted with the wide extent of the psyche, and no longer remain inside the confines of the conscious alone, can we know that our consciousness is entangled in *mūlādhāra.*

The symbols of the cakra, then, afford us a standpoint that extends beyond the conscious. They are intuitions about the psyche as a whole, about its various conditions and possibilities. They symbolize the psyche from a cosmic standpoint. It is as if a superconsciousness, an all-embracing divine consciousness, surveyed the psyche from above. Looked at from the angle of this four-dimensional consciousness, we can recognize the fact that we are still living in *mūlādhāra.* That is the *sūkṣma* aspect. Observed from that angle we ascend when we go into the unconscious, because it frees us from everyday consciousness. In the state of ordinary consciousness, we are actually down below, entangled, rooted in the earth under a spell of illusions, dependent—in short, only a little more free than the higher animals. We have culture, it is true, but our culture is not suprapersonal; it is culture in *mūlādhāra.* We can indeed develop our consciousness until it reaches the *ājñā* center, but our *ājñā* is a personal *ājñā,* and therefore it is in *mūlādhāra.* Nonetheless, we do not know that we are in *mūlādhāra,* any more than the American Indians know that they are living in America. Our *ājñā* is caught in this world. It is a spark of light, imprisioned in the world, and when we think, we are merely thinking in terms of this world.

But the Hindu thinks in terms of the great light. His thinking starts not from a personal but from a cosmic *ājñā.* His thinking begins with the brahman, and ours with the ego. Our thought starts out with the individual and goes out into the general. The Hindu begins with the general and works down to the individual. From the *sūkṣma* aspect everything is reversed. From this aspect we realize that everywhere we are still enclosed within the world of causality, that in terms of the cakra we are not "high up" but absolutely "down below." We are sitting in a hole, in the pelvis of the world, and our *anāhata* center is *anāhata* in *mūlādhāra.* Our culture represents the conscious held prisoner in *mūlādhāra.* Looked at from the *sūkṣma* aspect, everything is still in *mūlādhāra.*

Christianity also is based on the *sūkṣma* aspect. To it, too, the world is only a preparation for a higher condition, and the here and now, the state of being involved in this world, is error and sin. The sacraments and rites of the early church all meant freeing man from the merely personal state of mind and allowing him to participate symbolically in a higher condition. In the mystery of baptism—the plunge into *svādhiṣṭhāna*—the "old Adam" dies and the "spiritual man" is born. The transfiguration and ascension of Christ is the symbolical representation and anticipation of the desired end, that is, being lifted above the personal and into the suprapersonal. In the old church Christ represents the leader, and hence the promise of what the mystic or initiate could also contain.

But to non-Christians of the West, the here and now is the only reality. The *sthūla* aspect, the rootedness in *mūlādhāra*, must first be fully lived in order for us to be able to grow beyond it afterward. Before we get that far, we are not to know that we are caught in *mūlādhāra*. Only in this way can we develop our personal consciousness to the level of the *ājñā* center, and only in this way can we create culture. It is indeed only a personal culture, as I have said, but behind the culture stands God, the suprapersonal. And so we attain to the *sūkṣma* aspect. Only then do we see that what seemed to us the summit of our endeavor is merely something personal, merely the light-spark of consciousness. Then we realize that taken from the standpoint of the psyche as a whole, it is only our personal consciousness that has attained *ājñā*, but that we, from the aspect of the cosmic cakra system, are still in *mūlādhāra*.

It is best to understand this by a metaphor. You can imagine the cosmic cakra system as an immense skyscraper whose foundations go deep down in the earth and contain six cellars, one above the other. One could then go from the first up to the sixth cellar, but one would still find oneself in the depths of the earth. This whole cellar system is the cosmic *mūlādhāra*, and we still find ourselves in it even after we have reached the sixth cellar—our personal *ājñā*. This we have to keep in mind always, otherwise we fall into the mistake made by theosophy and confuse the personal with the cosmic, the individual light-spark with the divine light. If we do this we get nowhere; we merely undergo a tremendous inflation.

Taken from the standpoint of the cosmic cakra system, then, we can see that we are still very low down, that our culture is a culture in *mūlādhāra*, only a personal culture where the gods have not yet awakened from sleep. Therefore we have to awaken Kundalini in order to make clear to the individual spark of consciousness the light of the gods. In the thought world and in psychic events we can reach this other state of mind, we can look at ourselves from the *sūkṣma* aspect, but then everything is reversed. Then we see that we are sitting in a hole and that we do not go down into the unconscious, but that in gaining a relation to the unconscious we undergo a development upward. To activate the unconscious means to awaken the divine, the *devī*, Kundalini—to begin the development of the suprapersonal within the individual in order to kindle the light of the gods. Kundalini, which is to be awakened in the sleeping *mūlādhāra* world, is the suprapersonal, the non-ego, the totality of the psyche through which alone we can attain the higher cakras in a cosmic or metaphysical sense. For this reason Kundalini is the same principle as the *Soter*, the Saviour Serpent of the Gnostics. This way of looking at the world is the *sūkṣma* aspect. The *sūkṣma* aspect is the inner cosmic meaning of events—the "subtle body," the suprapersonal.

The *parā* aspect, which Professor Hauer called the metaphysical, is for us a purely theoretical abstraction. The Western mind can do nothing with it. To the Indian way of thinking such hypostatized abstractions are much more concrete and substantial. For example, to the Indian, the brahman or the *puruṣa* is the one unquestioned reality; to us it is the final result of extremely bold speculation.

Mrs. Baynes: What does Professor Hauer mean by the metaphysical aspect?[6]

Dr. Jung: That again is the *sūkṣma* aspect. We can speak of it only in symbols. Such symbols, for instance, are water and fire, the metabasis into the unconscious.

Mrs. Crowley: Is there a connection between the *saṃskāra* and the creative principle? And is the puer aeternus related to them?[7]

Dr. Jung: The *saṃskāra* can be compared to *mūlādhāra*, for they are the unconscious conditions in which we live. The *saṃskāra* are inherited germs, we might say—unconscious determinants, preexisting qualities of things to be, life in the roots. But the puer aeternus is the sprout that buds from the roots, the attempt at synthesis and at a release from *mūlādhāra*. Only by synthesizing the preexisting conditions can we be freed from them.

Dr. Reichstein: Are the *saṃskāra* archetypes?

Dr. Jung: Yes, the first form of our existence is a life in archetypes. Children live in this form before they can say "I." This world of the collective unconscious is so wonderful that children are continually being drawn back into it and can separate themselves from it only with difficulty. There are children who never lose the memory of this psychic background, so extraordinary are the wonders it holds. These memories continue to live in symbols. The Hindus call them the "jewel world" or "manidvipa," the jewel island in the sea of nectar. With a sudden shock the child passes from this marvelous world of the collective unconscious into the *sthūla* aspect of life or, expressed in another way, a child goes into *svādhiṣṭhāna* as soon as it notices its body, feels uncomfortable, and

[6] Hauer defined his concept of the metaphysical as follows: "I make a distinction between the theology of tantric yoga . . . meaning their way of looking at the gods, the way they figure them, etc., and metaphysics, which is the philosophical aspect of that theology" (*HS*, 25–26). Under this he included the distinctions between the *sthūla*, *sūkṣma*, and *parā* aspects.

[7] On the puer aeternus, see Marie-Louise von Franz, *Puer Aeternus* (Santa Monica, 1981); and *Puer Papers*, edited by James Hillman (Dallas, 1979).

cries. It becomes conscious of its own life, of its own ego, and has then left *mūlādhāra.* Its own life now begins: its consciousness begins to separate itself from the totality of the psyche, and the world of the primordial images, the miraculous world of splendor, lies behind it forever.

Mrs. Crowley: Is there any connection between *citta*[8] and Kundalini?

Dr. Jung: Citta is the conscious and unconscious psychic field, collective mentality, the sphere in which the phenomenon of Kundalini takes place. *Citta* is simply our organ of knowledge, the empirical ego into whose sphere Kundalini breaks.[9] Kundalini in essence is quite different from *citta.* Therefore her sudden appearance is the coming-up of an element absolutely strange to *citta.* If she were not entirely different from *citta* she could not be perceived.

But we ought not to speculate too much about these concepts, because they belong to a field of thought which is specifically Eastern. Therefore we have to be very sparing in our use of these concepts. In general our psychological terms are quite adequate for our use. It is better for us to make use of the tantric concepts only as technical terms, when our own terminology falls short. Thus, for instance, we are obliged to borrow the concepts *mūlādhāra,* or *sthūla* and *sūkṣma* aspects, from tantric yoga, because our own language has no expressions for the corresponding psychic facts. But a concept like *citta* we do not need. Also, the concept of Kundalini has for us only one use, that is, to describe our own experiences with the unconscious, the experiences that have to do with the initiation of the suprapersonal processes. As we know from experience, the serpent symbol then occurs very often.

[8] Woodroffe stated: "Citta in its special sense is that faculty (Vṛtti) by which the Mind first recalls to memory (Smaraṇa) that of which there has been previously Anubhava or pratyaṣka Jñāna—that is, immediate cognition." In Arthur Avalon (pseud. Sir John Woodroffe), *The Serpent Power* (London, 1919), 64. For Hauer, "*Citta* is absolutely everything that is in our inner world. . . . Everything is under the power of *citta* and therefore *citta* is 'soul' is the sense of being the complete inner cosmos. . . . If I understand the psychology of Dr. Jung deeply enough, I feel that his conception of soul has something of this conception of *citta*" (*HS,* 33). Zimmer defined *citta* as "whatever is experienced or enacted through the mind." In Heinrich Zimmer, *Philosophies of India,* edited by Joseph Campbell (London, Bollingen Series XXVI, 1953), 321. Surendranath Dasgupta stated, "The states or vṛttis of citta are described as of five kinds: (1) right cognition, (2) illusory knowledge, (3) imagination, (4) sleep, and (5) memory." In Dasgupta, *Yoga Philosophy in Relation to Other Systems of Indian Thought* (Calcutta, 1930), 273. Feuerstein stated, "The word *citta* is the perfect passive participle of the verbal root $\sqrt{}$*cit,* meaning "to recognize, observe, perceive" and also "to be bright, to shine." It is applied wherever psychomental phenomena connected with conscious activity are expressed. In *The Philosophy of Classical Yoga* (Manchester, 1980), 58. For a commentary on the difficulties of translating this term, see Feuerstein, *The Philosophy of Classical Yoga*; and Agehananda Bharati, *The Tantric Tradition* (London, 1992), 44–47.

[9] In his commentary on Pantajali's *Yoga Sutra,* Jung translated *citta* as consciousness. *Modern Psychology 3,* 122.

APPENDIX 1

INDIAN PARALLELS[1]

11 October 1930

On this last seminar day a concept will be given of what the seen means, of how it is to be understood. This series of pictures has not been shown as a model. We must not bypass the European world and our own preconditions in order to create a therapeutic method out of such a process. The revival of inner images must develop organically.

Here one could field the objection whether this case would also have developed in this way if Dr. Jung, who himself knew about these things, had not been present. In other words: whether some kind of thought transmission or influence of the most subtle kind did not take place. To this one may only respond that, as is known, one cannot experiment with fate. It is impossible to determine how an event would have played itself out had this or that moment been different. In the case of spiritual development it is possible to exclude the subjective factor only through finding out whether things have taken place in the same way at other times and at different places. Dr. Jung tried to seek out such parallels. They can be demonstrated in the literature of all periods. Besides, Dr. Jung has in his possession various series of corresponding imaginal developments that originate from human beings of other parts of the world. This would constitute proof. But there is still another much more striking proof: a great culture has held these matters and symbols as its religious and philosophical teachings for more than two thousand years—namely India. Here we find the historical parallels to the series of images which

[1] For the source of this lecture, see the preface, p. xi. Jung's manuscripts headed "Tantrism" and "Chakras" closely correspond to the report of this seminar. The first page of the first manuscript consists of a list of Woodroffe's publications, and references and citations from Zimmer's *Artistic Form and Yoga in the Sacred Images of India*, translated by G. Chapple and J. Lawson (Princeton, 1984), 26–62. This suggests that these works formed Jung's main source for his general conception of tantric yoga. 2 and 3 closely correspond to the opening sections of this seminar. In a few places the terminology in this seminar has been made consistent with that used in the preceding seminars.

arose spontaneously in the circle of Jungian patients. Thereby proof is also given that these inner processes are not influenced by Dr. Jung's point of view but rather correspond to a primordial structure of the psyche.

The parallels are above all found in Indian tantrism (tantra means book). Tantrism is a movement which sprang up at a time when medieval Buddhism was deeply mixed with Hindu elements; that is to say, when Hinayana-Buddhism (the small vehicle) foundered in India and developed into Mahayana-Buddhism (the great vehicle) in Mongolia. That period of Buddhism when the Mahayana branch split off is one of peculiar syncretism: Hinduism redressed Buddhism through the practice of meditation in such a way that several intermediary forms were hardly recognizable as Buddhism any longer. The religious form of Shivaism contained mainly tantric ideas. The middle-Buddhist yoga practice divides into two trends: *sādhana* and *vajrayāna.*

In the magic rituals of *sādhana* practice mantras (power words) play a role. By way of the mantra it is possible to call forth the god. The emergence of the vision of the god is supported by a yantra[2] (mandala). A yantra is a cult image, in the center of which the god is depicted. Through intensive contemplation of the god, it comes alive. The viewer enters into the god, and the god is in the viewer (identification with the god, deification of the viewer). This method may be used to attain unity with the All, but also for sheer magic with worldly aims (fakir trickery).

Contrary to this is the *vajrayāna* branch. *Yāna* means vehicle, or way. *Vajra* is ambivalent and has both a divine and a phallic meaning. It can signify: lightening, power, libido, divine energy, intelligence, power of consciousness. Or else it is the thunderbolt and stands mystically for the *liṅga.* Its female counterpart is *padma-lotus,* which stands mystically for the *yoni.* In worship one frequently finds symbols of the unification of *vajra* and *lotus.*

As a consequence of the ambivalent meaning of *vajra,* a *school of the right hand* and a *school of the left hand* have developed. The former sees in *vajra* the divine energy. It represents the philosophical direction and loses its way from time to time in excessive spirituality. The school of the left hand, which is rather frowned upon, is the advocate of the sexual point of view. For it, *vajra* is the expression of the fulfillment of personal sexuality. (In the battle between these two viewpoints, one easily recognizes the parallels with the science of psychology today.)

[2] Concerning the yantra, Zimmer noted: "This word is a very broad designation for an instrument or tool, a device or a mechanism a person uses for carrying out a specific task. The sacred image is a device of very efficient construction used for both magical and ritualistic spiritual functions" (*Artistic Form and Yoga in the Sacred Images of India,* 28).

Mahayana teaches that all things are embryos of the Buddha; they are embryos of the *tathāgata*, the complete. All things are formed out of the same energy; *vajra* is immanent in everything. Thus also the fourth body (subtle body) of the Buddha is a manifestation of the lightening power in the form of bliss; it is *vajrasattva* or *ānanda*—bliss. (Nietzsche: "Since all pleasure wants eternity, wants deep, deep eternity."[3]) In this state of bliss and in the form of *vajra* the *tathāgata* embraces its Śakti. This is the eternal cohabitation of the god with its female form, its offspring, its emanation, its matter. This belief occurs above all in Shivaism.[4] The worshiped god is Śiva, the many-armed. He is the hunter on the mountains, the lightening, the hidden power of creation. He is purely contemplative. His spouse is Śakti, the emanation of power, the active creative power. This idea corresponds to an old Upanishad concept of *puruṣa* and *prakṛiti*. (Śiva and Śakti = *puruṣa*; and *prakṛiti* = *liṅga* and *yoni*.) Śiva is also conceived and portrayed in images of worship as *śiva-bindu* (*bindu* = point), that is, as the latent point-shaped power of creation. Surrounding *śiva-bindu*, around the center, rests the Śakti in the shape of a wheel or cakra. This is the primal form of the mandala. Such a cakra is also called a *padma-lotus*. To this relate the mystical syllables *Om mani padme hum*, which are best translated as something like: "Oh, by the gem in the lotus." They mean the highest perfection and the first beginning at the same time. Contained therein is everything that can be said. For us such speculations are the ultimate point at which one may arrive, whereas for the Indian they are simply the starting point, or point of departure. He begins with the internal, whereas we constantly live in the external. The visible world is for him *Māyā*, appearance, illusion, *Māyā-śakti*, that is, the product of Śakti.[5] Consciousness is *Māyā*, a veil which consists of the projection of earlier experience (*saṃskāras*). The tabula rasa of childlike consciousness is predetermined through the experience of foresight—through the collective unconscious, we would say. But the Indian says: Śakti has consciousness in itself. (Herein lies a key to the inconceivable.) The first childhood dreams contain the *saṃskāras*, the archetypes. It is thus in no way surprising that we find obvious cakras or mandalas in chil-

[3] Richard Hollingdale renders this sentence as "Joy wants the eternity of all things, *wants deep, deep, deep eternity*!" Friedrich Nietzsche, *Thus Spake Zarathustra* (London, 1985), 332.

[4] [Note to the 1932 edition: In 1910 there were approximately three million followers, particularly in South India.]

[5] [Note to the 1932 edition: Excentric spirituality as well as raw sexuality are to the insightful *Māyā*, appearance. Buddha therefore begins one of his sermons by speaking of the two ways that exist: that of worldliness and that of ascetism. But both are false: the middle way is true, the eightfold way of right thinking and right action. But what is "right" in each case he does not say, for that can emerge only from the respective situation.]

dren's drawings.[6] Small children are very old; later on we soon grow younger. In our middle age we are youngest, precisely at the time when we have completely or almost completely lost contact with the collective unconscious, the *saṃskāras.* We grow older again only as with the mounting years we remember the *saṃskāras* anew.

Within the *vajrayāna* branch a peculiar form of yoga practice has developed, the Śakti or Kundalini yoga. (Kundala = coiled up; Śak = having power, being able). Śakti-Kundalini or Devī-Kundalini is a goddess. She is the female principle, the self-manifesting power which surrounds the gem at the center. She is the *śabdabrahman,* the word of creation. Like a snake she coils around the center, the gold seed, the jewel, the pearl, the egg.[7] The Kundalini serpent is, however, also a Devī-Kundalini, a chain of glittering lights, the "world bewilderer."[8] By creating confusion she produces the world of consciousness, the veil of *Māyā.* It is the anima, the Devī-śakti, which has conceived the world.[9] (This is, of course, a view which corresponds to male psychology. Seen from the woman's point of view the animus devises the world.)

Śiva emanates Śakti. Śakti begets *Māyā. Māyā* is desire and thereby error: she is the fire of error. The desiring consciousness confronts the purely contemplative consciousness. The visual portrayal of this emanation can take place horizontally as well as vertically. In the first case the earlier-mentioned mandalas appear. *Māyā* is there depicted as a glowing circle of fire (honeycomb blaze). In the second case one finds portrayals in which are indicated the darkness and confusion below and the pure power and light above.[10] This vertical arrangement of levels of consciousness in the image of worship corresponds to the teaching of the different cakras in the human body.[11] In the oldest *Upanishads* the heart (four ventricles!) is the seat of the soul or of knowledge, of waking con-

[6] [Note to the 1932 edition: Cf. the projection of a child's drawing from the Rothe circle, about which Frau Sigg gave a lecture.]

[7] [Note to the 1932 edition: Cf. the Orphic mysteries: the world serpent surrounds the egg.]

[8] [In English in the original.] In his copy of Arthur Avalon's (pseud. Sir John Woodroffe) *The Serpent Power* (London, 1919), Jung had marked the phrase "the Devī Kuṇḍalī . . . the world bewilderer" (37).

[9] In his copy of *The Serpent Power,* Jung had marked the following passage: "Kuṇḍalī Śakti is Cit, or consciousness, in its creative aspect as Power. As Śakti it is through Her activity that the world and all human beings therein exist" (254).

[10] [Note to the 1932 edition: In Egypt (one finds the representation of) a coiled-up serpent below, with Isis above with a crown of light.]

[11] [Note to the 1932 edition: a) According to the Persian sufis, three cakras are distinguished: 1) the mother of the brain, or the spherical heart; 2) the cedar heart; and 3) the lily heart. b) Cf. the Mexican book of fables, *Popol Vuh.*]

sciousness. It is the root of all limbs and the seat of *prāṇa*, the breath of life. *Prāṇa* is *vāju*. *Vāju* comes from *mūlādhāra*, the root support. The *Hangsa Upanishads* teach: in the heart region there is an eight-leafed lotus. The eight leaves correspond to the compass and portray both moral and psychic states. At the center lives Vairagya, passionlessness, disinterest, and detachment (cf. Meister Eckhart).

According to another teaching brahman can be attained from four cardinal points: these appear separately in the head, neck, heart, and navel. In the *Dhyanabindu Upanishads* it is said, "The great and powerful with the four arms, that is, Vishnu, should be worshiped in the navel." In the cakras the elements are cleansed with the help of Kundalini. In Kundalini yoga six cakras, or centers, are distinguished. The first cakra lies near the perineum and is called *mūlādhāra*. The second is named *svādiṣṭhāna* and is located in the small pelvis.

The third has its seat in the naval region: it is called *maṇipūra*. *Anāhata* is located near the heart diaphragm. In the neck lies *viśuddha*. The uppermost center, *ājñā*, lies in the head between the eyebrows. Still higher than these corporeal cakras lie some metaphysical cakras: hence the *mana* center and above that the *soma* cakra. This teaching of the cakras should not be misunderstood as concrete and corporeal like the theosophers tend to do today. These centers are not corporeal entities. When one speaks of them, it is understood "as if" they were situated somewhere in the navel, and so on. Two serpent lines lead from *mūlādhāra* to the *ājñā* cakra.[12] And indeed, one begins in the left testicle and runs around the cakras to the right nostril. The other has its beginning in the right testicle and ends in the left nasal opening. This pair of paths are called *iḍā* and *piṇgalā* (*iḍā* =moon, female; *piṇgalā* = sun, masculine). The one lying to the left is the moon or water stream, the one to the right is the sun or fire stream. Besides these, there is also a middle stream, *suṣumṇā* (cf. the last picture of the patient).[13] The liberation through knowledge and insight takes place along these paths. The knower becomes brahman.

[12] Jung is referring to the *nāḍīs*. For a discussion of these, see Mircea Eliade, *Yoga: Immortality and Freedom*, translated by Willard R. Trask (Bollingen Series LVI; reprint, London, 1989), 236–41; and Georg Feuerstein, *Yoga: The Technology of Ecstasy* (Wellingborough, 1990), 259–62.

[13] *Bericht über das Deutsche Seminar von Dr. C. G. Jung* (1930), figure 30. In the preceding seminars, Jung had commented on the visions of Christiana Morgan. The illustration in question (not reproduced in *The Visions Seminar*) depicted a naked woman standing on a ridge with outstretched arms under a stream of light with a crescent moon. A vertical black line runs from her genitals to the top of her body. Jung commented: "This strip depicts the way of the snake, the Kundalini" (92; my translation).

THE INDIVIDUAL CAKRAS (figures 2–7)

mūlādhāra is the lowest, the center of the earth. It has its seat in the perineum. What is in *mūlādhāra* is unconscious, latent, dormant. *Śiva-bindu* lies at the middle point; around it Kundali-śakti is coiled up as a snake. *Bindu* corresponds to the self-generated *liṅgam* around which the serpent lies. A shell surrounds both; this shell is *Māyā*. When Kundalini awakens, consciousness of the world arises. In herself, Śakti is of course also conscious beforehand; she creates the world through imagination corresponding to the copies of *saṃskāras*. Kundalini, however, awakens only when hunger drives her. This hunger arises as a consequence of spiritual discipline, through the appeasement of pairs of opposites.[14] When the external process has finally come to rest, the internal begins. Kundali-śakti springs up, whereby her head becomes light. This is the process of becoming conscious.[15] The symbolic animal of the *mūlādhāra* cakra is the elephant, the image of firmness and strength, the earth. The *yoni* is in the *mūlādhāra* mandala represented as *traispura*, a female triangle united with the *liṅgam*, which is also termed the leaf.[16]

The second center is *svādiṣṭhāna*, the seat of error and desire. It is located in the small pelvis corresponding to the genital region. *Svādiṣṭhāna* corresponds to the water sphere and rules the bladder. Its animal is a water monster. The mandala portrays a red six-leaved lotus and the moon.

The *maṇipūra* cakra has its seat in the navel region. This is the place of fire and of pairs of opposites. These generate emotions and passions. Through concentrating on the navel, anger is suppressed. *Maṇipūra* "is lustrous as a gem."[17] *Maṇipūra* is at the same time the center of the re-

[14] [Note to the 1932 edition: In the mystery play of the patient, the Indian stands untouched in the middle between fire and water.] See *Interpretation of Visions* vol. 1, 8 December 1930, 147.

[15] [Note to the 1932 edition: "When a yogi, whose mind is under control, is able to confine the moon in her own place, and also the sun, then the moon and the sun become confined, and consequently the moon cannot shed its nectar, nor can the sun dry it. . . . Then the Kundali awakens for want of food and hisses like a serpent. Afterward, breaking through the three knots, she runs to Sahasrāra and bites the moon, which is in the middle of it."]

[16] [Note to the 1932 edition: Cf. the portrayals of the cakra mandalas (figures 2–7). A young Muslim whom Dr. Jung tested for his knowledge of the Koran cited three forms of the appearance of the *Chidr*: 1) it appears as a man; 2) it appears as white light; and 3) it is in everything that surrounds you and that you touch—in the stone, in the wood, and also in here. And there the native pointed to a young sprouting verdure.]

[17] Woodroffe, *The Serpent Power*, 119.

gion of the flesh, the corporeal human being, the meat eater. (Śakti Laktini with breasts red from blood and running with animal fat.) The ram, vehicle of Agni, is its animal.

Anāhata is the fourth center. It pertains to the heart, or rather to the midriff. Here, in the air, *vāju pranaśakti* (*prāṇa* = *pneuma*) has his seat. Here lives *puruṣa*, the conscious human being. From there one sees the *ātman*, and the yogi now knows, "I am it." In *anāhata* the prospective spirit is born; it starts becoming conscious. The accompanying symbol is the *kalpataru* tree, which fulfills all wishes. Below it is the *manipitha* altar.[18]

The fifth cakra is *viśuddha*: it lies in the neck, particularly in the larynx. Here lies the seat of speech, and thereby the spiritual center. It is "the purple center of the white ether [*akasha*] which sits on the white elephant." Śakti-śākinī is now white, and Śiva appears in androgynous form, half white, half golden. Together they celebrate the mystical union. *Viśuddha* is the lunar region and at the same time the "gateway of the great liberation" through which man leaves the world of error and the pairs of opposites. *Akasha* means the fullness of the archetypes; it concerns a renunciation of the world of images, a becoming-conscious of eternal things.[19]

Ājñā is the sixth and highest corporeal center. (*Ājñā* = knowledge, understanding, command). It is located between the eyebrows.[20] Here the command of the leader, the guru, is received from above. In the *ājñā* mantra the lotus is portrayed with two white leaves.[21] The *yoni* triangle is reversed: it is white, and in the middle of it, *itara-liṅga* sparkles like lightening. *Ātman* here shines like a flame. It is the pure, universal power in the form of a phallus. The mantra attached to the *ājñā* cakra is *Om*. In the sixth cakra lies the seat of *mahat* (mind[22]) and *prakṛiti*. Here the "subtle body,"[23] the diamond body, develops (cf. *The Secret of the Golden*

[18] [Note to the 1932 edition: "Thy blissful form, O Queen, manifests in *Anāhata* and is experienced by the mind inward turned of the blessed ones, whose hair stands on end and whose eyes weep with joy."]

[19] [Note to the 1932 edition: The anthroposophical expression of the *akashic records* is misleading, since it is not the case of the inheritance of certain isolated experiences but of that of the psychic possibilities of having such experiences.]

[20] [Note to the 1932 edition: cf. the vision of the patient, 54. Likewise, Jung and Wilhelm, *The Secret of the Golden Flower*.] In the vision in question, a ray of light strikes a child on the forehead, imprinting a star. See *The Visions Seminar*, vol. 1, 9 December 1930, 151.

[21] [Note to the 1932 edition: The vision of a yogi: white fire that rises into the brain and flares up and beyond as a blaze whose wings reach out both sides of the head.]

[22] In English in the original.

[23] In English in the original.

Flower)—that being which Goethe termed "Faust's Immortal." It is portrayed individually as *taijasa* and collectively as *hiranyagarhba,* the golden seed (Orphic: the world egg), the "great self." At the hour of death, *prāṇa* is removed from the *yoni* into the *ājñā* cakra, from which it passes over into the godhead, into timelessness, into *nirvāṇa*—into those cakras situated above the corporeal, in the "house without foundation," on the "island in the ocean of nectar."

Now followed the display of a series of unconscious images which were painted by different patients and which illustrate the Western parallels to the preceding observations concerning Indian psychology.

TRANSLATED BY MICHAEL MÜNCHOW

APPENDIX 2

JUNG'S COMMENTS IN HAUER'S GERMAN LECTURES

5 October 1932

Dr. Jung wants to make some remarks on meditation technique: the process of meditation has a clear parallel in psychological analysis, though with the difference that Professor Hauer gives us a completed conceptual framework, seen from above, as if floating in ether. If we place it on a foundation which, to begin with, we possess through our own experience, it will become more readily understandable. To be sure, it is difficult to compare the somber, earthbound figures of our unconscious with the Indian representation. To meditate on the cakras we first have to extricate the original experience; hence we cannot adopt the ready-made figures of yoga, and the question still remains whether our experiences fit into the tantric forms altogether. It all thereby depends on whether we possess this matter which India already has. That is why we have to come up with our own methods which can familiarize us with corresponding contents.

Ten or fifteen years ago, when patients brought me the first "mandalas," I did not yet know anything about tantra yoga. At this time Indologists were not familiar with it either—or, whenever it became known, it was scorned not only by the Europeans but also by wide sections of the Indian population. Its seeming oddity was only sniffed at. But we have to forget this sniffing at it now.

It is a fact that with us these things come individually and immediately out of the earth, but as small, ridiculous beginnings which we find hard to take seriously.

Example: we are dealing with a (female) patient with whom, after six years of sporadic analysis, I had finally, if very hesitatingly, to take the "yoga path." She was a practicing Catholic. Catholics have a stillborn unconscious, because the church has already entirely formed, regulated, and squeezed the nature of the unconscious. There is early evidence for this. Archbishop Athanasius of Alexandria,[1] for example, in his biography of St. Antonius, gives his monks instructions about what from the unconscious is good and bad. He says that the devils can also speak "words of truth" and that they can talk about things that are true. But, he states,

> It would be a disgrace for us, if those who revolted against God should become our teachers. Let us arm ourselves with the armour of justice and let us put on the helmet of redemption, and at the time of battle let us shoot mental arrows from a faithful mind. Because the devils are nothing, and even if they were something, their strength would comprise nothing which could resist the might of the cross.[2]

Also, the religious exercises of Ignatius of Loyola[3] are Christian counterparts to the Indian meditations or to our fantasies from the unconscious. The religious exercises are meditations according to church instruction; their purpose is the rehearsal of the symbols of faith. By it the vanishing of all thoughts and fantasies that are dogmatically unacceptable is provoked.

By means of such an attitude a complete paralysis developed in my patient—everything was already there on the outside, and hence had become invisible inside. I tried for six years to analyze her back into the church, so to speak, until she confessed what she would not have confessed to a confessor: that she believed neither in God nor in the pope but that nonetheless she would die in the fold of the church. Despite her age (she was fifty-five years old at that time), it made her suffer that everything in her was dead and dark, for after all she was still alive, and this life was asserting its rights. I was in a fix, because I saw that the living spirit wanted to get its way in spite of everything, and then came the original experience.

[1] [Note to the 1933 edition: See Jung, *Psychologische Typen*, 2d ed., 78ff.] (I.e., *CW*, vol. 6, §§82ff.)

[2] In *CW*, vol. 6, §82, this passage is cited from "Life of St. Anthony," in *The Paradise or Garden of the Holy Fathers*, compiled by Athanasius, archbishop of Alexandria, et al., translated by E.A.W. Budge (London, 1904), 24ff. The passage here has been directly rendered from the German.

[3] In 1939–40 Jung devoted his Eidgenössische Technische Hochschule seminars to a commentary on the spiritual exercises of Ignatius of Loyola, which followed from his commentary on Eastern texts. See *Modern Psychology 4*.

I instructed her thus to observe whether images were appearing before falling asleep, and I asked her about dreams. Until then she had been dreaming, but from the time of my question onward she did not dream any more. Therefore I told her to lie down and close her eyes, and now she had a vision: she saw a dark wall. She had to hold on to this image, concentrate on it (*dhārāṇa*), contemplate it—"impregnate it," so that it could become animated.

As she did so, the wall was divided into trees—it became a dark jungle, then figures started to move beneath the trees. It was in New Mexico, and the figures were an entire tribe of [American] Indians. The Indian archetype of the American had been animated in her.

A lake appeared before the forest. (The forest, the original home of humanity, represents the unconscious. The lake, with its even surface impenetrable to the eye, is also an image for it.) The Indians loosened canoes from the lakeside, loaded women and children into them, and crossed the lake. On the other side was a desert; the Indians put up their tents there, made a fire, cooked, ate, and then retired to the tents. They evidently went to sleep, even though it was broad daylight and the sun stood motionless in the sky. Only the chief remained outside and turned his face to the sand desert.

Here you see the world of *citta*—figures which the patient has not made and that live their own lives "willfully," according to their own laws.

The patient now repeatedly concentrated on the chief, but he did not move. Nothing at all happened any more. The patient had evidently arrived at the dogmatic wall, which puts before the individual experience of the unconscious all punishments of hell.

At least the relief was great enough that she could live for a year through the effect of the image, which she never lost from sight now. At the same time, there also developed attempts to break off—she saw, for example, heavy transport vehicles in a sandstorm, or horsemen in a snowstorm. These images are a side-elucidation of the danger, in which she found herself through the contact with the unconscious. But such a break is not permitted, because the story has to be brought to its end. The patient has to stick with it and try to make progress with the Indian.

After a year she came back to analysis; and one day she was particularly impressed by the calm, dry, clear desert air in which the Indian was standing. Suddenly she felt a bit of humidity in the air which had not been there before. Something had finally moved, and it stirred her to the extent that again she could continue to live for a year.

When after this time she came back to me, she told me that the Indian was not there any more; he had faded. Where had he gone? She had a second vision, and the first one had been dissolved in the second: a white serpent appeared to her in splendor and imperturbable majesty, wearing feathers and a diadem.

Personally she was in no way aware of what this image signified. It is the well-known representation of the Mexican air and wind god Quetzalcoatl in his shape as a feathered serpent (the Plumed Serpent). He is the redeemer-god of the Indian, who embodies for the psyche of the American person the unconscious spirit.

This vision impressed my patient tremendously and gave her the courage, after ten years, finally to make her general confession to me—with which the therapeutic effect was, of course, achieved.

What had actually happened? The humidity had descended as dew and had fertilized and burst the wrapping of the Indian. He now showed her his actual meaning, his undogmatic pagan face. From the point of view of the church, it was the appearance of a devil, who had merely assumed the form of the redeemer to mislead the Christian. Thus the Spanish conquerors of Yucatan already interpreted the crosses that they found all over the country as a seduction of the devil. The early Christians, as well, who recognized the similarity between the myth of Dionysus and the life of Christ, thought that the devil had invented this *Anticipatio Christi* expressly to confound them.

What the patient actually did during her analysis was really *pūjā*—persisting in prayer—which then caused the transformation. *Laya*, the redissolution of the figures, would for us correspond to the intellectual process of comprehension. The patient has to know what has happened to her; she has to understand her own myth. The image would capture and detain us, if we would not dissolve it through comprehension. Only when we have assimilated it to the height of consciousness can new figures emerge.

6 October 1932

Dr. Jung: What one could still add here, from the psychological side, is the purely empirical results of the analysis.[4] In every typical course of an analysis greater awareness emerges through realizing repressions, projections, and so on. The analytical process thus occasions a broadening

[4] These remarks follow a discussion of the process of the development of consciousness in yoga. *Tantra Yoga*, 50–51.

of consciousness, but the relation of the ego to its objects still remains. The ego is intertwined in conflict with the objects—one is still a part of a process. Only in the continuation of the analysis does the analogy with yoga set in, in that consciousness is severed from its objects (*Secret of the Golden Flower*). This process is linked up with the process of individuation, which begins with the self severing itself as unique from the objects and the ego. It is as if consciousness separated from the objects and from the ego and emigrated to the non-ego—to the other center, to the foreign yet originally own. This detachment of consciousness is the freeing from the *tamas* and *rajas*, a freeing from the passions and from the entanglement with the realm of objects. This is something which I cannot prove philosophically any further. It is a psychical experience, which in practice is expressed as a feeling of deliverance. What has caused one to be previously seized with panic is not a panic any more; one is capable of seeing the tension of opposites of the world without agitation. One does not become apathetic but is freed from entanglement. Consciousness is removed to a sphere of objectlessness. This experience has its effects in practical life, and indeed in the most palpable way. It is illustrated probably most beautifully in the tale of Buddha being threatened by Mara. Mara and all his demons assail him, but the throne of Buddha is empty—he is simply not sitting there any more. Or as *Rig Veda* I, 164, has it: "Two closely united friends both embrace one and the same tree. One of them eats the sweet berry, the other looks down only composedly."[5]

*

Dr. Jung: One has to take into account here the differences between the cases in question, because what the symbols mean is entirely dependent on the particular state of consciousness of the individual.[6] The tree is the tree of life. If it is standing up it is an indication of an unfolding and progressing life. When the "yoga path" is taken, one can find this symbol at the beginning. It also appears when doubts exist about the value of the path. The "yoga path" is the path of the plant—a plant function as opposed to an animal one. Ego consciousness is, so to speak, like an animal that can speak and move freely. The tree, however, signifies the not-being-able-to-make-way and the rootedness of the plant. When someone realizes this, he suddenly has the feeling: "Now I am imprisoned." The

[5] Cf. *The Rig Veda: An Anthology*, translated by Wendy Doniger O'Flaherty (London, 1981), 78, where a slightly different rendition of the same passage is given.

[6] Hauer and Gustav Heyer had related accounts of dreams that featured trees. *Tantra Yoga*, 52.

image of the uprightly growing tree then placates his fear, which sees something frightening in the unavoidable.

When the path has already been taken, however, and the conviction of growth has been consolidated, then the Christian prejudice comes: what grows *has to* grow upward. Then the image of the tree can appear with the roots on top, showing that its growth does not go up into the sky but downward into the depth.

There is also the tree with roots on top and at the bottom. Here it is emphasized that one gets to roots wherever one goes. This is what someone dreams who wishes or hopes for too much. He is being told, "Everything around you is earth, and with the earth you are supposed to form a union."

Conversely, the tree can have crowns on top and at the bottom; here everything is leaf and blossom and fruit—"heaven above, heaven below." Also, when the development apparently leads downward, the tree will still bear blossoms and fruit. I could substantiate this for each of the cases.

8 October 1932

Dr. Jung: Professor Zimmer has depicted the material as relatively simple to us.[7] I find it highly complicated—an ocean of individual differences, so ill defined that one cannot touch it anywhere! Individual problems cannot be understood in uniqueness; thus one is thankful for all references, such as Zimmer's book *Artistic Form and Yoga in the Sacred Images of India,* or the translation of the tantric texts by Avalon, which show that there have always been people with such problems. The Indian conceptual world was thus for me a means to clarify personal experiences.

In 1906 I found in a mentally ill patient for the first time the image of a serpent, creeping up on her back, its head divided into a crotch. In 1909 I even gave a lecture on this case without being aware of its general signification.

After the war a twenty-eight-year-old girl came to see me, wanting to be cured within ten hours. She said that she had a black serpent in her belly. She came to see me because of this serpent, for she thought that it should be awakened. Her problem was that she was not on earth. She was

7 Zimmer had given an account of yoga practice as a process of self-transformation. *Tantra Yoga,* 97–100.

only intuitive, entirely without a sense of reality. She was living in a secret brothel without being aware of it; she did not hear her own steps and had never seen her body. She dreamed that she was inside or on top of balloons, from which I had to shoot her down. One day she came and said that the serpent in her belly had moved; it had turned around. Then the serpent moved slowly upward, coming finally out of her mouth, and she saw that its head was golden. This is the shortest Kundalini path of which I have heard. To be sure, it was not experienced but only intuited; but already this had a curing effect for the time being. This case is a simple example of the spontaneous appearance of the Kundalini.

I got to know about the cakras only later, but even then I did not say anything about it, so as not to disturb the process in my patients.

The cakras are symbols for human levels of consciousness in general. Ethnically and psychologically we can distinguish three different psychical localizations, of which the first corresponds more or less to *mūlādhāra-svādhiṣṭhana*, the second to *maṇipūra* and *anāhata*, and the third to *viśuddha* and *ājñā*. The psychology of the lower centers is analogous to the one of primitives—unconscious, instinctive, and involved in participation mystique. Life appears here as an occurrence, so to speak, without ego. One is not aware that one wants or does things; everything happens as it were in the third person.

The next localization is in the region of the diaphragm, thus *maṇipūra-anāhata*, with oscillations up and down, above and beneath the diaphragm. Beneath the diaphragm, all occurrence is self-evident. In *maṇipūra* is the emotional human being, who again and again is inundated and becomes constantly the victim of his passions.

Only above the diaphragm is it: I want. In the heart—*anāhata*—is the first notion of the self, of the absolute center, the substance to which life is related. This notion of the self is the flame in *anāhata*. Here the rational functions start. We have figures of speech that still now express this. We say "cross my heart," or we beat our chest when we refer to ourselves. The Pueblo Indian thinks in his heart, as does the Homeric person, whose spirit is located in the diaphragm (*Phren*—the emotional and thinking soul). Our psychical localization is admittedly in the head, but the gesture is still archaic, and when emotions become involved, our psychology slips down to *maṇipūra*.

But most of the time we do not notice this. We believe ourselves to live in the *ājñā* center; we are convinced that we are masters in our own home. But if we believe that our thoughts are our epiphenomenology and that *we* have had them, we all too easily forget how often our thoughts have *us*. By thinking that psyche and brain are identical we become godlike, but our emotions bring the lower centers in us again into effectiveness.

In history we can also watch the Kundalini process. First the belly-consciousness of the primitive developed, and he only noticed what set heavy on his belly or in his stomach. Paul still said, "The belly is your God." Then the diaphragm-consciousness of the Homeric person developed, and he felt his emotions. This was expressed in states of respiratory tension and in changes in the heartbeat.

Only the modern Western person has noticed that the head can also be affected. Before that, it had not been much more than a button on a feeling body. How much this was really the case, we can see clearly in the representations of humans on the rock paintings of Negroes, which Leo Frobenius, for example, has reproduced in his book *Erythräa.*[8] You will find images there of humans with extraordinarily long bodies on which, to some extent very small, or by way of suggestion, human or animal heads are placed.

Only the contemporary person can say: "Now I am thinking." The *viśuddha* center expresses the *word,* and what surpasses this would be the center of abstraction.

I would like to point to one more important analogy. In all cases which involve such symbols, we may not forget the course of the sun as a main motive. The analogy to Kundalini is the sun serpent, which later in Christian mythology is identified with Christ. The twelve disciples are thought of as stations of the annual cycle supported by the zodiac serpent. All these are symbols for the change of the creative power. In *mūlādhāra* is the night sun, and beneath the diaphragm the sunrise. The upper centers starting from *anāhata* symbolize the change from midday up to sunset. The day of sun is the Kundalini passage—ascent and descent—evolution and involution with spiritual signs. The course of the sun is the analogy to the human life course.

The cakras, moreover, are, like all symbolic step formations, also the steps of mysteries, where the beginner steps into the dark (*katabasis*) and comes up again as deus sol via seven steps, as Apuleius describes it in *The Golden Ass.*

The greatest difficulties for my comprehension were caused by the god in *bindu* and Śakti. With us, the anima always first appears so grotesque and banal that it is difficult to recognize the Śakti in it. But then, what is God? He is the pale reflection of the ever-invisible central god in

[8] Leo Frobenius, *Erythräa: Länder und Zeiten des heiligen Königsmordes* (Berlin, 1931).

bīja, which one cannot grasp, who is like the rabbit which the hunter never hunts down. That is the self—incomprehensible, because it is bigger than the ego. This self has a faint reminiscence in us—that is the god in *bindu*. The god in *bindu* is our relation to the self, the will in the ego, the daimon, which forces us through need to take the path—the small individual god—the inner Śiva.[9]

TRANSLATED BY KATHERINA ROWOLD

9 Hauer then stated that although he thought Jung's account of the psychophysical centers was correct, it left out the metaphysical aspect. *Tantra Yoga*, 103.

APPENDIX 3

HAUER'S ENGLISH LECTURE

8 October 1932

Professor Hauer: Would you like to ask any questions about yesterday's discussion?

Dr. Shaw: May I say that it seems to me that if we can only awaken the Kundalini when we get to the beginning of the sixth stage on the road through the cakras,[1] where we are not able to see her, that we would be as far out of reality as the East. We should have something simpler, a mixture of earth.

Professor Hauer: As I told you, my conception rests upon the classical text of the *Ṣaṭ-cakra-nirūpaṇa* and on a number of the *Upanishads,* where it is quite clear to me that the full awakening can take place only after the yogin has gotten to the end of *viśuddha*—he must be purified, cleansed—and to the beginning of *ājñā,* the stage where the great intuitions appear.

I said yesterday that it was a hypothesis. You must work on it not with the help of Avalon or the modern Indian writers but from the original texts which give us the historical development of perhaps a thousand years. Most of our writings now are of a very late date, and the original meaning is concealed. In the course of the historical evolution all sorts of things have accrued and been superimposed on the original. My intention is to get at the original always because I am sure that is nearer to us than the yoga evolved in India as it fares now, or a hundred years ago.

It is the same with the classical yoga. I have to take it out of the yoga

[1] Hauer had stated: "As to the question when it [Kundalini] is to be awakened, I think the texts have been misunderstood by the commentators not only in the West but also in the East. They all speak as if she could be awakened at any time from the beginning onward. But that is not so. Kundalini can be awakened only after the yogin has mastered all the limbs of yoga up to *samādhi,* the eight limb or step of yoga. Only after he has finished the whole course, and has achieved all the changes within that are to be worked by yoga, only then can he awaken Kundalini" (*HS,* 96).

Sutras,[2] with the help of Vyasas's commentary, the Yogabhāsya. What I have explained to you is Kundalini at the highest stage. In the evolution of the yogin there is always the union of both the man and woman powers. This union is symbolized by the triangle and the *liṅga,* as you know already. We have the fact that there is always woman power working in the growth of knowledge through man power, but only at three stages does the aspect of woman power appear under the symbol of the triangle. That means there are epochs in our inner development in which woman power plays a very important role. And certainly the erotic aspect of woman power has something to do with the awakening of knowledge. I call that the gross Kundalini—instead of the very sublime, subtle, spiritual Kundalini. A number of yoga texts, Hatha yoga, and the yogins themselves, in speaking about the awakening of Kundalini, really mean the awakening of that creative element in woman power which accompanies man power all through. But in the *Ṣaṭ-cakra-nirūpaṇa,* as I have shown, only the subtle, sublime woman power is symbolized by Kundalini. So for the West, and even for India as it is now, we may say that the awakening of Kundalini is just the awakening of the power that is influencing man's development all through; but this is not *the* Kundalini. We must be clear about the fact that there are the two aspects of the woman power, and that when the Kundalini is crawling up a certain distance, we have not awakened the real Kundalini.

Mrs. Crowley: That explains it! I could not understand why the two processes were not going on simultaneously—because that is the thing that awakens her.

Professor Hauer: I want to put it very emphatically that the awakening of Kundalini, as we usually talk about it, is only a preliminary to the awakening which is waiting in *ājñā.* We are certainly still very far from it, if we take the evolution of our psychic state in general, but it lies ahead of us.

Now, the return of the Kundalini after she has united with Śiva (which means to be united with the inner self, you know) symbolizes the fact that intuition has dawned upon man; when the union of these two powers has taken place in *ājñā,* then all the regions of the psychic life are permeated by that power. So now she can go down even to the lowest, to the erotic, region. It is a different thing if a man lives an earthly life after he has awakened the Kundalini; it may *seem* to be the same, but it is *absolutely different from his former experience, it is new.* We may look at a Japanese parallel for a moment. I wonder whether you know the book *Ten Essays*

[2] The reference is to the yoga sutras of Pantanjali, which Hauer translated in his *Der Yoga als Heilweg* (Yoga as a way of salvation) (Stuttgart, 1932).

in Buddhism by Suzuki. In it is an essay with pictures called "The Ten Cow-Herding Pictures," the cow being the symbol for the last reality. After long seeking, the disciple finds the cow, which means that he gets hold of his innermost reality. Then a most important feature, which is not clearly worked out in yoga, is that after he has found the cow he no longer cares for her; he sleeps and does not look after her, *he just knows she is there.* That is, after he has had the highest intuition, he does not always go on looking at it: he lets it drop into the subconscious again as if there were nothing in it. So he lies there asleep, the sun shining in his face; and he gets up and goes to town:

> *Entering the City with Bliss-Bestowing Hands.* His humble cottage door is closed and the wisest know him not. No glimpses of his inner life are to be caught; for he goes his own way without following the steps of the ancient sages. Carrying a gourd he goes out into the market, leaning against a stick he comes home. He is found in company with wine-bibbers and butchers, he and they are all converted into Buddhas.
>
> Bare-chested and barefooted, he comes out into the market
> place;
> Daubed with mud and ashes, how broadly he smiles!
> There is no need for the miraculous power of the gods,
> For he touches, and lo! the dead trees come into full bloom.[3]

Now perhaps Dr. Jung will say something about the psychological side.

Dr. Jung: I came here really in order to answer certain questions. Of course, I am not competent to put these things more clearly in the particular realm of which Professor Hauer speaks, but if you have any questions in regard to the psychological point of view, I would be glad to answer them. I cannot imagine what is clear to you and what is not. There is naturally great difficulty in linking up this peculiar terminology and ideology with our psychological language and processes.

For instance, to take your question "How can Kundalini be aroused?" It seems to you as if one already had to possess the thing one could possess only afterward in order to awaken Kundalini.

Dr. Shaw: It is as if it were doing just what Dr. Jung says we should not do. He always stresses so much the value of the earth, the necessity for both the spiritual and the earthly.

Dr. Jung: Yes, but that is what the yoga says too—it is right in the body, not in the air.

[3] D. T. Suzuki, *Essays in Zen Buddhism* (first series) (London, 1980), 376.

Professor Hauer: Of course, there is a certain reaction against classical yoga in tantric yoga. Classical yoga wants to stop when the highest intuition is reached; it has altogether a tendency toward letting the world go, while tantric yoga is just the reaction against that, in the idea that the Kundalini has to return to *mūlādhāra.* You must also think historically here in order to understand the danger and the necessity of that high spiritual life.

Mrs. Crowley: I should like to know Dr. Jung's psychological opinion about the difference between the *puruṣa* and the *ātman* as you presented it.[4]

Dr. Jung: From a psychological point of view you hardly can make a difference between them. They may be all the difference in the world, but when it comes to psychology they are the same. Even in philosophy those two concepts have been used in the same way. At least the difference is too subtle for it to play any role in psychology.

Mrs. Crowley: Is the ultimate experience of the *ātman* (the self) intuitively seen before the *puruṣa*?

Dr. Jung: If you think in those Hindu terms, you lose yourself in ten thousand aspects; it is exceedingly complicated. To look at it from a psychological point of view is much simpler. It is even much too simplified when put into words, for, as a matter of fact, when you go through it yourself, you see how terribly involved and complicated the whole process is—you begin to understand why the Hindus have invented so many symbols to explain that apparently simple thing. But you put it a very different way psychologically. What analysis does, then, is first a reduction. It is analyzing your attitude. You must become conscious of many resistances and personal things which suppress your genuine mental activity or your psychological processes. All these inhibitions are so many impurities, and your mind must be purified before the psychological process of transformation can begin.

Therefore yoga says one's *citta* (mind) must be purified before one can even think of beginning the way of the Kundalini. It is the same in analysis. You must clarify the mind until you have perfect objectivity, until you can admit that something moves in your mind independently of your will—for instance, until you can acknowledge a fantasy objec-

4 Hauer had stated that *ātman* and *puruṣa* were both terms that could be translated as the self. The former term was used in the *Upanishads* and tantric yoga, and the latter in classical yoga: "The *puruṣa* in classical yoga is just an entity by itself; there are innumerable such *puruṣas* in the world, and the divine ego is just one of them . . . whereas in tantric yoga the aspect is somewhat different; in *ātman* there is a part of the Absolute, it is the appearance of the absolute on one point of the whole" (*HS*, 43–44).

tively. You must remove a lot of inhibitions before you are capable of admitting that, and until then no objective psychological process can take place. But when you can admit that the psychical contents have autonomy, that the idea comes not because you invented it but by its own autonomous action, then you can see how the thing moves. Then the objective process can begin. Then later the self, the *puruṣa*, can be awakened.

Mrs. Crowley: Exactly that. There is a great difference between the two ways.

Dr. Jung: There is the preparatory way and then the real awakening. You speak of the realization of the *ātman*, but that is the result. And the difference between *puruṣa* and *ātman* I would advise not to make for practical purposes.

Mrs. Crowley: Except that as you explain it, there seems to be a very distinct difference.

Dr. Jung: I was speaking of the *citta*. The first part is an elaboration of the *citta*, and the second part is the awakening of Kundalini, and only in the awakening does the self appear—namely, in the subsequent stages of the psychological process that begin when you are capable of objectification. There the *puruṣa* appears, but not in the first part.

Professor Hauer: There is no real difference between *ātman* and *puruṣa*; they are synonymous terms. The only difference—and there lies the difficulty—is that the self is mirrored in different ways, which is very much what Dr. Jung has said. You cannot see the self clearly in *citta* at first. It is as if it were mirrored in moving water. But then it gets more and more clear, and in *anāhata* there is the same self that was seen below in flashes, but it appears now as the self that cannot be doubted any longer. Down below, as long as the mirror or the water was moving, it might be doubted, but now you know it is there; you cannot lose it, though it is still surrounded by that creative activity, the red color, which you have still to go through. Up above it is mirrored in tranquility; it is absolutely clear. *Citta* is really no more than a mirror of the *puruṣa*. There are no *kleśa* at that stage. And when that happens there is an absolute presence, the real presence of the self, and then appears the identity of the *ātman* with the *paramātman*. It is a question of being mirrored in a different way in a *citta* which is developing.

Miss Hannah: I am in an awful muddle as to what the difference is between the Western approach and the Eastern. The East apparently goes through the jaws of the monster, the makara.

Dr. Jung: Professor Hauer gives you a very clear picture of how this problem is tackled in the East,[5] and if you study analytical psychology you know how it is tackled in the West.

Mrs. Sawyer: I think that the confusion comes from people trying to make the two fit, the East and the West, yoga and analysis.

Dr. Jung: My term for the process which tantric yoga calls the awakening of Kundalini is psychic objectivity. For instance, those visions we are dealing with in the English seminar are experiences on a different plane: they are to be considered not from the *sthūla* aspect but from the *sūkṣma* aspect. These things happen in the nowhere; they are universal and impersonal—and if you do not understand them as impersonal, you simply get an inflation through your identification with the universal. So the whole process begins with the fact that certain things in the mind are purely impersonal. You are not responsible for their existence; they drop down from heaven or come up from hell, and you cannot account for them in any way. Certain fantasies, certain dreams, are very clearly out of an impersonal sphere, and they are not produced by any intentional purpose. These are contents which can be experienced only if you assume that you can dissociate yourself and play a role.

Therefore people always have a tendency to perform mystery plays, to step out of the ordinary frame of their existence and assume a role. Even the most primitive aborigines in central Australia have the very elaborate idea that when they perform their totem rites, it is not as themselves but as their ancestors in the alcheringa times. They identify themselves with the divine heroes. I am no longer Dr. Jung, I am Zarathustra, and then I can say the most outrageous things because I speak with the voice of the centuries—I am talking under the cloak of a great ancestor, and afterward I take off my paint and am an ordinary citizen again. Now, such a thing could never live if it did not answer a psychological need; it is simply another reality because it works. Our rationalism simply cannot understand naturally how it is possible but it does work.

For instance, there is the idea that everybody must lead a normal life and have at least two children. But many people do not have two children, or they have many more, or they do not dream of having children

[5] Hauer had stated: "In following the course of this life, you come across that sea monster, the makara; somewhere you will come face to face with a tremendous danger, and you cannot go past it. This monster is pictured in the cakra as covering the whole width of the crescent (the crescent in *svādiṣṭhana* stands for Śiva), and the jaws of the monster are open. Now, if you come from the right you may attack the monster from behind. You don't fall into its jaws and may be able to grapple with it, whereas if you come from the left, you will fall into its jaws. It is a question of the right way" (*HS*, 84).

at all. So real life is very irregular, and many things live which should not live—monasteries, nunneries—they all live, and quite productively, though it is against the bourgeois rationalism of the nineteenth century.

And so that impersonal kind of experience, where you can experience as if you were not yourself, as if you were a stage thing, is the intrinsic element in all mystery plays, and that condition is artificially brought about. I have often told you of the Mithraic mysteries, in which, in the initiations, people were changed into *milites*, the soldiers of the god, and lions, and the *heliodromoi*, the sun runners of the god.[6] These were simply different stages of impersonal experience. For instance, a Roman innkeeper who has been made a *milēs* is afterward not that alone. Of course not—he is what he always has been, but he has experienced himself on a higher level that was not identical with the three-dimensional world: an impersonal level where he was allowed to look out the window into another dimensional way, onto psychical reality.

The proof of that idea is that it works automatically—it drops upon us like the fires of Sodom and Gomorrah and can destroy our lives, even. You think you are quite all right and that the world is all right, and suddenly you cannot cross the street any longer because you have agoraphobia. You cannot have invented it, it simply takes you by the neck. And who does it? We say it is merely a disease, but that is only a word. You can just as well say that it is an evil spirit causing the fear. That is an example of the autonomy of the psychic world, and the proof that such things can live there. Therefore I advise all people who have such a neurosis: go into it now, live it, and then you have it in your hands and it has not got you any longer.

Now, the Kundalini yoga is a symbolic formulation of the impersonal experience in the Eastern way. It would cause us a great deal of trouble to understand in our Western way what the East tries to convey to us through its symbolism. Professor Hauer would surely be the last to encourage us in taking these things literally. It is only living when one understands it in the Western way, where it is less simple and also less involved. When you are not clear about things, you always say they are very simple. The simplest people in the world are really the great world confusers. These things are by no means simple, but it is as well if you have some straight psychological analogy that will help you to see the connection between the Eastern and the Western experience.

Miss Hannah: The Eastern way seems a trifle dogmatic.

Dr. Jung: Think of the thousands of years, the thousands of individuals,

[6] Cf. Jung, *Analytical Psychology*, 98–99.

and the thousands of very good intellectual heads that have worked at it. Of course it becomes dogmatic.

Miss Hannah: Is psychology already dogmatic?

Dr. Jung: Yes, when people say there is no such thing as the unconscious, and you say, "That is heresy." Then you are getting dogmatic under your skin, and you do not notice it—like going black in Africa.[7]

Miss Thiele: Professor Hauer said yesterday that no European had ever actually awakened the Kundalini in a higher sense except possibly Suso,[8] but would it be possible with the help of the analytical process to get to the stage at which one might?

Professor Hauer: In a thousand years perhaps.

Dr. Jung: You must never forget that India is a very peculiar country. The primitive man has lived there since time immemorial and has grown up in absolute continuity. We have not grown up in continuity. We were cut off from our roots. Moreover the Hindu is a very different race. Not only is it Aryan but there is a great deal of the aboriginal influence of Dravidism. Therefore there are very old chthonic things in the tantric yoga. So we must admit that this particular yoga philosophy is strange to our very blood, and whatever we may experience will take an entirely different turn. We can never take those forms over literally. That would be a terrible mistake, for to us they are artificial processes.

Remark: I thought some of the process according to our Western conception was similar to that of the Indian yoga.

Dr. Jung: Yes, analytical psychology is, of course, an attempt of a similar sort. We did not know that there was such a close analogy with tantric yoga when we were elaborating the beginnings of it. The tantric texts were not translated, and even the experts on that sort of thing knew very little of the tantric yoga. Only recently has it become known, through Sir John Woodroffe's translations. Our attempt is a perfectly genuine naive attempt in the same field—of course, with different means, according to our different temperaments and attitude.

Professor Hauer: You know, you must compare the preparatory work which is done now by analytical psychology with the stages of yoga four or five hundred years before it became a system. It first became a system at the time of Buddha, or not long before. What is being done by analytical psychology was done by the thinkers and brahmins of about five hundred years before Buddha. The names have been lost. We see only little

7 On Jung's fears of "going black" during his visit to Africa, see *MDR*, 302.

8 In answer to Dr. Shaw's question "Do you mean that no one has awakened Kundalini?" Hauer replied: "No one in the West, I think, but I do not know. . . . I do think that Suso, the German mystic of the Middle Ages, had the same kind of experience" (*HS*, 99).

flashes of insight coming up, so to speak. One little thing after the other has been added to their understanding, perhaps, and then there appeared one great mind who created the system whose function it was to bring into order the minds or souls of that epoch. But only for a time—say, for a few hundred years. That is the process of psychic adaptation, which is going on through the whole history of mankind. Christianity, for example, is no longer valid for us all, so it does not work. In a few hundred years there will be another system. This will disappear just as tantric yoga has disappeared. All these systems are human attempts to grapple with the great problem of life by symbols and sentences which are not only for you and me but for the whole community. The leading character of symbols that are valid for a whole community can be brought about only through the work of centuries. Then each individual need not do all the original work; it has been done for him—and we get a common psychic and spiritual culture. But in a few hundred years that epoch is finished. The symbol changes, or their life changes, and the danger lies in carrying on with that symbol as valid in the new epoch.

As I look at analytical psychology, it is working from the bottom toward a great building, certainly. Then it will become in a few centuries a most rigid dogma, and the destroyers will come and say it is all wrong. However, we may be sure that every system has gotten at some truths, which are lasting. We see that there is something true in the Christian; there are absolute realities which cannot be dispensed with. And yet we must find a new system of truths and symbols. It is the same in India. Historically tantric yoga is only an adaptation of the thousand-year-old yoga to a new psychic situation, and that situation has disappeared from India. If they try to work out life there according to tantric yoga they may go perhaps just as far wrong as we. Take Gandhi. New symbols must be for the whole community, and Gandhi is the man who, with a quite new method, has created those symbols out of the new psychic and spiritual state. As I told you, when he goes to the ocean and shows a lump of salt to his people, it is as good as a cakra. They need no cakra. Take the spinning wheel. Why should they concentrate on a cakra when they see Gandhi with a spinning wheel? They contemplate it and are carried to a higher plane of thought—the idea of sacrifice, and so on. That is a new "tantric yoga," if you like. And yet, as in Christianity, there are also in tantric yoga elements which cannot be lost, symbolized truths that are eternal and universal. And those we study, those are valuable. That is the pedagogical value of the cakras. And then there are parallel experiences that are made everywhere and always. I have intentionally not talked of the psychological parallels of tantric yoga to analytical psychology, for I would mix things up, I suppose. I just put this yoga before you, and you yourselves can make the comparisons.

Mrs. Crowley: The comparison was illustrated last night in the mandalas done in the Western way that Dr. Jung showed.[9] To me it was like seeing cakras in the making, the beginning of things in comparison with the Hindu ones which were already developed.

Professor Hauer: The Indian ones are perfect. Those shown yesterday are just rough material, out of which perhaps a cakra will grow. And these illustrations show how in spite of all the differences, the human soul has a good deal of uniformity always and everywhere.

Dr. Jung: Well, those are cakras.

Professor Hauer: I mean a cakra that is valid for a whole community.

Dr. Jung: Yes, that all needs cooperation, the elaboration of thousands of people and untold centuries.

Mrs. Crowley: But what was so startling was that the analogy was so complete in the cakras as Dr. Jung developed them one after the other.

Dr. Jung: Just there, tantric yoga is a really invaluable instrument to help us in classification and terminology, and to create concepts of those things. That is why the study of tantric yoga is so fascinating.

Mr. Baumann: Professor Hauer said that the yogin had to reach the *ājñā* cakra for the Kundalini to be awakened.

Professor Hauer: In that subtle sense, that spiritual sense, let us say.

Mr. Baumann: In analysis there is a preparatory stage—one must get rid of personal inhibitions and so on—and then you reach the impersonal. I think it is possible—it really happens, that patients make impersonal drawings when they are still in the first stage.

Dr. Jung: Oh yes, you can make the most marvelous drawings and you are nowhere at all. Particularly artists. Anybody can make drawings, even little children, and it means precious little. You see, the drawing must be an expression of a fact, of a psychological experience, and you must know that it is such an expression, you must be conscious of it. Otherwise you might just as well be a fish in the water or a tree in the woods. For every plant makes marvelous mandalas. A composite flower is a mandala, it is an image of the sun, but the flower does not know it. The human eye is a mandala, but we are not conscious of it. So it requires long and painstaking work in analysis to get people to the point where they become conscious of the impersonal character of the problem. And that impersonal thing is really the Western analogy to the Eastern mind. Kundalini

9 "Westliche Parallelen zu den Tantrischen Symbolen" (Western parallels to tantric symbols), in *Tantra Yoga.* Jung had used many of these mandalas in his "Commentary on 'The Secret of the Golden Flower,'" in *CW,* vol. 13.

is an impersonal thing, and it is extremely difficult for our Western mind to grasp the impersonal in our mind as an objective happening.

I will give you an example. I was once treating a writer, a very clever fellow. He was intelligent and very rational and explained everything to the rule: everything had its natural cause, and everything was reasonable. He had had a great deal of analysis with people of all the different schools, and he used to explain his dreams according to the principles of causal reduction. Of course, you can say of practically every figure or fact or emotion that it comes from some definite experience, and hardly ever do you come across something which has not been in your experience before. Naturally one goes on as long as one can with this kind of thinking. I thought that finally the dreams would bring up something that could not be reduced, and after a long time of working together, he did have dreams in which figures appeared that he could not trace. For instance, he dreamed a great deal of women, as they played an important role in his life. Formerly he was able to trace them in reminiscences, to say, "She looks something like Mrs. So-and-So," so we were able to stitch the whole thing together. But then a woman appeared whom we could not stitch together. He took the utmost pains to find the memory images, and finally he had to give up; he found absolutely no association, and he had to admit that he was unable to show a reasonable origin for that figure. So I said, "Here we are at the end of your principle of causal reduction. Now I propose something entirely different—that this thing has not had its origin in your personal experience but is coming in all by itself, just as if somebody were walking into this room whom we had not invited, or as if she were stepping out of the wall—she walks, she talks—she must be a ghost." Naturally he had resistance against that proposition. He said things could not come into his mind which had not been there. He had that depreciation of the psychic world which is part of our Western attitude. But he had to admit that something very definite had come up in his mind which he had not invented and which caused him great emotion in his dreams. That was the beginning of the recognition of the objective autonomous factor and the beginning of the psychological process. It was as if a real woman had come into his life—he did not know why she existed, but he had to deal with her existence. I invented the term *anima* in order to designate such figures, which, according to our Western prejudice, should not be.

Now, this is the moment where the analogy with the Kundalini process begins, when something stirs up and develops all by itself. If that process is followed up on, one arrives at results which can be expressed in terms of tantric yoga. We are grateful to tantric yoga because it gives us the most differentiated forms and concepts by which we are able to express the chaotic experiences that we are actually undergoing. As Professor Hauer rightly puts it, we are at the beginning of something, and in the beginning things are exceedingly individual and chaotic. Only after centuries do they begin to settle down and crystallize into certain aspects; and then, of course, dogma inevitably follows.

Mr. Baumann: Dr. Jung mentioned yesterday receiving a mandala in a letter from a patient in which there were fish around the center. It made a great impression on me when she said: "I hope I may find a state where I am like a center, with the fishes whirling around me."[10]

Dr. Jung: No, it was to find a way a center around which she could move like those fish in harmonious order; she would not be the center. That is our Western idea. It is a mistake to think that we are the center. We think we are gods of our world, and therefore the tantric yoga idea that one becomes a god is dangerous for us. We start with that prejudice. But we are really devilish, awful things; we simply do not see ourselves from the outside. We think we are very wonderful people, highly respectable and moral, and so on, but in reality we are bloody pirates. What the European thinks of himself is a lie. I learned my lesson from the Red Indian and from the Negro. Look at our world, and you see what we are. But our prejudice being that we are gods, when anybody dreams of a center he quietly and instinctively puts himself in it. You remember, possibly, the picture that I showed you last evening—the central stone and the little jewels round it. It is perhaps interesting if I tell you about the dream in connection with it. I was the perpetrator of that mandala at a time when I had not the slightest idea what a mandala was, and in my extreme modesty I thought, *I* am the jewel in the center, and those little lights are surely very nice people who believe that they are also jewels, but smaller ones. That is what we do—we are always following the example given by Anatole France in *L'Isle des Pingouins* (The island of penguins).[11] St. Malo had baptized the penguins in the heavenly concilium, and when they asked St. Catharine what they should do about the penguins' souls, she said to God: "Donnez-leur une âme mais une petite" [Give them a soul, but a small one]. That is our principle. I gave them a little soul; I

[10] It is likely that Jung showed the mandala by a woman, with fish radiating out from a central circle, reproduced in "Commentary on 'The Secret of the Golden Flower,'" in *CW*, vol. 13, figure A2. The remarks that Baumann cited are not contained in the report of Jung's lecture in *Tantra Yoga.*

[11] Anatole France, *Penguin Island,* translated by E. W. Evans (London, 1948).

admitted as much as that. I thought very well of myself that I was able to express myself like that: my marvelous center here, and I am right in my heart.

Then I had a dream.[12] I was in Liverpool, where I have never been, actually. It was very dark and dirty; it rained dirt; and I was walking up a street with certain other Swiss fellows in raincoats. We were talking together, but it was very disagreeable, and I was thinking of a place where I could get shelter from the rain and the cold.[13] We came to a sort of plateau, a level part of town, where there was a huge and beautiful park. I did not recognize it at first, but it was the mandala which I demonstrated yesterday. There were intersecting paths, and in the center was a little lake, in the center of that was an island, and upon the island was a magnolia tree of that rosy hue, a beautiful tree. And the tree was standing in full sunshine—it was a most glorious picture on a dark rainy night, that marvelous tree in full bloom; I was fascinated by it. Then suddenly I discovered that my companions did not notice it; they just walked on and began to talk about another Swiss who was living at the corner of a street in Liverpool on the left side of the park. I pictured the place: there was one single street lamp at that corner, and he was living there in an apartment house. They said: "He must be a damned fool to live in Liverpool in such a dirty place." But I thought he must be a tremendously intelligent fellow, and I knew why he was living there—he knew the secret of that island; he had found the right place.[14] Now, Liverpool is the center of life—liver is the center of life—and I am not the center, I am the fool who lives in a dark place somewhere, I am one of those little side lights. In that way my Western prejudice that I was the center of the mandala was corrected—that I am everything, the whole show, the king, the god. We have come down from that notion. The Hindu, being a primitive man, has no such idea. He never imagines he is not a man to begin with; therefore in the end he can never become a god. But we have anticipated the divinity, so we have to come down.

[12] An account of this dream is found in *MDR*, 223–24. There it is dated 1927. Additional details from this account are in the notes that follow.

[13] "I had the feeling that we were coming from the harbour, and that the real city was actually up above, on the cliffs. We climbed up there. It reminded me of Basel, where the market is down below and then you go up through the Totengässchen ("Alley of the Dead"), which leads to a plateau above and so to the Petersplatz and the Peterskirche" (*MDR*, 223).

[14] "On one detail of the dream I must add a supplementary comment: the individual quarters of the city were themselves arranged radially around a central point. This point formed a small open square illuminated by a larger street lamp, and constituted a small replica of the island. I knew that the 'other Swiss' lived in the vicinity of one of these secondary centres" (*MDR*, 223–24).

Professor Hauer: I will say just a few words more about the form and symbolism of the cakras, repeating certain points we have already discussed. All those mathematical figures in the cakras, in my opinion, indicate the life of the cosmos and the psychic life as ordered by laws. Then the idea of the lotus is that the whole psychic life is embodied in an organic center. You remember that on each petal is a letter. The letters are hummed in meditation, and while humming one should realize the meaning of each, which is told to you only by a guru. The letters symbolize the growing organic aspect hidden in that particular region. This is not conscious. Hidden away in each petal is a force which must be realized and brought into connection with the center. The metaphysical and the metapsychical[15] idea is that in the very center of the psychic organism, which is in the very center of the cosmic organism, there is a subconscious sound force that regulates life unconsciously, and one should realize the meaning of that sound power by meditation. It must come up into the conscious, and if one can let it work in consciousness it becomes stronger.

The *bīja*[16] also should be realized in meditation. The inner working force in this *bīja* is not a clearly developed personality; it is never named. The *bīja* simply symbolizes a subconscious power in that element of which it is the symbol—this is working in one's psychic foundation—but it can work with real force only when it is realized by meditation. As you know, I call that power the *bīja-deva.*[17] Out of this is projected or grows the *bindu-deva*, which is the same force but projected out of the unconscious into clear consciousness. But it does not come as clearly into consciousness as the Śakti, the woman power. I think there is no question about it—it has become evident to me—that this is the anima. That hidden man force is combined with the woman force and should work within us, according to the tantric yoga, and that is realized consciously in different periods of our lives. This symbolism figuring a great truth I call a *leading* symbol, a symbol that has a leading character, such as can only be found in the course of many centuries.

There is also a color symbolism, of course. You know that red means

[15] "Metapsychique" was the term proposed by Charles Richet for the branch of studies now known in the English-speaking world as parapsychology. See his *Traité de Metapsychique* (Paris, 1922).

[16] Hauer defined the *bīja* as follows: "The *bīja* is the germ of a cakra; the word *bīja* means germ" (*HS*, 80).

[17] Hauer had stated: "I distinguish the *bīja-deva* from the *bindu-deva.* (These expressions I have coined myself on the basis of the cakras as I understand them.) The *bindu-deva* is always a psychic and spiritual working force . . . ; the *bindu-deva* is the ruling divinity of that force" (*HS*, 81).

blood, the powers deep down in the earth. And white means the higher intuition. Then wherever you find the golden color, you get the idea of clear insight, though it is not the highest insight. Thus the golden color in *mūlādhāra,* which is also in the letters on the petals; there is somehow a subconscious working force of insight in this region. Within the erotic life a power of insight is working. The erotic seems a way to insight into the nature of things, and that grows into the spiritual aspect above. Then the strange thing is that in *maṇipūra* you have blue letters on blue-gray petals, and in *anāhata* the red color of the pericarp is repeated in the letters on the leaves. Red represents the musical tone there. *Anāhata,* in my opinion, symbolizes the creative life—the petals of the lotus are red, and the power of insight is in the center in that golden triangle. The musical undertone of that region is alive somehow—life has a different reality; a blood reality comes from the outside and tries to work its way in and harmonize the two.

I give you this explanation as a suggestion of how to work on these things. I may cite here a word of Lao-tzu: "The meaning that you can think out is not the meaning."[18] Take all I say in this light. Forget everything I tell you, and begin as *you* must begin. There are different approaches to these things. Of course, I have certain grounds for my explanation, but you must work it out as a riddle that you try and solve. There may be more than one meaning, just as there might be two correct meanings of a dream, through what we may call the coincidence of things in our psychic and our outer life. The outer event and the psychic event may be quite different, yet they have a similar character and may be symbolized by the same dream. Perhaps one finds the outer and has not yet found the inner. It may be the same with cakras: the meaning of one symbolism runs into another and is discovered only by deep insight. As I told you, that energetic life is all moving, and only by dipping into that movement can you get at it. Here we reach things which are rather difficult to talk about, and the color symbolism is a great help. You sink into the color, so to speak, and then you find its meaning.

Take the *anāhata* cakra again. In the center is the triangle, and around that is the *bīja* of *yaṃ.* Then there is the hexagram, consisting of two interlocked triangles, in dark smoke color, and that is surrounded by the coloring of the rising sun, and outside that are the twelve red petals of a

[18] A rendition of the commencement of the *Tao Tê Ching.* Arthur Waley translates the opening lines as: "The way that can be told is not an unvarying way; the names that can be named are not unvarying names." *The Way and Its Power: A Study of the Tao Tê Ching and Its Place in Chinese Thought* (London, 1934), 141. (*Tao* has sometimes been rendered as "meaning.") Jung had a copy of this translation.

still finer red. You remember that the number of the petals increases in each cakra after the *mūlādhāra*—life unfolds more and more. So it is a living music of colors. Now try and *feel* the meaning; or you may use the intellect as well. All sorts of associations may come up. This *bīja yam* is the air or storm *bīja,* and all around it is the tremendous dark smoke-colored hexagram, and this beautiful red issues from that. My explanation is that no real creative power would be there unless there were storm and chaos. Therefore this is the storm mandala, all dark, and expressing the psychic state. It may also be a cosmic state; most probably it is. Then it breaks through the creative power in the middle, and the glowing red color appears.

Question: May I ask the significance of the absence of the symbol for man power in some cakras?

Professor Hauer: Man and woman power are clearly defined symbols in *mūlādhāra,* in *anāhata,* and in *ājñā.* The same symbols do not appear in *maṇipūra, svādhiṣṭhāna,* and *viśudhha,* though we know the power is always there. The three stages when man and woman power work together in full strength are the three stages of the erotic life, the creative life, and the intuitive life, so here we have the *yoni* and *liṅga.* But there are intermediate stages. I take *svādhiṣṭhāna* as the region or the psychic state where we lose ourselves in life—we have no goal, we just want to live. Then there are the different aspects; every cakra has three aspects. We have the *sthūla* aspect of the flow of water in all that circling round of water in our bodies, and this *sthūla* aspect is expressed in nature by the sea. Our bodies are only a small counterpart to the whole, the microcosm in the macrocosm. The *sthūla* of the psychic state would be the experience of just losing ourselves in life, and here the woman power plays a part, for in a hidden way, it is not a regulating force. *Maṇipūra* I take as the life on which rests the working of our whole bodily structure. Here is the fire of digestion. This cakra looks like a tremendous engine. It would express the economics of our body and of our whole being. And here also woman does not play a visible role; she remains hidden. Then above, in *viśudhha,* you reach the stage of the wise man who has gotten beyond creative work, one who lives in the pure light of knowledge. (You remember that beautiful blue circle outside the white *bīja ham,* surrounded by the dark lotus petals.) But in order to get to the last stage of intuition, she again comes in, as I have told you in describing Kundalini.

Now the different animals. The elephant always means the carrying power in India. It comes again in the *viśudhha* for the same reason. Then there is the sea monster in *svādhiṣṭhāna,* of which I have tried to explain the symbolism. And you have the gazelle in the heart lotus. We know from a text in the *Hathayogapradipika* that the meaning of it is the versatile and fugitive mind. There always is, in that creative region, a tendency in the intellect to run away; you have to fetter the gazelle of the heart lotus, and there is the danger of just making jumps in any direction.

These are suggestions toward a method of getting at the symbolism both through intellectual processes and through feeling. But I think Dr. Jung will have something to say about its meaning.

Dr. Jung: I can only express my extreme gratitude to you for giving us the symbolism so beautifully and so clearly. If these things mean something rather different to me, it is of course because my approach to the question of the cakras was a different one. You know that my first experiences in the field were made at a time when there was no chance of getting at the teaching of the cakras. When I first touched on the subject, it seemed to me utterly hopeless; I had the feeling that it was the specific symbolism of an entirely exotic people, which conveyed nothing to us. But then I had an extraordinarily difficult case which caused me great trouble.[19] The patient was a girl born in India of European parents. There was no mixture of blood, she was as European as you are. But the first six years of her life had been spent in India, where she had had a Malay nurse who was quite uneducated. There was no teaching of this sort, these things were completely unknown to her, but somehow these Eastern ideas got into her unconscious. She could not adapt to European conditions because her instincts refused all along the line; she would not marry, she would not be interested in ordinary things, she would not adapt to our conventions. She was against everything, and so naturally she became very neurotic.[20] First she exploded two analysts,

[19] Jung provided an extended commentary on this case in his "The Realities of Modern Psychotherapy" (1937), in *CW*, vol. 16 (this was added to the second edition of *CW*, vol. 16, as an appendix), and reproduced and commented on several of her paintings in "Concerning Mandala Symbolism" (1950), in *CW*, vol. 9, part 1, figures 7–9, §§656–59. Some significant comments have been appended in the notes that follow.

[20] In "The Realities of Modern Psychotherapy" Jung stated: "The patient had been born in Java. . . . In her dreams there were frequent allusions to Indonesian motifs" (§557). In "Concerning Mandala Symbolism" he stated: "The patient was born in Dutch India, where she sucked up the peculiar local demonology with the mother's milk of her native *ayah*. . . . Brought up in India until her sixth year, she came later into a conventional European milieu, and this had a devastating effect on the flowerlike quality of her Eastern spirit, and a prolonged subsequent psychic trauma was set up" (§657; translation modified—Hull substituted "Dutch East Indies" for "India"). In "The Realities of Modern Psychotherapy" Jung noted that she was twenty-five when she came to see him, and listed the following additional symptoms: "[She] suffered from a high degree of emotivity, exaggerated sensitivity, and hysterical fever. She was very musical; whenever she played the piano she got so emotional that her temperature rose and after ten minutes registered one hundred degrees

then she came to me and almost succeeded in blasting me, because I had to explain to her that I could not understand her dreams at all, two thirds of them were absolutely dark to me on account of the peculiar Eastern psychology. She kept on working bravely, and I did the same, despite the fact that I could not understand—and here and there we got a little flash of something. She developed an entirely new set of symptoms,[21] beginning with a dream which made a tremendous impression on her: that out from her genital organs came a white elephant. I was completely baffled, I had never heard of such nonsense—and yet she was so impressed that she began to carve the elephant in ivory. Then organic symptoms appeared: she had ulcers in the womb, and I had to send her to a gynecologist. For months the thing would not heal; they tried everything under the sun, and whenever she had a somewhat obstinate dream things became worse. For at least five months her condition remained like that, and then another set of symptoms began. She developed polyuria, an impossible amount of fluid; she could hardly hold the urine.[22] Then the same amount of fluid also developed in the colon and intestines, and caused such a rumbling that when I was outside the room and left the door open I could hear it. It sounded like a little river pouring down a staircase, and it lasted about ten minutes. With that there were acute attacks of diarrhea—again floods of water with apparently no provocation; it just happened. At the same time she really loved a man but could not think of marrying him. And then the thought entered her head that I, or circumstances, might persuade her to marry and have a baby, but that was impossible. For a whole year she fought against this idea, until she developed an entirely new symptom. She felt as if the skull had become soft on top, as if the fontanelle was opening up—like a child with an open skull—and that something like a bird was descending from above with a long beak and going into her through the skull, meeting something that was coming up from below. When that happened, the whole thing cleared up, and she married and had babies. That was the

Fahrenheit or more. She also suffered from a compulsive argumentiveness and a fondness for philosophical hairsplitting that was quite intolerable despite her high intelligence" (§546).

[21] In "The Realities of Modern Psychotherapy" Jung stated: "The first took the form of an indefinable excitation in the perineal region" (§551).

[22] In "The Realities of Modern Psychotherapy" Jung stated: "Psychologically, the symptom meant that something had to be 'ex-pressed.' So I gave her the task of expressing by drawings whatever her hand suggested to her. She had never drawn before, and set about it with much doubt and hesitation. But now symmetrical flowers took shape under her hand, vividly coloured and arranged in symbolic patterns. She made these pictures with great care and with a concentration I can only call devout" (§553).

symptomatology of the case, and it was that which forced me to look into things; I had the idea that something of the sort existed in the East. It was soon after Avalon's book *The Serpent Power* was published,[23] and there I found the parallel. You see, first was the elephant in *mūlādhāra*, second was *svādhiṣṭhāna*, the water region, and after that the emotional center, *maṇipūra*; and then it did not go on continuously—something came from above, and this brought about the dissolution. At first it was absolutely dark to me; I could not understand what had happened. But subsequently I understood that this was the awakening from above, and she could then disentangle herself from the maze of the exotic jungle. She could objectify the Indian psychology that had been grafted upon her with the milk she drank from that *ayah* and through the suggestion of her surroundings. She became liberated by the objectivity and could accept European life. And, quite naturally, she objectified her whole development in the most beautiful mandalas. Now, mandalas are really cakras, though in our experience there are not just six but innumerable mandalas. But they really should be arranged like the cakras, one above the other. The first ones are usually connected with *mūlādhāra*, and then they gradually come up, and wind up with analogies to the *ājñā* center, or even the *sahasrāra*, the highest, the seventh center—they are really an equivalent in a way.

Since then I have had a number of experiences, and found a certain regularity in them: it was quite clear that a certain set of mandalas, or psychological conditions, belonged to the psychology of the *mūlādhāra* region, namely, a sort of complete unconsciousness in which one lives merely instinctively. Then the next is the region of the diaphragm, and the third is the heart. Now, among the Pueblo Indians in New Mexico I made friends with an interesting fellow who was the chief of religious ceremonies. He confessed to me that they believed all Americans were crazy because they said they thought in the head, whereas the Indians knew that the normal thing was to think in the heart. I stared at him and

[23] *The Serpent Power* was published in 1919. The copy in Jung's library is the first edition. In "The Realities of Modern Psychotherapy" Jung stated: "It is, as you see, quite impossible that the patient knew the book beforehand. But could she have picked up a thing or two from the *ayah*? I regard this as unlikely, because Tantrism, and in particular Kundalini Yoga, is a cult restricted to southern India and has relatively few adherents. It is, moreover, an exceedingly complicated symbolic system which no one can understand unless he has been initiated into it or has at least made special studies in this field" (§559). Jung overestimated the obscurity of Kundalini yoga—for instance, Swami Vivekânanda had included an account of the cakras and the means of awakening the Kundalini in his *Yoga Philosophy: Lectures Delivered in New York, Winter of 1895–1896*, 5th ed. (New York, 1899), without, however going into detail concerning their iconography.

then remembered, of course, that it was only in relatively late periods of civilization that the head was discovered to be the seat of the mind. And the Pueblo Indians are already civilized—they are really descendants of our fathers of the Aztec; they have a certain culture. The Greek in Homeric times located his thinking a bit below the heart, in the diaphragm. Another word for diaphragm is *phren*, the Greek word for mind; and the same root is in the name of the mental disease schizo*phren*ia, which means a splitting of the mind. So in the Homeric days, the physical localization of the mind was in the region of the diaphragm. They were conscious to the extent that they could notice psychological contents inasmuch as those influenced the breathing. And certain Negroes put the seat of their emotions and thoughts in the belly. They are conscious insofar as they notice contents which affect the functions of the abdominal intestines. When we have disagreeable thoughts or feelings, our stomachs get upset. We still get jaundice when we repress a violent anger, and every case of hysteria has trouble in the digestive organs, because originally the most profound and important thoughts were down there. So those are three localizations of consciousness that are still to be traced historically, as it were.

The intervening cakras that are characterized by the absence of the union of the *liṅga* and the *yoni* can be traced, too. I have made some observations lately concerning *viśudhha*, for instance. The *anāhata* cakra, of course, is the air center, which obviously coincides with the fact that the lungs are situated there; and as it is situated above the diaphragm, it means that a higher state of consciousness is reached. The heart is always associated with feelings or with mind; therefore, as I also have seen by practical experience, *anāhata* would be a center of consciousness, of feeling and thoughts, which can be blown out in the breath. For feelings also come out in the breath; you can express them—you press, and out comes the feeling in the form of sound. That was the original method of calling to the gods. We have a description of it in the Mithraic liturgy, where it says: "Hold both your sides and press them with all your might and shout like a steer," so that the gods may hear you.[24] You see, that is a kind of conscious feeling and thought expression. Now, this is very primitive, but most of us are really still about there. We express feelings and thoughts as if we were just spitting them out, without realizing in the least what we are doing. You know, many people have not the faintest idea what they are saying, or what they are doing to other people by thus exhaling their thoughts and feelings. I see that all the time. So the think-

[24] Cf. Albrecht Dietrich, *Eine Mithrasliturgie* (A Mithras liturgy) (Leipzig, 1903).

ing and feeling life at this stage is not yet so conscious that it deserves to be called consciousness, which probably accounts for the fact that the self is only beginning to be visible from the *anāhata.*

The next stage is the purified condition. You see, the air belongs to the earth. We are walking about here in the air, but above is the ether region, which we do not reach, and that is abstract thought expressed in human language. The ethereal region is the human larynx: speech comes apparently from the throat, and speech is the life of the word. The word that leaves one carries the meaning; it is doing things. We are often tremendously astonished when people flare up and misunderstand what one says—"and then I said, and she said"—one feels oneself to be entirely innocent; one simply had a thought and cannot understand what happened afterward. So man has slowly learned that the word has existence; it is like a winged being that takes to the air and has magic effects, an abstract being, absolutely purified from the admixture of the lower regions.

Then the strange thing is, I have seen representations of the *ājñā*, the highest thing you can imagine, something which is even beyond the winged word. One can imagine that one could put oneself into a word and *become* a word, like Jesus, who became the Logos. He detached himself from God the Creator and took a flight into the world, shining like a light. One could become such an impossible detached thing that one no longer touches the earth. One would be as creative as a being with golden wings in a globe or an egg—completely detached. I have really seen such a representation. You remember, the *ājñā* cakra is the mandala with the two petals, which looks like the winged seed of certain trees. It is quite purified from any earthly admixture; it has almost no substance and is quite purely white light. So one gets the impression of something that really has taken to wings. And I think that the idea of the winged egg, or the homunculus in the second part of *Faust*, the artificial little man that flies about in his retort, is really the anticipation of such a possibility—a man who has created himself again in a new form, as the old alchemist produced a little man in his retort. That, again, I take as a symbol for the *ājñā* center.

Now this is, of course, an entirely empirical approach. In our Western symbolism it sounds banal or grotesque, far from the absolute perfection of the East, with its specific style, its specific beauty. We are at this stage in the rough experience and the raw ordinary material; we are far from any differentiation—we are only just beginning to see that we also have certain experiences that approach that kind of symbolism. We also know something about color symbolism—for instance, that the different stages are always symbolized by different colors. We know all those red things belong to a region below the diaphragm where there is no air, and when the red gets lighter it is a bit above the diaphragm, and when it disappears and blue prevails, we are approaching the icy regions of detached consciousness. And we know that dark colors mean obscurity, or evil, or fear, or heavy matter. And light colors always give the idea of differentiated things, of things that are easy, sometimes even cheap, and detached. So we have quite a series of colors with almost typical meanings.

All those other peculiarities of the Eastern cakras—the letters, the sounds, the mantras, the differentiated gods—all that is, of course, lacking in our experience completely. But it is absolutely regular that every mandala has a center, where there is something that one cannot grasp; one tries, but it is most evasive. You see, man has forever felt something which evades his grasp and is aloof; and which is not an ordinary thing, it is always demoniacal. For instance, when a certain animal always eludes him, when he never succeeds in catching it, the Red Indian says, "That is no good animal; it is a doctor animal and ought never to be caught at all." A doctor animal is like a werewolf; it is divine or demoniacal. So in our psychology the things we cannot grasp are usually the things to which we give a sort of divine attribute. Therefore the center of a mandala, which is the object of drawing the whole mandala, is the very thing that escapes, that cannot be tied down; one is forever deceived about it. In the center is the invisible god.

Moreover, in each mandala one inevitably finds the male and the female elements clearly indicated, as here in the *devī* or Śakti. And you remember that Kundry, for instance, in the Parsifal legend is also represented with fangs, like Śakti;[25] in the lower localizations of our psychology there is a most terrible and bloodthirsty thing. Emotions on that level are not mitigated by any kind of reason; there people have emotions and tear everything to bits because they themselves are torn into shreds, the woman by the *animus* and the man by the *anima.* We must allow for a new kind of cakra. In the case of a woman we should put in the *animus.* The *animus* is also a thing with fangs. Here, too, we have parallels, in that these figures are never in the center and will not be, because they are things that are already known—they are the illusions, or *Māyā,* of gods. In the psychology of a Western mandala, the god is the most excentric ego power, "my" power, just as the *bindu-deva* and the Śakti are usually on one side, away from the center. It is "my" power, but it is moved by the invisible divine power in the center; in the center is the great one, and the other is the smaller one. As Faust says, man is the

[25] On the significance of the Parsifal legend for Jung, see John Haule, "Jung's Amfortas Wound," *Spring: A Journal of Archetype and Culture* 53 (1992): 95–112.

small god of the world. I am only the *bindu*, but the *bīja* letter, the real thing, is the self, and whatever I do is moved or caused by the *bīja-deva*. So one understands right away that part of the Eastern symbolism, despite the fact that in our mandalas it is never in such a form because we don't know what the gods are. We have not the faintest idea of God, we have only a philosophical conception of the *summum bonum* as the Christian God in heaven, which we cannot imagine properly, and therefore we cannot put it into our mandalas. Well, that is the main thing I wanted to say. One could talk, of course, for a couple of centuries, but other people must do that—I won't live so long.

Professor Hauer: I have been most interested, it has been most enlightening—and I think that if we take just the psychic elements, these experiences may help us a long way toward the creating of new mandalas. I would not agree, perhaps, with every explanation, but to a great extent with the fact that there are first physiological centers, then psychic centers, and so on. I suppose it would be a great thing for the Indian yogins to listen to Dr. Jung; it would help them to get those cakras into motion again, they have made them into a metaphysical condensation and do not see and feel so much, just the psychic aspect, and it is very important to have that side. But then, of course, the development in India was the other way, toward metaphysics. There were two causes, I think, for the creation of the heart mandala. First, through certain experiences in the heart; the great intuitions did not come through thinking, it is said thousands of times in the *Upanishads*. They felt that the deepest intuition—which stands always for the creative power in India—was from the heart. Then I am sure that physiologically the breathing had some influence on the composition; and last, of course, they went on to the metapsychical and metaphysical. And I think the study of the symbolism of tantric yoga may help us to push forward in the direction of the metapsychical and metaphysical. For as I look at it, every center has a psychic and a physical aspect, as well as the metaphysical and metapsychic aspects. That is indicated in the letters and so on, and also in the *bījas*. Further, the gods are psychic as well as metapsychic and metaphysical. So I would say that if we work together from different sides, the yogin coming from above, let us say—

Dr. Jung: And I from below!

Professor Hauer: Then the great event may happen, as with that girl, your patient. When the two things come together, the child will be born. So I hope something will come out of the work we have done here.

APPENDIX 4

ṢAṬ-CAKRA-NIRŪPAṆA

Preliminary verse

Now I speak of the first sprouting shoot (of the Yoga plant) of complete realization of the Brahman, which is to be achieved, according to the Tantras, by means of the six Cakras and so forth in their proper order.

Verse 1

In the space outside the Meru, placed on the left and the right, are the two Sirās, Śaśi and Mihira. The Nāḍī Suṣuṁnā, whose substance is the threefold Gunas, is in the middle. She is the form of Moon, Sun, and Fire; Her body, a string of blooming Dhātūra flowers, extends to the middle of the Kanda to the Head, and the Vajrā inside Her extends, shining, from the Meḍhra to the Head.

Verse 2

Inside her is Citriṇī, who is lustrous with the lustre of the Praṇava and attainable in Yoga by Yogīs. She (Citriṇī) is subtle as a spider's thread, and pierces all the Lotuses which are placed within the backbone, and is pure intelligence. She (Citriṇī) is beautiful by reason of these (Lotuses) which are strung on her. Inside her (Citriṇī) is the Brahmanāḍī, which extends from the orifice of the mouth of Hara to the place beyond, where Ādi-deva is.

Verse 3

She is beautiful like a chain of lightening and fine like a (lotus) fibre, and shines in the minds of sages. She is extremely subtle; the awakener of pure knowledge; the embodiment of all Bliss, whose true nature is pure Consciousness. The Brahma-dvāra shines in her mouth. This place in the entrance to the region sprinkled by ambrosia, and is called the Knot, as also the mouth of Suṣuṁnā.

Verse 4

Next we come to the Ādhāra Lotus. It is attached to the mouth of the

Suṣuṁnā, and is placed below the genitals and above the anus. It has four petals of crimson hue. Its head (mouth) hangs downwards. On its petals are the four letters from Va to Sa, of the shining colour of gold.

Verse 5

In this (Lotus) is the square region (Cakra) of Pṛthivī, surrounded by eight shining spears. It is of a shining yellow colour and beautiful like lightening, as is also the Bīja of Dharā which is within.

Verse 6

Ornamented with four arms and mounted on the King of Elephants, He carries on his lap the child Creator, resplendent like the young Sun, who has four lustrous arms, and the wealth of whose lotus-face is fourfold.

Verse 7

Here dwells the Devī Dakinī by name; her four arms shine with beauty, and her eyes are brilliant red. She is resplendent like the lustre of many Suns rising at one and the same time. She is the carrier of the revelation of the ever-pure Intelligence.

Verse 8

Near the mouth of the Nāḍī called Vajrā, and in the pericap (of the Ādhāra Lotus), there constantly shines the beautifully luminous and soft, lightening-like triangle which is Kāmarūpa, and known as Traipura. There is always and everywhere the Vāyu called Kandarpa, who is of a deeper red than the Bandhujīva flower, and is the Lord of Beings and resplendent like ten million suns.

Verse 9

Inside it (the triangle) is Svayaṁbhu in His Liṅga-form, beautiful like molten gold, with His head downwards. He is revealed by Knowledge and Meditation, and is of the shape and colour of a new leaf. As the cool rays of lightening and of the full moon charm, so does His beauty. The Deva who resides happily here as in Kāśī is in forms like a whirlpool.

Verses 10 and 11

Over it shines the sleeping Kuṇḍalinī, fine as the fibre of the lotus-stalk. She is the world-bewilderer, gently covering the mouth of Brahmadvāra by Her own. Like the spiral of the conch-shell, Her shining snake-like form goes three and a half times round Śiva, and Her lustre is as that of a strong flash of young strong lightening. Her sweet murmur is like the indistinct hum of swarms of love-mad bees. She produces melodious poetry and Bandha and all other compositions in prose or verse in sequence or otherwise in Saṁskṛta, Prākṛta and other languages. It is she who maintains all beings of the world by means of inspiration and expiration, and shines in the cavity of the root (Mūla) Lotus like a chain of brilliant lights.

Verse 12

Within it reigns dominant Parā, the Śrī-Parameśvarī, the Awakener of eternal knowledge. She is the Omnipotent Kalā who is wonderfully skilful to create, and is subtler than the subtlest. She is the receptacle of that continuous stream of ambrosia which flows from the Eternal Bliss. By Her radiance it is that the whole of this Universe and this Cauldron is illumined.

Verse 13

By meditating thus on Her who shines within the Mūla-Cakra, with the lustre of ten million Suns, a man becomes Lord of speech and King among men, and an Adept in all kinds of learning. He becomes ever free from all diseases, and his inmost Spirit becomes full of great gladness. Pure of disposition by his deep and musical words, he serves the foremost of the Devas.

Verse 14

There is another Lotus placed inside the Suṣuṁnā at the root of the genitals, of a beautiful vermilion colour. On its six petals are the letters from Ba to Puraṁdara, with the Bindu superposed, of the shining colour of lightening.

Verse 15

Within it is the white, shining, watery region of Varuṇa, of the shape of a half-moon, and therein, seated on a Makara, is the Bīja Vaṁ, stainless and white as the autumnal moon.

Verse 16

May Hari, who is within it, who is in the pride of early youth, whose body is of luminous blue beautiful to behold, who is dressed in yellow raiment, is four armed and wears the Śrī-vatsa, and the Kausubha, protect us!

Verse 17

It is here that Rākiṇī always dwells. She is of the colour of a blue lotus. The beauty of Her body is enhanced by Her uplifted arms holding various weapons. She is dressed in celestial raiment and ornaments, and Her mind is exalted with the drinking of ambrosia.

Verse 18

He who meditates upon this stainless Lotus, which is named Svādiṣṭhāna, is freed immediately from all his enemies, such as the fault of Aha kāra and so forth. He becomes a Lord among Yogīs, and is like the Sun illumining the dense darkness of ignorance. The wealth of his nectar-like words flows in prose and verse in well-reasoned discourse.

Verse 19

Above it, at the root of the navel, is the shining Lotus of ten petals, of the colour of heavy-laden rain-clouds. Within it are the letters Ḍa to Pha, of the colour of the blue lotus with the Nāda and Bindu above them. Meditate there on the region of Fire, triangular in form and shining like the rising sun. Outside it are three Svastika marks, and within, the Bīja of Vahni himself.

Verse 20

Meditate upon him (Fire) seated on a ram, four-armed, radiant like the rising Sun. In his lap ever dwells Rudra, who is of a pure vermilion hue. He (Rudra) is white with the ashes with which he is smeared; of an ancient aspect and three-eyed, His hands are placed in the attitude of granting boons and dispelling fear. He is the destroyer of creation.

Verse 21

Here abides Lākinī, the benefactress of all. She is four-armed, of radiant body, is dark (of complexion), clothed in yellow raiment and decked with various ornaments, and exalted with the drinking of ambrosia. By meditating on this Navel Lotus the power to destroy and create (the world) is acquired. Vāṇī with all the wealth of knowledge ever abides in the lotus of His face.

Verse 22

Above that, in the heart, is the charming Lotus, of the shining colour of the Bandhūka flower, with the twelve letters beginning with Ka, of the colour of vermilion, placed therein. It is known by the name of Anāhata, and is like the celestial wishing-tree, bestowing even more than (the supplicant's) desire. The Region of Vāyu, beautiful and with six corners, which is like unto the smoke in colour, is here.

Verse 23

Meditate within it on the sweet and excellent Pavana Bīja, grey as a mass of smoke, with four arms, and seated on a black antelope. And within it also (meditate) upon the Abode of Mercy, the Stainless Lord who is lustrous like the Sun, and whose two hands make the gestures which grant boons and dispels the fears of three worlds.

Verse 24

Here dwells Kākinī, who in colour is yellow like unto new lightening, exhilarated and auspicious; three-eyed and the benefactress of all. She wears all kinds of ornaments, and in Her four hands She carries the noose and the skull, and makes the sign of blessing and the sign which dispels fear. Her heart is softened with the drinking of nectar.

Verse 25

The Śakti whose tender body is like ten million flashes of lightening is in the pericarp of this Lotus in the form of a triangle (Trikoṇa). Inside the triangle is the śiva-Liṅga known by the name of Bāṇa. This Liṅga is like shining gold, and on his head is an orifice minute as that in a gem. He is the resplendent abode of Lakṣmī.

Verse 26

He who meditates on this Heart Lotus becomes (like) the Lord of Speech, and (like) Īśvara he is able to protect and destroy the worlds. This Lotus is like the celestial wishing-tree, the abode and seat of Śarva. It is beautified by the Haṁsa, which is like unto the steady tapering flame of a lamp in a windless place. The filaments which surround and adorn its pericarp, illumined by the solar region, charm.

Verse 27

Foremost among Yogīs, he is ever dearer than the dearest to women, He is pre-eminently wise and full of noble deeds. His senses are completely under control. His mind in its intense concentration is engrossed in thoughts of the Braham. His inspired speech flows like a stream of (clear) water. He is like the Devata who is the beloved of Lakṣmī and is able at will to enter another's body.

Verses 28 and 29

In the throat is the Lotus called Viśuddha, which is pure and of a smoky purple hue. All the (sixteen) shining vowels on its (sixteen) petals, of a crimson hue, are distinctly visible to him whose mind (Buddhi) is illumined. In the pericarp of this lotus there is the Ethereal Region, circular in shape, and white like the full Moon. On an elephant white as snow is seated the Bīja of Aṁbhara, who is white of colour.

Of His four arms, two hold the noose and goad, and the other two make the gestures of granting boons and dispelling fear. These add to His beauty. In His lap there ever dwells the great snow-white Deva, three-eyed and five-faced, with ten beautiful arms, and clothed in a tiger's skin. His body is united with that of Girija, and He is known by what His name, Sadā-Śiva, signifies.

Verse 30

Purer than the Ocean of Nectar is the Śakti Sākinī who dwells in this Lotus. Her raiment is yellow, and in Her four lotus-hands She carries the bow, the arrow, the noose, and the goad. The whole region of the Moon without the mark of the hare is in the pericarp of this Lotus. This (region) is the gateway of great Liberation for him who desires the wealth of Yoga and whose senses are pure and controlled.

Verse 31

He who has attained complete knowledge of the Ātmā (Brahman) becomes by constantly concentrating his mind (Citta) on this Lotus a great Sage, eloquent and wise, and enjoys uninterrupted peace of mind. He sees the three periods, and becomes the benefactor of all, free from disease and sorrow and long-lived, and, like Haṁsa, the destroyer of endless dangers.

Verse 31A

The Yogī, his mind constantly fixed on this Lotus, his breath controlled by Kuṁbhaka, is in his wrath able to move all the three worlds. Neither Brahmā nor Viṣṇu, neither Hari-Hara nor Sūrya nor Gaṇapa is able to control his power (resist Him).

Verse 32

The Lotus named Ājñā is like the moon (beautifully white). On its two petals are the letters Ha and *Kṣa*, which are also white and enhance its beauty. It shines with the glory of Dhyāna. Inside it is the Śakti Hākinī, whose six faces are like so many moons. She has six arms, in one of which She holds a book; two others are lifted up in the gestures of dispelling fear and granting boons, and with the rest She holds a skull, a small drum, and a rosary. Her mind is pure (Śuddha-Cittā).

Verse 33

Within this Lotus dwells the subtle mind (Manas). It is well-known. Inside the Yoni in the pericarp is the Śiva called Itara, in His phallic form. He here shines like a chain of lightning flashes. The first Bīja of the Vedas, which is the abode of the most excellent Śakti and which by its lustre makes visible the Brahma-sūtra, is also here. The Sādhaka with steady mind should meditate upon these according to the order (prescribed).

Verse 34

The excellent Sadhāka, whose Ātmā is nothing but a meditation on this Lotus, is able quickly to enter another's body at will, and becomes the most excellent among Munīs, and all-knowing and all-seeing. He becomes the benefactor of all, and versed in all the Śāstras. He realises his unity with the Brahman and acquires excellent and unknown powers. Full of fame and long-lived, he ever becomes the Creator, Destroyer, and Preserver, of the three worlds.

Verse 35

Within the triangle in this Cakra ever dwells the combination of letters which form the Praṇava. It is the inner Ātmā as pure mind (Buddhi), and resembles a flame in its radiance. Above it is the half (crescent) moon, and above this, again, is Ma-kāra, shining in its form of Bindu. Above this is Nāda, whose whiteness equals that of Balarāma and diffuses the rays of the Moon.

Verse 36

When the Yogī closes the house which hangs without support, the knowledge whereof he has gained by the service of Parama-guru, and when the Cetas by repeated practice become dissolved in this place which is the abode of uninterrupted bliss, he then sees within the middle of and in the space above (the triangle) sparks of fire distinctly shining.

Verse 37

He then also sees the Light which is in the form of a flaming lamp. It is lustrous like the clearly shining morning sun, and glows between the Sky and the Earth. It is here that the Bhagavān manifests Himself in the fullness of His might. He knows no decay, and witnesseth all, and is here as He is in the region of Fire, Moon, and Sun.

Verse 38

This is the incomparable and delightful abode of Viṣṇu. The excellent Yogī at the time of death joyfully places his vital breath (Prāṇa) here and enters (after death) that Supreme, Eternal, Birthless, Primeval Deva, the Puruṣa, who was before the three worlds, and who is known by the Vedānta.

Verse 39

When the actions of the Yogī are, through the service of the Lotus feet of his Guru, in all respects good, then he will see above it (i.e., Ājñā-Cakra) the form of Mahānāda, and will ever hold in the Lotus of his hand the Siddhi of Speech. The Mahānāda, which is the place of dissolution of Vāyu is the half of Śiva, and like the plough in shape, is tranquil and grants boons and dispels fear, and makes manifest pure Intelligence (Buddhi).

Verse 40

Above all these, in the vacant space wherein is Śaṇkhinī Nāḍī, and below Visarga is the Lotus of a thousand petals. This Lotus, lustrous and whiter than the full moon, has its head turned downward. It charms. Its clustered filaments are tinged with the colour of the young Sun. Its body is luminous with the letters beginning with A, and it is the absolute bliss.

Verse 41

Within it (Sahasrāra) is the full Moon, without the mark of the hare, resplendent as in a clear sky. It sheds its rays in profusion, and is moist and cool like nectar. Inside it (Candra-maṇḍala), constantly shining like lightening, is the Triangle and inside this, again, shines the Great Void which is served by all the Suras.

Verse 42

Well concealed, and attainable only by great effort, is that subtle Bindu (Śūnya) which is the chief root of liberation and which manifests the pure Nirvāna-kalā with Anā-Kalā. Here is the Deva who is known to all as Parama-Śiva. He is the Brahman and the Ātmā of all beings. In Him are united both Rasa and Virasa, and He is the Sun which destroys the darkness of nescience and delusion.

Verse 43

By shedding a constant and profuse stream of nectar-like essence, the Bhagavān instructs the Yati of pure mind in the knowledge by which he realizes the oneness of the Jīvātmā and the Paramātmā. He pervades all things as their Lord, who is the ever-flowing and spreading current of all manner of bliss known by the name of Haṁsah Parama (Parama-haṁsah).

Verse 44

The Śaivas call it the abode of Śiva; the Vaiṣṇavas call it Parama Puruṣa; others again, call it the place of Hari-Hara. Those who are filled with a passion for the Lotus feet of the Devī call it the excellent abode of the Devī; and other great sages (Munis) call it the pure place of Prakṛti-Puruṣa.

Verse 45

That most excellent of men who has controlled his mind and known this place is never again born in the Wandering, as there is nothing in the three worlds which binds him. His mind being controlled and his aim achieved, he possesses complete power to do all which he wishes, and to prevent that which is contrary to his will. He ever moves towards the Brahman. His speech, whether in prose or verse, is ever pure and sweet.

Verse 46

Here is the excellent (supreme) sixteenth Kalā of the Moon. She is pure, and resembles (in colour) the young Sun. She is as thin as the hundredth part of a fibre in the stalk of lotus. She is lustrous and soft like ten million lightening flashes, and is down-turned. From Her, whose source is the Brahman, flows copiously the continuous stream of nectar (or, She is the receptacle of the stream of excellent nectar which comes from the blissful union of Para and Parā).

Verse 47

Inside it (Amā-Kalā) is Nirvāṇa-kalā, more excellent than the excellent. She is as subtle as the thousandth part of the end of a hair, and of the shape of the crescent moon. She is the ever-existent Bhagavatī, who is the Devatā who pervades all beings. She grants divine knowledge, and is as lustrous as the light of all the suns shining at one and the same time.

Verse 48

Within its middle space (i.e., middle of the Nirvāṇa-kalā) shines the Supreme and Primordial Nirvāṇa-Śakti; She is lustrous like ten million suns, and is the Mother of the three worlds. She is extremely subtle, and like unto the ten-millionth part of the end of a hair. She contains within her the constantly flowing stream of gladness, and is the life of all beings. She graciously carries the knowledge of the Truth (Tattva) to the mind of the sages.

Verse 49

Within her is the everlasting place called the abode of Śiva, which is free from Māyā, attainable only by Yogīs, and known by the name of Nityānanda. It is replete with every form of bliss, and is pure knowledge itself. Some call it the Brahman; others call it the Haṁsa. Wise men describe it as the abode of Viṣṇu, and righteous men speak of it as the ineffable place of knowledge of the Ātmā, or the place of Liberation.

Verse 50

He whose nature is purified by the practice of Yama, Niyama, and the like, learns from the mouth of his Guru the process which opens the way to the discovery of the Great Liberation. He whose whole being is immersed in the Brahman then rouses the Devī by Hūṁ-kāra, pierces the centre of the Liṅga, the mouth of which is closed, and is therefore invisible, and by means of the Air and Fire (within him) places her within the Brahmadvāra.

Verse 51

The Devī who is Śuddha-sattvā pierces the three Liṅgas, and, having reached all the lotuses which are known as the Brahma-nāḍī lotuses, shines therein in the fullness of Her lustre. Thereafter in Her subtle state, lustrous like lightening and fine like the lotus fibre, She goes to the gleaming flame-like Śiva, the Supreme Bliss and of a sudden produces the bliss of Liberation.

Verse 52

The wise and excellent Yogī rapt in ecstasy, and devoted to the Lotus feet of his Guru, should lead Kula-Kuṇḍalī along with Jīva to Her Lord the Para-śiva in the abode of Liberation within the pure Lotus and meditate upon Her who grants all desires as the Caitanya-rūpā-Bhagavatī. When he thus leads Kula-Kuṇḍalinī, he should make all things absorb into Her.

Verse 53

The beautiful Kuṇḍalī drinks the excellent red nectar issuing from Para-śiva, and returns from there where shines Eternal and Transcendent Bliss in all its glory along the path of Kula, and again enters the Mulādhāra. The Yogī who has gained steadiness of mind makes offering (Tarpaṇa) to the Iṣṭa-devatā and to the Devatās in the six centres (Cakra), Dākinī and others, with that stream of celestial nectar which is in the vessel of Brahmāṇḍa, the knowledge whereof he has gained through the tradition of the Gunas.

Verse 54

The Yogī who has after practice of Yama, Niyama, and the like, learnt this excellent method from the two Lotus Feet of the auspicious Dikṣā-guru, which are the source of uninterrupted joy, and whose mind (Manas) is controlled, is never born again in this world (Samsāra). For him there is no dissolution even at the time of Final Dissolution. Gladdened by constant realization of that which is the source of Eternal Bliss, he becomes full of peace and foremost among all Yogīs.

Verse 55

If the Yogī who is devoted to the Lotus Feet of his Guru, with heart unperturbed and concentrated mind, reads this work which is the supreme source of the knowledge of Liberation, and which is faultless, pure, and most secret, then of a very surety his mind dances at the Feet of his Iṣṭa-devatā.

TRANSLATED BY SIR JOHN WOODROFFE

INDEX

Schmitz, Oskar, xx
School of Wisdom, xix
sea monster (makara), 13, 18, 92, 93n
The Secret of the Golden Flower, xx, xlv, 12, 14, 77–78
self, 14–15, 29, 39, 49, 57, 61, 85, 87
The Serpent Power (Woodroffe), xxvi, 106
serpents: feathered, 82; symbolism of in analysis, 84–85. *See also* Kundalini serpent
sexual revolution, and tantrism, xxiii
sexual symbolism, in tantric texts, xliii
Shivaism: description of, 73; tantric basis of, 72
Shrichakrasambhara (Patanjali), xxvii, 12
Śiva, 15, 18, 39, 57, 74, 87, 89, 93n
Solar Phallus Man, 37
soma cakra, 75
Soter (Saviour Serpent of the Gnostics), 68–69
sound, in meditation, 101
Spiegelberg, Friederich, xl
spirit, 37
spiritual development, 71
sthūla aspect: definition of, 6n; discussion of, 7–9, 66; of higher cakras, 64; as personal aspect, 62–63, 65; philosophy of, 60; Western language concepts of, 70
subconscious; in Kundalini yoga, xxxix; sound force in, 101
sūkṣma aspect: conscious understanding of, 64; definition of, 6n; discussion of, 7–10; Hindu acceptance of, 65–66; philosophy of, 60; as suprapersonal aspect, 62, 69; Western language concepts of, 70
sun serpent, 86
suprapersonal process: in analysis, 66–67; creation of values, 65; discussion of values, 62; and *sūkṣma* aspect, 62, 69
suṣumṇā nāḍīs: ascent of Kundalini through, xxv; importance of, xxiv
Suzuki, Daisetz: collaboration with Jung, xx; *Ten Essays in Buddhism*, 89–90
svādiṣṭhāna: baptism symbolism of, 66–67; as beginning of psychic life, 63–64; center of, 75; color symbolism of, 17; description of, 76, 113–14; discussion of, 15; Hauer's description of, 13n; level of, 62; leviathan as symbol of, 51; and *sthūla* aspect, 69; water symbolism of, 17
swastika: Hauer's symbolism of, xli; Jung's discussion of, 43
symbolism: of alchemy, 37; in analysis, 83; of animals, 51–56, 74, 76–77, 84–85; of baptism, 16–17, 30–32, 66–67; of breath, 44; of color, 17, 101–3, 108–9; of elements, 16–17, 35, 37, 42, 44–45, 66; of gender, xxiv, 103; of mandalas, 3; of plants, 77, 83; of psyche, 61, 67
symbols, definition of, 61

taboos, in tantrism, xxiii
tantric texts, language of, xliii
tantric yoga: chthonic nature of, 95; vs. classical yoga, 91; evolution of, 96; obscurity of, 12; origins of, 43; repute of, xxviiin
tantrism: as countercurrent to Christianity, xlv; and Kundalini yoga, xxii–xxv; origins of, 72; overview of, xxii–xxiii; taboos of, xxiii
tattva: discussion of, 9, 11; libido as example of, 8
Ten Essays in Buddhism (Suzuki), 89–90
Theosophy, 68
totem rites, and impersonal experience, 93
transformation, of images, 82
Transformation and Symbols of the Libido (Jung), xix
The Travel Diary of a Philosopher (Keyserling), xix
trees, symbolism of, 83

unconscious, 13, 17–21, 27–28, 32–33, 35–36, 59, 62, 66–70, 79, 85, 104; activation of, 68; and archetypes, 9; difficulties of experiencing, 27; localization of, 85; in religious instruction, 80; spirit of, 82; stillborn in Catholics, 80; unleashing of, 33, 35–36. *See also* collective unconscious
underground symbolism, 18
unfathomable things, 109
unicorn, symbolism of, 52
Upanishads, xix. *See also* Dhyanabindu Upanishads; Hangsa Upanishads

The Collected Works of C. G. Jung

Editors: Sir Herbert Read, Michael Fordham, and Gerhard Adler; executive editor, William McGuire. Translated by R.F.C. Hull, except where noted.

1. PSYCHIATRIC STUDIES (1957; 2d ed., 1970)
   On the Psychology and Pathology of So-Called Occult Phenomena (1902)
   On Hysterical Misreading (1904)
   Cryptomnesia (1905)
   On Manic Mood Disorder (1903)
   A Case of Hysterical Stupor in a Prisoner in Detention (1902)
   On Simulated Insanity (1903)
   A Medical Opinion on a Case of Simulated Insanity (1904)
   A Third and Final Opinion on Two Contradictory Psychiatric Diagnoses (1906)
   On the Psychological Diagnosis of Facts (1905)

2. EXPERIMENTAL RESEARCHES (1973)
   Translated by Leopold Stein in collaboration with Diana Riviere
   STUDIES IN WORD ASSOCIATION (1904–7, 1910)
   The Associations of Normal Subjects (by Jung and F. Riklin)
   An Analysis of the Associations of an Epileptic
   The Reaction-Time Ratio in the Association Experiment
   Experimental Observations on the Faculty of Memory
   Psychoanalysis and Association Experiments
   The Psychological Diagnosis of Evidence
   Association, Dream, and Hysterical Symptom
   The Psychopathological Significance of the Association Experiment
   Disturbances in Reproduction in the Association Experiment
   The Association Method
   The Family Constellation
   PSYCHOPHYSICAL RESEARCHES (1907–8)
   On the Psychophysical Relations of the Association Experiment
   Psychophysical Investigations with the Galvanometer and Pneumograph in Normal and Insane Individuals (by F. Peterson and Jung)

(*continued*)

Further Investigations on the Galvanic Phenomenon and Respiration in Normal and Insane Individuals (by C. Ricksher and Jung)
Appendix: Statistical Details of Enlistment (1906); New Aspects of Criminal Psychology (1908); The Psychological Methods of Investigation Used in the Psychiatric Clinic of the University of Zurich (1910); On the Doctrine Complexes ([1911] 1913); On the Psychological Diagnosis of Evidence (1937)

3. THE PSYCHOGENESIS OF MENTAL DISEASE (1960)
The Psychology of Dementia Praecox (1907)
The Content of the Psychoses (1908/1914)
On Psychological Understanding (1914)
A Criticism of Bleuler's Theory of Schizophrenic Negativism (1911)
On the Importance of the Unconscious in Psychology (1914)
On the Problem of Psychogenesis in Mental Disease (1919)
Mental Disease and the Psyche (1928)
On the Psychogenesis of Schizophrenia (1939)
Recent Thoughts on Schizophrenia (1957)
Schizophrenia (1958)

4. FREUD AND PSYCHOANALYSIS (1967)
Freud's Theory of Hysteria: A Reply to Aschaffenburg (1906)
The Freudian Theory of Hysteria (1908)
The Analysis of Dreams (1909)
A Contribution to the Psychology of Rumour (1910–11)
On the Significance of Number Dreams (1910–11)
Morton Prince, "The Mechanism and Interpretation of Dreams": A Critical Review (1911)
On the Criticism of Psychoanalysis (1910)
Concerning Psychoanalysis (1912)
The Theory of Psychoanalysis (1913)
General Aspects of Psychoanalysis (1913)
Psychoanalysis and Neurosis (1916)
Some Crucial Points in Psychoanalysis: A Correspondence between Dr. Jung and Dr. Loÿ (1914)
Prefaces to "Collected Papers on Analytical Psychology" (1916, 1917)
The Significance of the Father in the Destiny of the Individual (1909/1949)
Introduction to Kranefeldt's "Secret Ways of the Mind" (1930)
Freud and Jung: Contrasts (1929)

(*continued*)

8. THE STRUCTURE AND DYNAMICS OF THE PSYCHE (1960; 2d ed., 1969)
On Psychic Energy (1928)
The Transcendent Function ([1916] 1957)
A Review of the Complex Theory (1934)
The Significance of Constitution and Heredity in Psychology (1929)
Psychological Factors Determining Human Behavior (1937)
Instinct and the Unconscious (1919)
The Structure of the Psyche (1927/1931)
On the Nature of the Psyche (1947/1954)
General Aspects of Dream Psychology (1916/1948)
On the Nature of Dreams (1945/1948)
The Psychological Foundations of Belief in Spirits (1920/1948)
Spirit and Life (1926)
Basic Postulates of Analytical Psychology (1931)
Analytical Psychology and *Weltanschauung* (1928/1931)
The Real and the Surreal (1933)
The Stages of Life (1930–31)
The Soul and Death (1934)
Synchronicity: An Acausal Connecting Principle (1952)
Appendix: On Synchronicity (1951)

9. PART I. THE ARCHETYPES AND THE COLLECTIVE UNCONSCIOUS (1959; 2d ed., 1968)
Archetypes of the Collective Unconscious (1934/1954)
The Concept of the Collective Unconscious (1936)
Concerning the Archetypes, with Special Reference to the Anima Concept (1936/1954)
Psychological Aspects of the Mother Archetype (1938/1954)
Concerning Rebirth (1940/1950)
The Psychology of the Child Archetype (1940)
The Psychological Aspects of the Kore (1941)
The Phenomenology of the Spirit in Fairytales (1945/1948)
On the Psychology of the Trickster-Figure (1954)
Conscious, Unconscious, and Individuation (1939)
A Study in the Process of Individuation (1934/1950)
Concerning Mandala Symbolism (1950)
Appendix: Mandalas (1955)

(*continued*)

The Complications of American Psychology (1930)
The Dreamlike World of India (1939)
What India Can Teach Us (1939)
Appendix: Documents (1933–38)

11. PSYCHOLOGY AND RELIGION: WEST AND EAST (1958; 2d ed., 1969)

WESTERN RELIGION

Psychology and Religion (the Terry Lectures) (1938/1940)
A Psychological Approach to Dogma of the Trinity (1942/1948)
Transformation Symbolism in the Mass (1942/1954)
Forewords to White's "God and the Unconscious" and Werblowsky's "Lucifer and Prometheus" (1952)
Brother Klaus (1933)
Psychotherapists or the Clergy (1932)
Psychoanalysis and the Cure of Souls (1928)
Answer to Job (1952)

EASTERN RELIGION

Psychological Commentaries on "The Tibetan Book of Great Liberation" (1939/1954) and "The Tibetan Book of the Dead" (1935/1953)
Yoga and the West (1936)
Foreword to Suzuki's "Introduction to Zen Buddhism" (1939)
The Psychology of Eastern Meditation (1943)
The Holy Men of India: Introduction to Zimmer's "Der Weg zum Selbst"(1944)
Foreword to the "I Ching" (1950)

12. PSYCHOLOGY AND ALCHEMY ([1944] 1953; 2d ed., 1968)
Prefatory Note to the English Edition ([1951?] added 1967)
Introduction to the Religious and Psychological Problems of Alchemy
Individual Dream Symbolism in Relation to Alchemy (1936)
Religious Ideas in Alchemy (1937)
Epilogue

13. ALCHEMICAL STUDIES (1968)
Commentary on "The Secret of the Golden Flower" (1929)
The Visions of Zosimos (1938/1954)
Paracelsus as a Spiritual Phenomenon (1942)
The Spirit Mercurius (1943/1948)
The Philosophical Tree (1945/1954)

14. MYSTERIUM CONIUNCTIONIS ([1955–56] 1963; 2d ed., 1970)
AN INQUIRY INTO THE SEPARATION AND
SYNTHESIS OF PSYCHIC OPPOSITES IN ALCHEMY
The Components of the Coniunctio
The Paradoxa
The Personification of the Opposites
Rex and Regina
Adam and Eve
The Conjunction

15. THE SPIRIT IN MAN, ART, AND LITERATURE (1966)
Paracelsus (1929)
Paracelsus the Physician (1941)
Sigmund Freud in His Historical Setting (1932)
In Memory of Sigmund Freud (1939)
Richard Wilhelm: In Memoriam (1930)
On the Relation of Analytical Psychology to Poetry (1922)
Psychology and Literature (1930/1950)
"Ulysses": A Monologue (1932)
Picasso (1932)

16. THE PRACTICE OF PSYCHOTHERAPY (1954; 2d ed., 1966)
GENERAL PROBLEMS OF PSYCHOTHERAPY
Principles of Practical Psychotherapy (1935)
What Is Psychotherapy? (1935)
Some Aspects of Modern Psychotherapy (1930)
The Aims of Psychotherapy (1931)
Problems of Modern Psychotherapy (1929)
Psychotherapy and a Philosophy of Life (1943)
Medicine and Psychotherapy (1945)
Psychotherapy Today (1945)
Fundamental Questions of Psychotherapy (1951)
SPECIFIC PROBLEMS OF PSYCHOTHERAPY
The Therapeutic Value of Abreaction (1921/1928)
The Practical Use of Dream-Analysis (1934)
The Psychology of the Transference (1946)
Appendix: The Realities of Practical Psychotherapy ([1937] added 1966)

17. THE DEVELOPMENT OF PERSONALITY (1954)
Psychic Conflicts in a Child (1910/1946)
Introduction to Wickes's "Analyses der Kinderseele" (1927/1931)

(*continued*)

Child Development and Education (1928)
Analytical Psychology and Education: Three Lectures (1926/1946)
The Gifted Child (1943)
The Significance of the Unconscious in Individual Education (1928)
The Development of Personality (1934)
Marriage as a Psychological Relationship (1925)

18. THE SYMBOLIC LIFE (1954)
Translated by R.F.C. Hull and others
Miscellaneous Writings

19. COMPLETE BIBLIOGRAPHY OF C. G. JUNG'S WRITINGS (1976; 2d ed., 1992)

20. GENERAL INDEX OF THE COLLECTED WORKS (1979)

THE ZOFINGIA LECTURES (1983)
Supplementary Volume A to the Collected Works.
Edited by William McGuire, translated by
Jan van Heurck, introduction by
Marie-Louise von Franz

PSYCHOLOGY OF THE UNCONSCIOUS ([1912] 1992)
A STUDY OF THE TRANSFORMATIONS AND SYMBOLISMS OF THE LIBIDO.
A CONTRIBUTION TO THE HISTORY OF THE EVOLUTION OF THOUGHT
Supplementary Volume B to the Collected Works.
Translated by Beatrice M. Hinkle,
introduction by William McGuire

Related Publications

THE BASIC WRITINGS OF C. G. JUNG
Selected and introduced by Violet S. de Laszlo

PSYCHE AND SYMBOL
Selected and introduced by Violet S. de Laszlo

C. G. JUNG: LETTERS
Selected and edited by Gerhard Adler, in collaboration with Aniela Jaffé.
Translations from the German by R.F.C. Hull
VOL. 1: 1906–1950
VOL. 2: 1951–1961

THE FREUD / JUNG LETTERS
Edited by William McGuire, translated by
Ralph Manheim and R.F.C. Hull

C. G. JUNG SPEAKING: Interviews and Encounters
Edited by William McGuire and R.F.C. Hull

C. G. JUNG: Word and Image
Edited by Aniela Jaffé

THE ESSENTIAL JUNG
Selected and introduced by Anthony Storr

THE GNOSTIC JUNG
Selected and introduced by Robert A. Segal

Notes to C. G. Jung's Seminars

DREAM ANALYSIS ([1928–30] 1984)
Edited by William McGuire

NIETZSCHE'S *ZARATHUSTRA* ([1934–39] 1988)
Edited by James L. Jarrett (2 vols.)

ANALYTICAL PSYCHOLOGY ([1925] 1989)
Edited by William McGuire

THE PSYCHOLOGY OF KUNDALINI YOGA ([1932] 1996)
Edited by Sonu Shamdasani

INTERPRETATION OF VISIONS ([1930–34] 1997)
Edited by Claire Douglas

Sonu Shamdasani is a historian of psychology at the Wellcome Institute for the History of Medicine, London. He is the editor of Théodore Flournoy's *From India to the Planet Mars: A Case of Multiple Personality with Imaginary Languages* (Princeton), of Michael Fordham's *Analyst-Patient Interaction*, and, with Michael Münchow, *Speculations after Freud: Psychoanalysis, Philosophy, Culture.*